An International Hit!

Helping people achieve their dream worldwide. *Dream It Do It* is also published in South Korea and India.

"A **powerful roadmap for success**.... "Dream CPR" will breathe new life into your buried dreams."
   — *Rebecca Johnson,*
The Rebecca Review

Book of the Month

"*Dream It Do It* offers readers a **clear, realistic path** toward reviving and achieving their most heartfelt dreams."
   — *spiritcrossing.com*

"A **thoroughly "user friendly"** self-help guidebook to rebuilding confidence, unleashing creativity, awakening our passions, and learning to take risks while keeping responsibilities in mind — all the better to pursue our personal dreams and goals in life. A motivational instructional to help one take control and steer one's life toward the future one desires, *Dream It Do It* **combines testimonials with solid advice for making things happen**, instead of just letting things happen."
   — *Midwest Book Review's Small Press Bookwatch*

"**Very well written** and **inspiring...**"
   — *Cheryl McCann, review–books.com*

Book of the Week

"*Dream It Do It* **will make your spirits soar** and inspire even the most discouraged readers to put their lives back together and achieve their most heartfelt dreams."
   — *OfSpirit.com*

See the full reviews and more at
http://www.dreamitdoit.net

Start a "Dream It Do It Club"® at your school or in your community

Seeking ways to help nontraditional students who didn't go to college straight from high school find their way in school and life, academic adviser Beverley Berlin Mas launched the first "Dream It Do It Club"® at Palm Beach Community College a few months after this book was first published in 2004.

Her own life story is one of the 37 featured in *Dream It Do It: Inspiring Stories of Dreams Come True*. Starting with seven members, her initial club has grown to nearly 700 members in early 2007 and is being replicated at all four campuses of her school. Members include students as well as men and women from the surrounding community. The clubs use *Dream It Do It* as their guide and basis for much discussion at monthly meetings that often feature a guest speaker.

Other activities include community service projects that have raised funds for a wide variety of groups and individuals in need, as well as assistance to individuals seeking to find and achieve their dreams.

Thanks to donations from community members who believe in what the Dream It Doers are accomplishing individually and as a group, Beverley's "Dream It Do It Club"® has established a scholarship fund that has awarded more than $8,000 in scholarships to club members.

Now you, too, can establish a "Dream It Do It Club" in your community or at your school.

For details on starting a "Dream It Do It Club,"® contact *Dream It Do It* co–author Sharon Cook by email at: sharon@dreamitdoit.net.

To order copies of *Dream It Do It* at a quantity discount for your "Dream It Do It Club,"® contact publisher Daniel Lauber by phone at 708/366–5200 (9 a.m. to 6 p.m. Central time) or via email at: dl@planningcommunications.com.

April 26, 2007

Whoever reads these pages, may the words inspire, uplift to follow your life's purpose. Always Believe in yourself.

Best Wishes Sharon

Thank you for your Donation!

Dream It Do It

Inspiring Stories of Dreams Come True

Sharon Cook &
Graciela Sholander

PLANNING/COMMUNICATIONS

River Forest, Illinois

For quantity discounts and permissions, contact the publisher:

PLANNING/COMMUNICATIONS

7215 Oak Avenue
River Forest, Illinois 60305 ① 708/366–5200
http://jobfindersonline.com, http://dreamitdoit.net

Cover design by Salvatore Concialdi
Interior design by Daniel Lauber
Text and photos edited by Jennifer Lee Atkin
Produced using Corel Ventura 10, PhotoPaint 11, KnockOut 2

Disclaimer of All Warranties and Liabilities

The authors and publisher make no warranties, either expressed or implied, with respect to the information contained herein. The authors and publisher shall not be liable for any incidental or consequential damages in connection with, or arising out of, the use of materials in this book.

Publisher's Cataloging–in–Publication Data
(Provided by Quality Books, Inc.)

Cook, Sharon (Sharon L.)
   Dream it do it : inspiring stories of dreams come
   true / Sharon Cook & Graciela Sholander.

   p. cm.

   LCCN: 2003111006
   ISBN–13: 978–1–884587–30–6 (paper)
   ISBN–10: 1–884587–30–5 (paper)

   I. Self–actualization (Psychology) — Case Studies.
   2. Spiritual biography   I. Sholander, Graciela. II.
   Title

   BF637.S4C66 2003   158.1

                         QB133–1590

Table of Contents

Dedication v

Acknowledgments vii

Foreword xi

1   Dream It 1

2   Dream CPR 5

   THE ELEMENTS OF DREAM CPR 8

      CONFIDENCE: TRUST YOURSELF 8

      COURAGE: SUMMON YOUR STRENGTH 8

      COMMITMENT: STAY FOCUSED 9

      CREATIVITY: IMAGINE YOUR REALITY 9

      PURPOSE: REACH HIGHER 10

      PASSION: LOVE WHAT YOU DO 10

      PERSISTENCE: KEEP TRYING 10

      RESILIENCE: BOUNCE BACK 11

      RISK: TAKE A LEAP OF FAITH 11

      RESPONSIBILITY: CHOOSE WISELY 12

   BECOMING A DREAM ACHIEVER 12

3   Confidence: Believe In Yourself 14

   HARRISON FORD: ACTING ON HIS OWN TERMS 15

   CALE KENNEY: WILD WOMAN ON SKIS 22

   NANCY ARCHULETA: FROM HIGH SCHOOL DROPOUT TO HIGH–TECH CEO . 27

   BUILD YOUR CONFIDENCE 32

4 Courage: Conquer Your Fears 37

MARIGOLD LINTON: BLAZING NEW TRAILS 38

LANCE ARMSTRONG: A TOUR DE FORCE 43

STEPHANIE NGO PHAM: STRANGER IN A STRANGE LAND 47

COURAGE TO MOVE FORWARD WITH YOUR DREAMS 50

5 Commitment: Devote Yourself 53

BARBARA VOGEL: ENCOURAGING STUDENTS TO STOP SLAVERY 55

TIGER WOODS: LEGEND IN HIS TIME 59

CYNTHIA HESS: CAREER PSYCHIC BY CHOICE 63

COMMIT YOURSELF TO YOUR DREAM 68

6 Creativity: Create a New Reality 71

BILL NYE: EXPERIMENTING WITH FUN 72

SUSAN TITCOMB AND DAVID MACKAY: RECIPE FOR SUCCESS 76

PHIL VISCHER: A HIGHER CALLING LEADS TO A BIG IDEA 80

CREATIVITY BREEDS DREAMS 85

7 Purpose: Find Your Reason to Dream 88

BEVERLEY BERLIN MAS: TURNING TRAGEDY INTO TENDERNESS 89

BINH NGUYEN RYBACKI: REMEMBERING THE FORGOTTEN CHILDREN ... 94

JIMMY AND ROSALYNN CARTER: POST–PRESIDENTIAL PEACEMAKERS .. 99

PURPOSE IS THE REASON BEHIND OUR DREAMS 104

8 Passion: Get Fired Up 107

GLORIA ESTEFAN: UNSTOPPABLE SINGING SENSATION 108

MICHAEL CLARKE DUNCAN: DITCH–DIGGER NO MORE 113

EILEEN COLLINS: WHERE NO WOMAN HAS GONE BEFORE 116

CARL NICHOLAS KARCHER: FROM HOT–DOG STAND TO FAST–FOOD EMPIRE 120

PASSION FUELS YOUR DREAMS 124

9 Persistence: Try and Try Again 127

BARBARA WALTERS: BREAKING BROADCAST BARRIERS 128

EDWARD A. BERGER: REVOLUTIONARY AIDS RESEARCHER 134

JANETTE FENNELL: SAFETY STANDARDS THAT SAVE LIVES 137

PERSISTENCE IN AN INSTANT GRATIFICATION SOCIETY 142

10 Resilience: Rise Up With Hope 145

RICHARD BLOCH: SHARING A WEALTH OF HOPE 146

MAYA ANGELOU: WRITING THE WRONGS 150

DOUG WEST: THE POWER OF CALM 155

SUSANNE BLAKE: FINDING SPIRITUAL SUSTENANCE............159

LEARN RESILIENCE TO RECOVER FROM BLOWS................164

11 Risk: Take a Chance 167

YO–YO MA: EXPLORING ARTISTIC FRONTIERS 168

CONNIE BRADY: PUTTING CHILDREN'S NEEDS FIRST 172

GEORGE FULLERTON: DEVELOPING A NEWFANGLED GUITAR.......175

DAVID HOWARD: FACING HIGH STAKES IN HIGH–TECH 179

TAKE A RISK TO GROW YOUR DREAMS....................184

12 Responsibility: Choose Wisely..............187

DOUG AND WENDY ISHII: MARRIAGE OF ART AND SCIENCE 189

CHRISTY CURTIS: FOLLOWING HER CONSCIENCE...............198

MARY O'DONNELL: PAVING A WOMEN'S ROAD TO RECOVERY.......201

DENNIS WEAVER: LEADING MAN FIGHTS FOR THE BACKDROPS 205

TAKE RESPONSIBILITY FOR YOUR DREAMS...................209

13 Nine Keys 211

14 Do It!.........................222

BREATHE LIFE INTO YOUR DREAM 223

GO FOR IT! 224

Appendix A........................227

VOICES OF THE FUTURE 227

Appendix B........................231

FOR MORE INFORMATION.........................231

Credits & Permissions 233

About the Authors................238

Dedication

To my sons, David and Robert,

And to all the dreamers and voices of the future.

With love always,
Sharon

To my children, Susanne and Spencer:

"You are the light of the world." Matthew 5:14

May your most special dreams shine brightly.

With love eternal,
Graciela

Acknowledgments

"WHEN YOU HAVE A DREAM YOU'VE GOT TO GRAB IT AND NEVER LET GO."
— CAROL BURNETT

We honor and thank every person who helped, supported, and accompanied us on this journey.

To each of you who shared your personal story of a dream come true, thank you. This book holds but a sampling of these incredible stories; yet all of you, by pursuing your dreams with dedication, have inspired and amazed us. Our lives have been enriched by knowing you.

Many thanks to every young person who shared your goals and dreams with us, and to your parents and teachers. May your dreams come true! Special thanks to Joyce Weybright, Reneé Rose, Flow Van Koten, and Muriel Ferris for your enthusiastic help with "Voices of the Future."

Our sincere appreciation to the many libraries and Internet sources that facilitated our research, and to every publicist, agent, representative, manager, photographer, librarian, and administrative assistant who provided valuable information and service.

Our heartfelt gratitude goes to our publisher, Daniel Lauber, for believing in our book and taking a chance on us, and to our editor, Jennifer Lee Atkin, for polishing our manuscript until it shone.

Thank you, readers — this book is for you. We honor you for your courage to embark on a new, exciting path.

From Sharon: Thank you to the trailblazers who were important to me in my life — my mother, Pearl Jeffreys, and my aunts

Imogene Gabbard, Aneita Jones, Merle Isaac, and Jean Snodgrass.

To my special friends — Claudia Waterman, Margaret Ward, Erlene Caudell, and Vince and Marge Bluhm, thank you for your faithful friendship and for being there for me through the ups and downs of this process.

To my dear co–author Graciela, words cannot express the love and respect I feel for you and the wonder I have for your gift of writing. Thank you for a creative alliance built upon mutual respect and cooperation. Thanks for your courage, your humor, and for hanging in there when the road was rough and uncertain. I thank your wonderful husband and children for their support.

To my precious family, Larry, David, and Robert, and my brother John, thank you from my heart for your love, devotion, and support to help me realize a dream that began when these words came to me in March 1999: "Oh, I have a dream stirring inside of me. It wrestles inside, bursting to shout. All I need is the courage to let it out. Then my dream can begin to sprout. At that moment I become the dream I desire to bring about. We are all children of dreams. We must inspire dreaming in our children, our future. This is what living is all about." I love you all.

From Graciela: To Donata and Mieczyslaw, thank you so much, Mom and Dad, for all you have given me. You followed your dreams when you immigrated to this great nation of opportunity, and so from you, I learned about the courage needed to venture boldly into the unknown and persistence needed to succeed. Thank you, my grandmother Natalia, from heaven you continue to guide and inspire me. Special thanks to my brother Robert, a true and loyal friend; and my mother–in–law, Carol, who knows firsthand the sheer joy of losing oneself in the creative process.

Many thanks to my extended family and friends for adding bright, colorful hues to my life. I'd like to especially thank writer Cynthia Boman Thompson, for your friendship and support; Pastor Dale Bauer, for the freedom to write a creative monthly column; the people at King of Glory for your friendship; and my children's dedicated teachers for whom I have the utmost respect.

To my dear co–author Sharon, thank you for giving me this project to write and wings to soar. Thank you for this magnificent opportunity, for teaching me so much, and for being my mentor and friend. You've challenged and inspired me to take creative risks.

To my cherished, beloved ones — my husband, Kevin, thank you for your unfaltering support, your steadfast love, and your integrity and goodness; and my precious children, Susanne and Spencer, you give me great joy and fill me with pride. Thank you, children, for your energy, creativity, enthusiasm, wisdom, and love. I treasure each of you and the life we share as a family.

Both Sharon and Graciela wish to express our everlasting gratitude to our Creator, from whom the Spirit of Creativity flows so abundantly to all of us children on earth. Peace to all.

Foreword

It is not unusual for either young people or adults to be urged to follow their dreams. As a social worker involved in all kinds of youth development programs, it is advice I have heard delivered, movingly and eloquently, many times over. And it is advice that I have delivered myself. But it is one thing to counsel people to dream. It is something else altogether to help people — regardless of their age or circumstances — to get both the support and the practical know–how they need to make their dreams come true.

Sharon Cook and Graciela Sholander decided in 1999 to do something that would empower people to follow their dreams. Sharon, a motivational speaker and author, saw that many people simply weren't fulfilled. As she traveled across the country to different speaking engagements, she saw over and over that many people were not passionate about their work or their lives. Sitting quietly one day, she experienced a burst of inspiration. She realized that with her trusted friend and colleague, freelance writer Graciela Sholander, she wanted to co–author a book showing people how to dream, how to begin turning dreams into reality, and how successful individuals have created the lives of their dreams. Graciela immediately saw the value such a book would bring to others. Both began to work on the project, compiling a book with a unique mix of true–life stories and information the reader can apply.

What these authors deliver on the exercise of dreaming is one part inspiration, one part example, and one part practical advice. On the pages that follow, you will be moved by words of dreamers from all walks of life. You will hear about the people, places, and things that first inspired and then sustained them. Whether the inspiration arose from artistry or science, humanitarianism or business, Graciela and Sharon have captured the moments of inspiration that spurred lifetimes of dedicated effort and profoundly satisfying outcomes.

These remarkable people and their collective stories exemplify the power of dreaming and the dedicated action required to transform a dream into reality. Some of the names will be familiar to you, well–known artists like Yo–Yo Ma, Gloria Estefan, and Harrison Ford. Other names, like Nancy Archuleta and George Fullerton, are likely to be entirely new. In either instance, I guarantee that you will enjoy getting to know them all and learning about the origins and fulfillment of their dreams. You will also take heart from the obstacles they met and overcame along the way. Entrepreneur David MacKay speaks for all of those profiled when he says: "There is no such thing as failure, only learning experiences."

Example is buttressed by practical guidance. The authors provide questions to trigger your mind and heart into revealing your own dreams. Their "Dream CPR" is a reminder of the essential attributes every dreamer must master for a dream to become reality.

One particularly strong piece of advice emerges from many of the stories — find and value mentors. I could not agree more. Many of the dreamers profiled in this book had a strong mentor who, along with caring relatives, helped them chart and stay on course to realize their ambitions.

As Graciela and Sharon demonstrate, dreaming is vastly more than a simple imaginative exercise. Dreamers who succeed rely on their focus, drive, passion, faith, and a strong sense of accountability. This book will inspire and equip you, as well as the young people you care about, not only to dream big, but to dream effectively.

Gail Manza
Executive Director
The National Mentoring Partnership

Dream It Do It

Inspiring Stories of Dreams Come True

Chapter 1

Dream It

"EVERYTHING WE SEE TODAY, MADE BY PAST GENERATIONS, WAS, BEFORE ITS APPEARANCE, A THOUGHT IN THE MIND OF A MAN OR AN IMPULSE IN THE HEART OF A WOMAN." — KAHLIL GIBRAN

There's a dream — maybe several dreams — inside each of us, just waiting to emerge. But far too often, the realities of daily life take a toll on our dreams. As we struggle to make a living and get by in this complicated world, many of us bury our dreams so deeply that we forget about them. Many of us dismiss our dreams as nothing but fantasies concocted to escape the weight of real life. Some people have even forgotten how to dream!

It doesn't have to be this way. We'll show you how to harness the immense power of dreaming, not to escape your life but to create the reality you want. And it's never too early or too late to get started.

Dreams are not vaporous, fanciful thinking. They are the building blocks of reality. Just about everything we see and hear around us started as somebody's dream. The same wonderful creative force that made spinning galaxies, fragrant roses, and beating hearts equipped us with magnificent tools — including imagination, vision, and the ability to dream.

We use these tools to shape our earthly existence. People dreamt up the homes we live in, the clothes we wear, the music we hear. People dreamt up satellites and computers, vaccines and pacemakers — they didn't just appear out of thin air. People continue to dream up and breathe fresh life into new creations in medicine, business, art, philosophy, education, humanitarianism — you name it, people first dreamt it and then made it so. In the course of fulfilling personal dreams, people bring purpose into their own lives and enrich us all with their inventions and innovations.

Ever wonder how some people manage to reach major milestones, achieve personal success, and create the lives of their dreams? We did, too. So we interviewed more than 120 people, some famous, some you've never heard of, who transformed their dreams into reality. We've dissected their lives to understand what it takes to reach a dream. And we present the inspiring true stories of 37 of these dream achievers so that you may glimpse into their lives and learn the secrets of their success.

You will meet a dedicated grade–school teacher whose dreams inspired her young students to free hundreds of mod-ern–day slaves. You will see how dreaming and doing led a molecular scientist to make a pivotal discovery, opening the way to promising new treatments for AIDS. You'll discover how a one–time high school dropout became the CEO of a prominent engineering firm. You'll learn how a vibrant amputee whose aspirations could not be denied became a champion skier. You will read about people who follow their dreams to create, innovate, and achieve in a wide range of fields and professions.

They are not supermen or superwomen. They are ordinary people who somehow accomplish the extraordinary. Reading their stories will help you apply to your own life the valuable lessons these dreamers and doers have mastered. One of life's most exciting challenges is discovering how to release and fulfill the magnificent dreams stored in our hearts and minds. The successful people whose stories appear in this book have unlocked that secret. They've created the lives of their dreams by daring to achieve their deepest aspirations.

You can, too — we'll show you how. You have within yourself the power to make your dreams come true. You can soar in life! And if the trials and tribulations of daily living have deflated your dreams, burying them deep into the recesses of your mind, we'll show you how to resuscitate them. We'll help you breathe new life into your dreams of old to create your dreams of today.

Remember the popular *Back to the Future* trilogy? In the first film, Michael J. Fox's character, Marty, accidentally travels back in time where he meets his parents as high school students. Marty's actions and choices have a lasting effect on his future parents — and when he finally manages to return to his own time, he finds his family life to be much happier and more fulfilling. In the final film, Doc delivers the trilogy's message: *Your future is yours to write.* Whatever may be swirling around you, you determine the course of your destiny by the choices that you make. A single action can completely alter your future, for better or worse.

What kind of future do you want for yourself, for your loved ones, for generations yet to come? More than anybody else and more than any of the circumstances that surround you, *you* have the largest say in what your future will be.

Your dreams are as unique as your individual fingerprints. Some people have elaborate dreams; others have simpler ones. Your dream could take a few months to fulfill or a lifetime. Ac-

Dream CPR Journal

Keep a journal while you read this book to jot down your thoughts and answers to questions that we will pose from time to time to help you revive your dreams. Your journal doesn't need to be fancy — you're not trying to impress anybody. This journal is just for you.

Have fun with your journal: There are no right or wrong answers, no set number of items that you must come up with when we ask you to make a list. What's important is that you take the time to answer each question or compile each list to your satisfaction. Above all, write from your heart.

complishing a dream is rarely an easy, straightforward matter. But with the inspiration, encouragement, and practical guidance we offer in *Dream It Do It*, the pathway to fulfilling your dreams will emerge and become navigable.

Like any journey, your dream quest begins with a single step. And the first step toward making your dreams come true is discovering — or perhaps we should say, *rediscovering* — the ten essential elements of Dream CPR.

chapter 2

Dream CPR

> "DON'T BE AFRAID OF THE SPACE BETWEEN YOUR DREAMS AND REALITY. IF YOU CAN DREAM IT, YOU CAN MAKE IT SO." — BELVA DAVIS

After spending three years closely examining scores of dream achievers, we must tell you right up front: Nobody pretends that it's easy to fulfill dreams. There is no single magic formula that will make all our dreams come true.

However, our analysis of dream achievers identified ten attributes that help people from all walks of life make their dreams come true. We've found that dream achievers master at least one of the essential elements we've identified. Most dream achievers master several.

We call these the "Ten Essential Elements of Dream CPR." Just as cardiopulmonary resuscitation, or CPR, saves lives by restoring a person's heartbeat and breathing, the essential elements of Dream CPR can revive your dreams of long ago. With Dream CPR, you'll be able to breathe new life into your aspirations and restore the pulse of your most heartfelt ambitions.

In Dream CPR:

C REPRESENTS THE ELEMENTS CONFIDENCE, COURAGE, COMMITMENT, AND CREATIVITY.

P STANDS FOR THE ELEMENTS PURPOSE, PASSION, AND PERSISTENCE.

R DENOTES THE ELEMENTS RESILIENCE, RISK, AND RESPONSIBILITY.

Despite what we've been taught, we don't have to be rich, famous, or distinguished to make our dreams come true. It takes qualities of far greater substance than these transient conditions to fulfill a dream. Consider the case of two ordinary brothers who achieved an extraordinary dream a century ago. Every space–age hero, from moonwalker Neil Armstrong to astronaut Sally Ride, owes a debt of gratitude to these two guys.

The brothers didn't have a lot of money to finance their big dream — both built and fixed bicycles for a living. They didn't have college degrees; in fact, neither graduated from high school. They pursued their dream in relative obscurity. Nobody with clout promoted or financed them. Some of their acquaintances thought they were out of their minds to attempt such an "impossible" feat.

Yet somehow, Wilbur and Orville Wright turned their audacious dream of powered human flight into reality. The Wright Brothers were first to design, build, and fly an engine–powered airplane without crashing. The now–historic, 12–second first flight Orville successfully completed over North Carolina's sandy shores on a windy December morn in 1903 ushered in the dawn of modern aviation. That maiden voyage altered the course of humanity, paving the way for commercial air travel, space exploration, and even satellite communications.

How did the Wright Brothers do it? Imbued in their character were the "Ten Essential Elements of Dream CPR."

They had **confidence** in their unique set of skills and strengths. They may not have been trained scientists or engineers, but they knew they were meticulous, detail–oriented problem solvers with mechanical aptitude and a keen ability to apply whatever they gleaned from books.

They also had ample **creativity** to design and build an airplane when none before had worked.

The brothers made a firm **commitment** to seeing their dream to fruition.

And they possessed tremendous **courage** to become human guinea pigs aboard their unproven flying contraptions!

The brothers shared a strong **passion** for achieving human flight — a fire first ignited by the unusual, helicopter–like toy they received as children.

Wilbur and Orville were elevated by a sense of **purpose** — by trying to achieve powered human flight, they were working toward something much bigger than themselves.

Persistence propelled them forward even when they were faced with far more work than they originally anticipated, like building their own airplane engine when others refused to construct one to meet their unconventional specifications.

Despite repeated failure, their **resilience** enabled them to bounce back stronger than ever with new ideas and solutions.

Their desire to achieve human flight was so strong that they were willing to **risk** everything — their savings, their reputation, even their personal safety — to attain success.

And despite the ridicule and doubts from others, Orville and Wilbur never abandoned their sense of **responsibility** — they knew that if ultimately they were to succeed, it was up to them to stay the course and go the distance.

Like other successful people, the Wright Brothers never stopped dreaming. And they never stopped *doing* — ever striving to turn their dream into reality.

The Elements of Dream CPR

> **"**I KNOW QUITE CERTAINLY THAT I MYSELF HAVE NO SPECIAL TALENT; CURIOSITY, OBSESSION AND DOGGED ENDURANCE, COMBINED WITH SELF—CRITICISM, HAVE BROUGHT ME TO MY IDEAS."
> — ALBERT EINSTEIN

The timeless qualities that served the Wright Brothers so well comprise Dream CPR, which we developed to help you breathe life back into your dreams. Dreamers and doers the caliber of the Wright Brothers are not just figures from the past. Successful dreamers are alive and well today. In fact, anyone can tap into these elements and, with the right guidance, make them their own.

CONFIDENCE: TRUST YOURSELF

Confidence amounts to believing in, trusting in, and relying upon yourself, including your judgment, your powers, and your abilities. It enables each of us to walk a path uniquely ours. You may have the support of mentors, role models, and teachers along the way, but nobody else, no matter how much you trust them, can tell you what your dreams are. Our dreams come from within us, and confidence lets us trust that we can make them come true. With confidence, we can trust our judgment like businesswoman Nancy Archuleta (Chapter 3) did: A former high—school dropout and teen mom, Nancy built a multimillion—dollar engineering company from the ground up.

COURAGE: SUMMON YOUR STRENGTH

Courage is the ability to face challenges. Courage gives us strength to hold on to our dreams in the midst of trying times. It gives us strength to overcome our own fears in the face of illness, a painful loss, or financial uncertainty. It's not always easy to be one of just a few people — or the only person — with a particular idea or vision, but courage gives us strength to continue forward with our plans. In 1954 , it took courage for a Native American girl to leave her home on the reservation and go to college; everybody around her told her she would fail. But Marigold Linton (Chapter 4) tapped into her courage to defy the naysayers. She not only earned a bachelor's degree, she went on to complete a doctorate degree and become a university professor.

COMMITMENT: STAY FOCUSED

Commitment — the act of devoting oneself fully to a goal — is what carries our dreams to fruition. It helps us focus on something that matters to us. Sometimes we become distracted, sidetracked, or discouraged while pursuing our dreams, so it's important to develop a high level of commitment to making our dreams come true right from the start. Elementary school teacher Barbara Vogel (Chapter 5) maintained such a steadfast commitment to her students that no critics or detractors could stand in her way. Barbara's unwavering support of her students' ambitious campaign has freed thousands of modern–day slaves halfway around the world.

CREATIVITY: IMAGINE YOUR REALITY

This is the marvelous quality that enables us to imagine and build — in short, to use our skills and talents to create. Without creativity, we'd be stuck: we'd never see anything new under the sun. With creativity, we have a powerful tool to first imagine the reality we want and then develop a plan to get there. The most creative people become some of our greatest innovators like Bill Nye (Chapter 6), who left a successful mechanical engineering career to establish himself in comedy. This unusual move led to the creation of "Bill Nye the Science Guy," a role he enjoys immensely. Today, he's in a position to help create a science–literate society and work on some of the most exciting scientific projects in the world.

PURPOSE: REACH HIGHER

Purpose is the reason why we strive for a particular goal. Going after a dream enables us to rise above the routine of everyday matters and reach for something higher, to find a greater purpose for our lives. After escaping her war–torn native Vietnam, Binh Rybacki (Chapter 7) rebuilt a stable life for herself in the United States as a computer specialist. But that wasn't enough for her — she felt compelled to help others in her homeland. Thus Binh found her purpose, and today she cares for thousands of orphaned children across the sea through her nonprofit organization. Purpose makes our dreams valuable and essential, no matter how unusual or unconventional they may seem.

PASSION: LOVE WHAT YOU DO

Passion — a compelling enthusiasm for an activity or purpose — defines and fuels our dreams. It is one of the most effective tools we have for creating a happy, meaningful, and fulfilling life. If you have ever felt such tremendous enthusiasm and desire for something that you would gladly spend all your waking hours working on it, that you would happily do without pay, then you have found your passion. Michael Clarke Duncan (Chapter 8) was a ditch–digger and bouncer with a passion for acting. With no theatrical background and nothing but a burning desire to act, he set out for Hollywood and beat the odds to reach his dream of becoming a movie actor — earning an Academy Award nomination along the way.

PERSISTENCE: KEEP TRYING

Persistence keeps us moving in the right direction. It's the quiet driving force that keeps us going even when we feel like quitting. Persistence means continuing firmly with a course of action despite obstacles and resistance. When the Wright Brothers could not find anyone to build the engine they needed to get off the ground safely, they persisted by building their own. Persistence and determination got journalist Barbara Walters (Chapter 9) to the top of television news at a time when network news was an exclusive boys' club, despite starting out as a writer with a speech impediment and no on-camera experience. With persistence, Barbara created her own breaks to become one of the most widely known and highly respected journalists on television.

RESILIENCE: BOUNCE BACK

Resilience, the ability to recover from adversity, makes us survivors. When pursuing a dream, sometimes we will get knocked flat on our backs. Or somewhere along the road, our dream might be snatched right out of our hands. When that happens, we can't afford to stay stuck in sorrow and defeat. We have to get back up and reclaim our dream. Writer and poet Maya Angelou (Chapter 10) has overcome great adversity, including racial discrimination and sexual assault that left her in a long self–imposed silence. But her resilience enabled her to march forward with grace, hope, and courage — to find her voice and become one of the most eloquent writers of our times.

RISK: TAKE A LEAP OF FAITH

The adage "nothing ventured, nothing gained" rings so true. Risk–taking opens greater possibilities. Following our dreams almost always requires us to take chances. There is no guarantee that we will succeed in our venture. But if we don't try, we will never know how far we can go. More than 20 years ago, electrical engineer David Howard (Chapter 11) began to dream about running his own computer business. But with kids to raise, a mortgage to pay, and a tough market to crack, the timing never seemed right — until the day he decided to take a leap of faith and become an independent consultant. That, in turn, led David to start his own successful software company.

RESPONSIBILITY: CHOOSE WISELY

Responsibility means we are accountable for something within our power. Each of us has dreams, and only we — not our teachers, friends, or family members — are responsible for what we do with these dreams. We each have a unique set of qualities and gifts, some that we were born with and others that we develop over time. What we do with these gifts is our choice. After enjoying a rewarding career in film and television, the late Dennis Weaver (Chapter 12) could have simply retired and lived a comfortable, secluded life. Instead, he chose to use his many gifts, including his ability to speak to crowds with ease, his public appeal, and his integrity, to motivate people to develop environmentally friendly business solutions.

Becoming a Dream Achiever

> "FOLLOW YOUR HEART, AND IT WILL TAKE YOU WHERE YOU NEED TO GO. IF YOU APPROACH ANYTHING THAT YOU FEEL VERY PASSIONATE ABOUT WITH THE PERSPECTIVE OF LOVE AND CARING FOR OTHERS, IT CAN HAPPEN." — JANETTE FENNELL, SAFETY ADVOCATE (CHAPTER 9)

Whether the dream achievers we interviewed are famous, like Harrison Ford and Jimmy and Rosalyn Carter, or known only within their professional circles, we found at least one Dream CPR element incorporated into every fiber of their being. For Harrison Ford, that element is confidence, although he definitely exhibits many other essential elements as well. For the Carters, it's purpose, but they've certainly also mastered courage, commitment, passion, persistence, resilience, risk, and responsibility.

The more Dream CPR essential elements you learn to master, the better equipped you will be to achieve your dreams. As you read the real–life accounts of dream achievers, you'll see that achieving dreams is a noble venture that doesn't require us to be selfish or self–absorbed. In fact, the most successful dream achievers are quite selfless — their stories show how achieving dreams leads to greater fulfillment, joy, and harmony for individuals, communities, and, ultimately, for society as a whole. Learning to integrate the Dream CPR essential elements more fully into our lives is one of the greatest gifts we can give to ourselves, our loved ones, and all of humankind.

Dream CPR Journal

List everything that you like to do.

Ask yourself: If I had only six months to live, what would I do today?

Remember, there is no single path to attaining dreams: We all must create our own individual road maps. But the stories presented here will guide you toward reviving your long–lost dreams and help you breathe life into your new ones. These stories will help you gain your footing as you set out on your exciting journey to becoming a successful dream achiever. We'll start by building the confidence so necessary for taking that first step.

chapter 3

confidence: Believe In Yourself

" IF ONE ADVANCES CONFIDENTLY IN THE DIRECTION OF HIS DREAMS, AND ENDEAVORS TO LIVE THE LIFE WHICH HE HAD IMAGINED, HE WILL MEET WITH A SUCCESS UNEXPECTED IN COMMON HOURS." — HENRY DAVID THOREAU

Let's fast–forward a moment. There you are, launching your dream. With gusto and energy you advance, making great strides. But then, without warning, turbulence hits. Progress grinds to a halt. People begin to question your dream. Some say outright that you will never reach it. Your own doubts surface: *What did I get myself into? How much longer can I hang on? Will I ever achieve my dream?* You have to choose. Do you keep going, or do you give up the dream? Sadly, many people quit when they run into trouble. But the confident dreamer continues to move forward, even in the face of doubt and discouragement.

The Dream CPR essential element *confidence* can help each of us hold tightly to a dream in the presence of uncertainty, turmoil, rejection, even tragedy. As you follow your life's ambitions, you'll see that confidence can shield you against dream–crushing ridicule and protect you against doubts.

Actor Harrison Ford, writer and champion skier Cale Kenney, and CEO Nancy Archuleta experienced plenty of doubt and upheaval in their lives. For years, Harrison simply could not break into Hollywood no matter how hard he tried. Cale's dreams seemed doomed when an accident took her leg. Nancy's dreams were placed on hold when she became pregnant at 15 and dropped out of high school. But by tapping into their confidence, these inspiring individuals clutched their dreams through the darkest storms and, ultimately, achieved their most heartfelt ambitions. Harrison's confidence helped him overcome Hollywood setbacks to become a phenomenally successful actor. Even with her left leg missing, Cale mustered the courage to try skiing and gained the confidence of a champion. Nancy rose above the struggles of her past to become CEO of one of the fastest–growing Hispanic–owned companies in the nation.

Having confidence means trusting our ability to achieve the goals we set. It means believing that our dreams will come true, even when life doesn't go as planned. We're all born with some level of confidence, and whenever we experience a measure of success, no matter how minute, our innate confidence grows. Then when the road gets rocky, the Dream CPR essential element *confidence* helps us hold on to our dreams, the way it helped Cale, Nancy, and Harrison.

Just like these confident dreamers, you have a unique vision that means something to you, even if nobody else understands it. And you, too, can tap into your confidence to keep following your dream in the midst of discouragement.

HARRISON FORD:
ACTING ON HIS OWN TERMS

He'd been a quiet, somewhat shy kid, and even today, public speaking makes him nervous. But time and again, Harrison Ford's natural confidence lifted him over daunting hurdles. He had the confidence to defy studio bigwigs who

said he couldn't act, and to stay true to himself rather than
sell out to Hollywood. Perhaps that's why his fans like him
so much — Harrison has the confidence to live out his
dreams without compromising himself.

It seemed that his dream was finally starting to come true.
Ever since that autumn day in 1964 when he drove his dilapidated Volkswagen van into sunny California, Harrison Ford had
toiled to become a professional film actor. Now, a year and a half
later, he was making his film debut playing a bellboy in the spy
flick *Dead Heat on a Merry–Go–Round.* The 23–year–old arrived at the Columbia Studios lot well–rehearsed and ready to
go. Looking debonair in his bellhop uniform but somewhat out of
place with his trademark half–smile, he delivered his line: "Paging Mr. Jones. Paging Mr. Jones."

Nobody on the set realized they were watching the young actor
take his first steps in a long, treacherous climb to international
stardom. In fact, if powerful studio producer Jerry Tokovsky had
gotten his way, that first film would have been Harrison's last.

"You ain't got it, kid. You ain't got it!" he admonished after
summoning Harrison into his office. The producer said that actor
Tony Curtis looked like a movie star even on his first performance delivering a bag of groceries. He made it crystal clear that
Tony had what Hollywood wanted but Harrison didn't.

Harrison's heart sank, but he had too much self–confidence
and integrity to stand there and take it. His anger bubbled to the
surface. With fire in his eyes, Harrison retorted that he thought
the point of Tony Curtis' performance was to get audiences to
think "grocery clerk," not "movie star." At that, the enraged producer threw Harrison out of the office, promising he wouldn't
work in another movie anytime soon.

And so it was. Harrison didn't land his second movie role for
another six months. Under contract with Columbia for a mere
$150 a week — half of which paid his rent — Harrison was at the
mercy of the studio executives' whims. He could have given up on
movies, packed up his few belongings, and moved back to the
Midwest. Instead he held his own, swimming upstream against a

torrent of rejection and humiliation. Harrison's confidence in his acting ability, along with his ambition to become a career film actor, propelled him forward.

Harrison had unknowingly stumbled into a shallow Hollywood empire that expected to hear, *Yes, sir. No, sir. Anything you say, sir*, from its initiate actors. His clashes with movie industry powerhouses held him back for years, but his confidence and integrity proved crucial to his phenomenal success in the long run. It wasn't until cinematic geniuses like George Lucas and Steven Spielberg came onto the Hollywood scene that Harrison had the opportunity to engage in intelligent, creative dialogue with directors and producers, and get his deserved break.

Born in Chicago in 1942, young Harrison had the good fortune to spend his formative years in a loving, stable household. The sunny personality of his mother, a former radio actress, created a positive environment while the outside–the–box thinking of his father, an advertising copywriter, encouraged Harrison to ask questions before drawing conclusions — in short, to think for himself. As a result, Harrison never hesitated to question authority, be it that of a professor or a producer.

Acting never really crossed Harrison's mind while he was growing up. In high school, he preferred behind–the–scenes roles: He joined the audiovisual club and provided technical help at his school's radio station. After graduating in 1960, he enrolled at Ripon College in Wisconsin and settled into a philosophy major. But Harrison's life took a drastic turn when he took a drama class during his junior year and then was cast as the lead in *The Threepenny Opera* at the Red Barn, Ripon's theater.

It wasn't quite love at first sight. During his inaugural performances, Harrison's legs shook and a trace of terror unmistakably crossed his face as he stood on stage looking out at the audience. But acting awakened something inside himself — he felt transformed, alive, empowered. Harrison impressed audiences and surprised himself by what he could accomplish on stage. He performed so well that he won the lead in the school's next production, *The Fantastics*.

But it was his extraordinary performance as a comical inventor in *The Skin of Our Teeth* that convinced Harrison to pursue acting in earnest. He left Ripon without a degree but with a newfound sense of purpose. In a 1986 interview with the Woodland Hills, California, *Daily News*, Harrison recalled that: "My only ambition was simply to work as an actor. But it didn't come naturally at all. I was shy. I had a fear of getting up in front of people ... It certainly helped when you could put on a mustache or dye your hair black and become somebody else."

Harrison's college performances led to a summer–stock acting opportunity with the Belfry Players in Williams Bay, Wisconsin, on the shores of Lake Geneva. As it turned out, California film director and acting coach William Fucik was directing at the Belfry that summer of 1964. Harrison was elated with the opportunity to become a paid actor and grateful for both compliments and criticism. The whirlwind season featured six plays in three months, and Harrison kept busy building sets when not rehearsing or performing. He made his professional acting debut with a small part in *Take Her, She's Mine*, then played the lead in *Little Mary Sunshine.* By the end of the summer, Harrison had shed much of his shyness and received enough praise from the director, audiences, and reviewers that he felt confident to take a colossal leap and give Hollywood a try. With great anticipation, Harrison and his bride, Mary, stuffed their belongings into their beat–up van and headed for California.

William Fucik, who saw tremendous potential in Harrison, graciously opened his ocean–view home to the young couple until they found their own place. He also groomed Harrison for the movies. The Midwesterner learned to surf in case a beach–party movie role came his way, and to ride horses in hopes of a Western. Harrison constantly memorized and rehearsed lines he heard on TV. And he did whatever was necessary to get by financially, from refurbishing boats to being an assistant buyer in a department store. He even delivered pizzas.

Almost a year passed before Harrison netted a contract with Columbia. Then he waited another six months for his first movie role, the bellhop bit that he hoped would lead to greater opportunities. So after Jerry Tokovsky's scathing criticism, it took a lot of confidence for Harrison to keep auditioning. Still, there was one thing Harrison never could overcome — that producer's lingering disdain. After earning small parts in only three movies, Columbia released Harrison from his contract. Once again, the young actor tapped into his confidence, signing with Universal Studios just three days later. Although his ambition was to appear in movies, Harrison accepted minor television roles at Universal to support his growing family.

It wasn't until March 1967 — two–and–a–half years after he'd moved to California — that Harrison finally landed a meaty part in the cowboy flick *Journey to Shiloh*. His performance earned him a trip to New York to audition for *Midnight Cowboy*, a movie that could have jump–started his career. Instead, he watched the lead go to Jon Voight. Harrison also auditioned for the lead in *The Graduate*, the role that launched Dustin Hoffman's film career. Disappointed but not defeated, Harrison kept auditioning.

As with Columbia, Universal released Harrison from his contract. As an independent actor, he managed to land an occasional role, but not enough of them to pay the bills. Harrison was in a difficult spot: Despite his talent, determination, and willingness to work hard, his acting career was floundering. He couldn't rely on acting to feed his family. In addition, every rejection Hollywood dished out was taking its toll. Harrison became moody, withdrawn, even depressed. He decided to take a break from acting and turn his carpentry hobby into a paying venture.

Through his Hollywood connections, Harrison was able to make a living building furniture and remodeling the homes of directors, agents, and entertainers — sometimes with a home improvement textbook in one hand and a hammer in the other. Ever the perfectionist, he taught himself to do beautiful work. Demand for his carpentry services grew, giving Harrison the success that had so far eluded him as an actor. That success helped restore his self–confidence. "Through carpentry, I fed my family and began to pick and choose from among the roles offered," he said in 1986. "I could afford to hold out until something better came along. But I never gave up my ambition to be an actor. I was frustrated but never felt defeated by my frustration."

His renewed confidence helped Harrison say "No thanks" when asked to appear in mouthwash commercials. The pay would have been better than he could earn as a carpenter and a small fortune compared to what he made as a part–time actor. But Harrison sensed that doing commercials before establishing himself as an actor would typecast him, jeopardizing his dream to be a film actor. He even declined an offer to play Archie Bunker's son–in–law, "Meathead," in *All In The Family*. Although later hailed as a groundbreaking exploration of race relations, Harrison, like many others at the time, felt the show's openly prejudiced lead character glorified bigotry and his conscience simply would not allow him to take part. Harrison preferred to continue as a carpenter.

It took tremendous confidence in himself to turn down lucrative TV commercials and sit–coms. Somewhere deep inside, Harrison knew that every failure, every rejection he had endured during his quest, was not in vain. He trusted that his break would materialize and his dream would come true — and if it didn't come anytime soon, he was fine building furniture for the stars while he waited.

It took eight years for Harrison to land a movie role that audiences would remember. In 1972, George Lucas cast the 30–year–old Harrison as Falfa, the overage hot–rodder in *American Graffiti*. Harrison was ecstatic. It seemed he was finally moving forward with his dream. But even after his stellar performance in *American Graffiti*, Harrison's struggles didn't end. Acting jobs were still slow in coming and Harrison had to keep working as a carpenter while he clung to his dream.

Then one day in 1975, when he least expected it, he got the chance of a lifetime.

George Lucas was looking for the right person to play Han Solo for his upcoming *Star Wars*. He wasn't interested in using anyone from *American Graffiti*; he wanted a fresh new cast. But after auditioning hundreds of actors, he remained empty–handed. None fit the part. Harrison the carpenter happened to be remodeling the offices where casting was taking place. Watching Harrison hammer nails and saw wood, George realized that his Solo had been right in front of him the whole time.

Now Harrison had a chance to show the world what he could do. His diverse acting skills, including character development and well–timed humor, gelled in *Star Wars*. When the film was released in 1977 to unprecedented box–office success, Harrison had reached his dream in earnest. He was a bona fide film actor.

Fourteen uncertain years of learning and perfecting his craft had finally paid off. Harrison had endured humiliation and persevered through fruitless auditions. Many others would have quit, but Harrison's confidence bred persistence and resilience, enabling him to hang on to his goals. Harrison knew something that shortsighted movie executives did not — that he could act. And he would, not in commercials or sit–coms but in movies that drew big audiences.

Star Wars led to Harrison starring as Indiana Jones in *Raiders of the Lost Ark*. Filming began in 1980 when Harrison was 37. Although it was hard work, he had a blast portraying Indy, even spending hours on end learning to expertly handle a bullwhip. Director Steven Spielberg valued Harrison's creative input: Harrison came up with Indy's classic line, "I don't know, I'm making this up as I go." And when Indy's love interest informed him he's not the same man she knew ten years ago, Harrison cleverly improvised with: "It's not the years, it's the mileage."

Not everything was fun and games. During filming, Harrison endured grueling heat, dysentery, and even a propeller plane running over his leg. In the memorable scene in which Indy outruns a gigantic boulder, the "fake" plaster–of–paris rock weighed several hundred pounds. Harrison had to do ten takes, risking his life each time, but he didn't mind working hard or doing his own stunts. He turned Indiana Jones into a human hero — adventurous yet vulnerable, strong but sensitive, confident enough to chase his dreams. Someone not unlike Harrison himself.

After the *Star Wars* and *Indiana Jones* trilogies, the tables had turned. Movie executives no longer chastised Harrison, they sought him. To date, he's appeared in more than 30 feature films, with the *Star Wars* and *Indiana Jones* movies still among the top–grossing ever made. He's received four Golden Globe nominations over the years, and he earned an Oscar nomination for best actor for his performance as the high–principled detective in *Witness*.

It was Harrison's confidence that carried him to the fulfillment of his dream — even during the lean times of his career when he was discredited, could barely pay his utility bills, and left one audition after another without a role. In the cutthroat world of Hollywood, Harrison Ford held on to enough confidence to reach his lofty dream without sacrificing his principles — and that's something to applaud.

CALE KENNEY: WILD WOMAN ON SKIS

We've all hit lows in our lives. Sometimes these lows can knock the dreams right out of us, threatening our very ability to dream. That's what happened to Cale Kenney. Her world turned upside–down in an instant when a tragic motorcycle accident took her left leg. But confidence enabled Cale to hold onto her last hope while battling excruciating pain. And confidence helped her achieve dreams she never even imagined before her debilitating accident, prompting her to become an athlete, an adventurer, and a writer. Cale shows us how large we can dream, despite our limitations.

Riding with her friend Mark on his motorcycle, 19–year–old Cale Kenney felt great. The petite blonde with the sunny smile and contagious joie de vivre had only a French final left, the last exam of her first year in college. Cale looked forward to acing her test, then enjoying a fun, relaxing summer break.

But she never got to take that exam. A car plowed into them head–on, killing Mark instantly and throwing Cale twenty feet into the air. She struck a telephone pole, shattering her pelvis and breaking both legs. An ambulance rushed Cale to the hospital where doctors and nurses worked on her around the clock. But they were powerless against gangrene: To save her life, they had to amputate. Cale lost everything on her left side from the waist down — her leg, her hip, and her pelvis. In one moment, her life changed forever.

Cale remained hospitalized for four–and–a–half months, battling excruciating physical pain. Her heart broke to pieces as she grieved the loss of her friend, her leg, and her way of life. But through the pain and sorrow, one thought stood out clearly: Cale wanted to go back to school and finish her college degree.

It was an ambitious dream. She knew that getting around campus on crutches would be arduous. Cale would have to re–master what she once took for granted — walking, climbing steps, getting out of bed without falling on her face. With only half her buttocks remaining, even sitting was difficult.

But she knew that she wanted to return to the stimulating exchange of knowledge and ideas that she missed immensely. With confidence and dogged determination, Cale turned to vocational rehabilitation to help her get back to school. By January — almost eight months after the accident — Cale was back on campus.

Her return was an amazing accomplishment, but those closest to Cale knew she wouldn't have had it any other way. Books and school had been her best friends her entire life. As a curious pre–kindergartner, she had fallen in love with the written word thanks to a creative elderly neighbor with a heart for children. "She had built a little library on her sun porch," Cale recalls. "And there we were, all the tattered kids in the neighborhood, given library cards by this neighbor to borrow her books. I remember thinking at the time that this was the neatest lady!"

The eldest of eight children, Cale had a difficult home life growing up in Revere, Massachusetts. She had to accept the death of a sister and deal with her father's schizophrenia. She served as her siblings' caretaker while her mother worked to support the family. Cale found respite across the street at the public library, where she could open her mind to greater possibilities. At the library, she could dream.

"I can't remember what book it was," she says, recalling one of her favorites, "but it had a reporter character who really caught my fancy. It was somebody whose curiosity gave them license to roam and explore the world. I thought that a reporter's experience was a privilege that the average person didn't have. I wanted that kind of adventurous life."

Compassionate librarians took Cale under their wings, and with their mentoring, she began to realize she was bright. Her ninth—grade IQ test scores verified what the librarians already knew — Cale was gifted. Previously overlooked in school, Cale moved up to the accelerated track and absolutely bloomed. She absorbed challenging material quickly and earned top grades, sending her confidence soaring.

Still, with her family living on the edge of poverty, Cale was convinced that college was out of the question. That changed after a high school teacher urged her to continue her education, and an aunt and uncle helped her apply for financial aid. With outstanding grades and financial assistance, she enrolled at the University of Massachusetts at Amherst. College turned out to be everything Cale ever wanted, and more. She thrived in an academically charged environment, both before and after the motorcycle accident.

Two years after losing her left leg and hip, Cale surprised everyone, including herself. The self—proclaimed bookworm who had never been an athlete took up skiing after a friend who was also a recent amputee urged her to try. At first Cale thought: "And break my remaining leg?" But after she saw disabled skiers in Vermont — some blind, others missing limbs — gracefully gliding down powder—white slopes, something tugged at Cale's soul. The skiers were so free. Cale longed to feel that freedom and grace.

Terrified, Cale mustered the courage to give it a try. Her first attempts were far from freeing or graceful. Just getting up on one ski proved virtually impossible. Every time Cale tried to stand, she fell right back down. Progress was slow and agonizing. Time and again, Cale wanted to quit. But her indomitable spirit would not let her give up. First she worked on balance, then she tackled maneuvering, and finally, she began to gain speed. Each small success boosted her confidence, giving her the energy to try again. Soon other skiers smiled whenever Cale sped past emitting her "wild woman" whoops that soon became her trademark. Cale felt she'd received a wake–up call to live life to the fullest. Skiing had brought back her spirit and restored her self–confidence.

By the time she earned her bachelor's degree with a major in English, Cale was a completely new woman. She had gradually re–invented herself into someone more adventurous than she had ever been before. By overcoming her physical limitations to fulfill not only her lifelong dream of completing college but also a new ambition to ski, Cale's self–confidence reached a higher level than she had ever known.

Cale then tapped into her confidence to follow another new dream: to live and ski in the Rocky Mountains. This would mean leaving friends and family, and the team of medical experts who had been treating her since the accident. Partly scared but ultimately up to the challenge, Cale moved halfway across the country to the friendly ski resort community of Winter Park, Colorado, in 1977. "Colorado has a wildness that really appeals to my nature," she explains with a laugh.

As a child, Cale had learned to get by with little. Now that ability came in handy. She lived in a mountain mobile home on just the $300 a month provided by Social Security Disability Income, plus whatever she could earn teaching ski classes. But she felt rich beyond her wildest dreams. Cale lived to ski, hitting the slopes every morning whether it was sunny or snowing or bitterly cold. "All of a sudden, I had this life that was just as glamorous and exciting as [the life] I had wanted with two legs," she says.

"And I felt that it was less likely that I would have found this society if I had not had my accident."

Skiing gave Cale the confidence to keep dreaming and to share her dreams with others. She confided in friends one dream she had long kept tucked away: to become a professional writer. Word reached the editor of the local newspaper, and Cale visited the offices of *The Winter Park Manifest*. "I went there," she recalls, "and said, 'You know, what you really need is a proofreader very badly!' Since they couldn't afford one, I volunteered my time."

Cale did such a spectacular job proofreading that the editor hired her as a staff reporter. Cale could hardly believe it — her childhood dream had come true. She covered local magic shows and ski races, and wrote about equipment for disabled skiers. When the ski resort had new chairlifts installed, Cale had the best view in town — on board a helicopter as it dropped giant poles into the ground. Cale quickly advanced from newspaper apprentice to sports reporter and columnist.

While becoming a journalist, Cale surprised herself again by becoming a ski racer. She could zip down a mountain on one ski at an amazing speed — faster than most people could on two skis. She began winning medals at competitions for disabled skiers, and she became the national champion in 1979. At the 1980 Winter Paralympic Games in Norway, Cale placed an impressive seventh. In 1982, she injured her knee just two days before the Alpine Ski World Championships for the Disabled in Switzerland. The injury terrified her. It put her back in the hospital for two weeks, followed by seven weeks in a wheelchair with her leg in a cast. She never wanted to experience that helplessness again and so she decided to retire from competition — after one more fling, that is. At the 1983 national championships in Squaw Valley, California, Cale won two silver medals. Then she retired from competitive skiing.

Cale's self–confidence kept pushing her to try adventurous things she had never considered back when she had both legs. She learned to sail. She boogie–boarded in Kauai's intense surf. She walked a mile down the Grand Canyon on crutches. And not only has Cale realized many of her own dreams, she has encouraged other women to do the same.

"I took a course called Writing The Wild Woman," she recalls. "When the instructor left town, I took over teaching that class. And that's when something occurred to me. I looked around and was struck by how these women were writing things that were so deep from their souls. They were good writers, but they were everyday people who weren't published. So I came up with the idea of publishing a literary magazine."

From a home-based desktop publishing setup, Cale launched *Howlings: A Magazine for the Wild Women of the West*, which became a vehicle for publishing the exceptional work of her students and other new writers. "The project was constantly growing and evolving," she says. "*Howlings* was a force in the community. I'd arrange readings for many of these writers in bookstores. There was a mixing of wonderful energies that went on, and I felt really good to be in the middle of it."

Cale has just embarked on an exciting new chapter in her life: In May 2003 she released her first book, *Have Crutch, Will Travel: The Adventures of a Modern-Day Calamity Jane*, a collection of true, humorous accounts from her fascinating life. Adding "author" to her impressive list of accolades, she's having a ball making friends at book signings and release parties.

Confidence has continually enabled Cale to envision and reach higher and higher ambitions. Cale shows all of us that big dreams can be achieved despite tragedy, physical limitations, or a lack of money. For Cale, the desire to reach a dream, the guts to pursue it, and the confidence that she can do it have enabled her to make all of her dreams come true.

NANCY ARCHULETA: FROM HIGH SCHOOL DROPOUT TO HIGH-TECH CEO

Without marketable skills or even a high school diploma, Nancy Archuleta's employment prospects were severely limited. Confidence helped the teenage mom go back to school, build a successful career in insurance, and create the financial security she dreamed of for herself and her children. Confidence later enabled her to become the CEO of a high-tech company. Her story shows us that we never have to settle for less.

As a spunky and smart little girl, Nancy Archuleta dreamed of an exciting life as an astronomer, astronaut, or world traveler. Many times she climbed the tall willow tree behind her house in Las Cruces, New Mexico, gazed confidently at the night sky, and proclaimed, "I can reach the stars. I can reach the stars!"

But as a teenager, Nancy felt terribly lonely and uncertain. Seeking love, she became pregnant at 15. Her peers' stares and snickers hurt, and Nancy soon dropped out of high school. After having her baby and marrying her boyfriend, she settled into the roles of mother and wife. More babies followed in rapid succession — she had four children by the time she was 20. "When people ask me about my teenage years, I ask, 'What are those?'" Nancy says now. "I really never was a teenager. When I became pregnant, I went directly to adulthood."

While her friends dated and went to dances, Nancy took care of babies and toddlers around the clock. Her husband offered little support. Young and sometimes angry to the point of violence, he had a hard time holding down a job. The family struggled financially and Nancy worried about her children. She wanted them to grow up in a safe environment, with enough food on the table and good clothes to wear to school.

Nancy looked for a job, but the best she could get was waiting tables at a doughnut shop for less than minimum wage. Unhappy with her prospects, Nancy began to revisit her childhood aspirations. She figured it was too late to become an astronaut or an astronomer, but not too late to build a respectable career that would provide financial security for her family and give herself a sense of accomplishment. Nancy dreamed of becoming a successful businesswoman.

The first step, enrolling in night school, was the hardest. But her parents cheered Nancy on as she returned to school and balanced her life as best she could. "I very seldom slept," she recalls.

"I learned to prioritize chores, work, school, and family life." With help from her mother and a close cousin, who took turns watching her children while Nancy worked and went to school, the former dropout earned her high school diploma. Her accomplishment boosted Nancy's confidence to a level that she hadn't known since childhood.

Her newfound success gave Nancy the confidence to take college courses. Each class she successfully completed propelled her to continue forward. "My self–esteem grew from going to school and getting good grades," Nancy says. "And as my self–esteem grew, so did my self–confidence. It happened over time, class by class, step by step."

By the time her marriage dissolved, the 27–year–old Nancy had completed college classes in business administration, psychology, and economics. This helped the newly single mom obtain a well–paying job as a Prudential Insurance agent. In this business environment, she discovered several things about herself that elevated her self–confidence further.

"I learned that I am good at reading people by tuning into my intuition," Nancy says. "Since a big part of business is building trust in relationships, this skill comes in handy. And I began to see that I have good negotiating skills." Within three years, she had been promoted to division manager, but Nancy set her sights even higher. Dreaming of having the independence and flexibility to better balance the demands of her work and her family, Nancy tapped into her confidence to open her own insurance agency. Nancy felt fulfilled: Her children and her business brought her both joy and a wonderful sense of purpose.

But at age 40, Nancy got the opportunity to pursue some of the excitement she had envisioned for herself as a child. In 1985, Nancy and several other business professionals were approached with an offer to invest in a start–up business — a printed circuit boards manufacturing company. It was a prosperous time for engineering, and Nancy was poised to seize the opportunity of a lifetime. She had always been fascinated with technology; here was a chance to invest in something that could take off flying. Nancy and three others signed on a line of credit for start–up financing for the business, which they named Mesilla Valley High Tech Industries, Inc. The businessman who had approached them with the idea became a consultant for the company.

At first Nancy and her fellow investors listened to their consultant, but it wasn't long before they began to feel used. He promoted the company as a woman–owned and minority–owned small business to gain access to government contracts, yet completely ignored the sound business ideas of the very women he was promoting. In fact, they felt he was making irrational business decisions. So Nancy and the other investors mutually agreed that with thousands of dollars at stake, the company needed a new leader, one who would steer clear of financial ruin. As the chair of the board, Nancy stepped in as the struggling start–up's president and CEO.

"I was voted in because I was the only one willing to step up to the plate," Nancy recalls. "I said, 'Give me six months. I'll pay off the line of credit. But in return, I'm to get all the stock.'" The other investors agreed to her terms. They weren't sure she could guide the company to financial stability, but with no other viable options to protect their investment, they were willing to let Nancy try.

"Everybody kept saying, 'You're just never gonna make it,'" Nancy recalls. "And every time somebody said that, I became more and more convinced that I was going to make it."

Listening to her intuition as she took the company reigns, Nancy quickly secured investment capital to pay off $50,000 of the company's total debt. Using the sound marketing and financial practices that she had learned in the insurance industry — not to mention the negotiating and management skills she had acquired as a mom — Nancy guided the company to financial health. And despite being a newcomer to the high–tech industry, Nancy found the confidence to take calculated business risks: In

1988, she decided to redefine the company as an engineering, technical, and management services provider for both private companies and government agencies. The move from the manufacturing sector to the service sector positioned the company perfectly to be in step with the new economy. In 1989, Nancy renamed the company MEVATEC, a catchy acronym for Million Electron Volts/Amps Technology, to convey the firm's power and productivity.

For more than 18 years, Chief Executive Officer Nancy Archuleta has led MEVATEC well. Named by *Hispanic Business Magazine* as one of the nation's fastest–growing Hispanic–owned companies in terms of gross revenues, MEVATEC in 1997 was awarded the largest U.S. Army small business contract ever, to the tune of $833 million. Now employing 450 people at 13 sites and serving customers such as NASA, Nancy is justifiably proud of her company's success.

She continues to apply valuable life lessons to running her company. "The first one," she says, "is that you always treat people with respect. Remember the golden rule: Do unto others as you'd have them do unto you. If you have a values system in place, then making decisions becomes easy. I don't treat my business any differently than I treated my children." Her matriarchal style of management has created a corporate culture focused on teamwork, enthusiasm, and mutual respect, where each employee is valued and creativity is fostered. Nancy encourages her employees, many of whom are disabled, to continually grow professionally through training, education, and increased levels of responsibility.

"My personal vision statement is a quote from Mohandas Gandhi: 'Let me be the change I wish to see in others,'" Nancy continues. "That to me is the essence of running a successful business." Through her involvement with the U.S. Small Business Administration's Mentor Protégée Program, Nancy models this success for other small–business owners, particularly women and minority entrepreneurs in the high–tech sector. MEVATEC also gives back to the community at large, setting an example of corporate responsibility through its generous donations of both time and money. Perhaps not surprisingly, the National Children's Advocacy Center tops the list of charitable organizations that Nancy's company supports.

The girl who dreamed of reaching the stars grew up to reach astronomical heights. As a successful CEO, Nancy's leadership and vision touch many lives: Organizations from Entrepreneur Expo to the U.S. Hispanic Chamber of Commerce have invited Nancy to share her inspiring story with audiences, and even co-medienne Joan Rivers has named Nancy as a personal role model. The one–time high school dropout could have ended up as a welfare mom, but instead she overcame the challenges of her youth to build the life of her dreams. Nancy not only built up her own self–confidence, she has inspired confidence in her children, her grandchildren, and many other people along the way.

Build Your Confidence

"SOME PEOPLE THINK SUCCESS IS JUST LUCK. THAT'S NOT TRUE. IT TAKES EFFORT AND LOTS OF HARD WORK. BUT IF YOU THINK POSITIVELY ABOUT YOURSELF, YOU CAN ACHIEVE YOUR GOALS." — CARL N. KARCHER, ENTREPRENEUR AND RESTAURANTEUR (CHAPTER 8)

Confidence helps each dreamer overcome discouragement to keep pursuing a dream. Likewise, following your dreams builds your confidence. It's a symbiotic relationship. After losing her leg, Cale Kenney was broken in both body and spirit. But through the fog of pain and sadness, she held on to one dream — to finish college. She knew she could do it if she put everything she had into pursuing that dream. Her self–confidence gave her strength to return to school, and going back to college gave her the confidence to create and go after new dreams.

A big part of building the confidence to follow your dream is to tell yourself that you can do it if you want to. It's your choice. Cale wanted to go back to college, even though hobbling around campus on crutches would be painful, even if sitting for every lecture would be torturous. Nobody would have blamed her if she had given up. But she wanted to return to college so badly that she told herself she could do it, even with limitations. And she did.

Just like Cale, you must trust yourself. You must want to achieve your dreams and believe in your ability. Harrison Ford kept believing in himself, even when a studio producer told him that he couldn't act. He wanted to be an actor, and he knew he could act, so he just kept trying. Ultimately, he succeeded.

Just like the producer told Harrison, "You ain't got it, kid," some people will try to tell you that you don't have what it takes to reach your dreams. Baloney. You've got what it takes, and you know it. Develop your confidence and tap into it when others doubt, ridicule, or belittle your dreams. Confidence is your shield against every awful thing anybody has said or will say — you can't, you're not good enough, or there's no way you can get it done, like the doomsayers who tried to convince Nancy Archuleta to give up. These words hurt, but we can't allow ourselves to believe such soul–killing lies.

Think back: Have you lost confidence in yourself because of what others have said? Have you forgotten a dream because somewhere along the road, you came to believe it could not be done? Have you ever given up a dream because you believed you couldn't reach it, or because you were sidetracked by life circumstances, or because of past failures? You're not alone. A lot of people have given up their dreams and lost confidence in themselves.

Everybody feels down in the dumps sometimes. Right now, you may be facing financial, emotional, health, or spiritual issues. But you must understand that this is temporary. It's difficult, but it's not forever. Cale was at rock bottom for months after her tragic motorcycle accident, but her confidence helped pull her back up. A frustrated Harrison felt shut out of Hollywood for years. Look at the confident actor now. No matter how bad things get, the confident dreamer can envision something better and start working to make that vision a reality.

It's time to reclaim your dream — and yourself. Let the Dream CPR essential element *confidence* be your ally. Boost your confidence by following these steps:

1 Revisit as many of your successes in life as you can recall. Use your own definition of "success," not somebody else's. Go way back. Remember your successes from grade school, high school, work, home, trips and vacations, at every stage of your life. Remember the times you felt justifiably proud of something you accomplished. Probe deeply. As these memories surface, write them down in your journal. No measure of success is too small to list.

2 Look over your list and pick out some of the highlights. For each item you've chosen, immerse yourself in the memory. Feel the pride and joy your success brought you. Feel how your confidence rose. Feel how that confidence gave you the energy to try new things. Remember how good success and confidence feel.

3 Reclaim your confidence to follow your dreams. Write down this affirmation: "I am creative and confident. I can accomplish the goals I set for myself. I reclaim my confidence. I reclaim my power to create." Take a moment every day to repeat this affirmation out loud. Copy it and post it throughout your home. Say it whenever your confidence needs a boost.

4 Practice setting and achieving goals. For each goal, continue trying until you reach it. For example, set a goal to walk a mile, then do it by going out every day and walking just a little bit further each time. Or set a goal to finish one chapter a day of a book you've been wanting to read, and set aside the time you need to achieve that goal. The more you integrate goals into your daily life and achieve them, the more your confidence will grow.

5 Use your imagination to help you believe in yourself. Close your eyes and picture yourself joyous and successful. If negative thoughts creep in, mentally push them away and focus on positive images. Envision yourself discovering and following your dream. Find a quiet moment to bring that image up each day, even several times a day. Believe, right down to the core of your being, that you are worthy of joy and success and that your dream is worth pursuing.

Now let your heightened confidence help you resuscitate your dream:

1 Examining your past dreams with renewed confidence, ask yourself: *Do they still hold value? Do any of your dreams still capture your imagination? Do you still long to follow your dreams, or some portion of them?* Take a moment to write your thoughts down in your journal.

2 Next, ask yourself: *What do I really want to do with my life now?* Your self–confidence will help you come up with honest answers. You're not trying to impress anybody. You're trying to open up the truth that lies within you. If you believe and trust yourself, you can speak straight from the heart, without worry of ridicule from anybody. Again, write your answers down.

3 Now read what you've just written in steps 1 and 2 above. Do you notice any trends? *How might you combine your long–held dreams with your current goals to create a new dream tailor–made for you?* Hang on to your confidence and focus on the positive as you tackle this last question and remember, there are no wrong answers. Whatever you come up with is of value to you on your dream quest.

4 Start with what you like and build from there. If you love animals, try volunteering once a week at your local humane society. After you're familiar enough with the people there, ask about employment opportunities, or at least obtain a glowing referral from these folks. The success and fulfillment you gain from doing what you enjoy will boost your confidence. This in turn will help you tackle new challenges.

5 With each measure of success, no matter how subtle, congratulate yourself. Feel your confidence grow. Continue to trust yourself. You are getting closer and closer to reaching your dream.

If you're unhappy with your life right now, remember: You don't have to be stuck forever. The sooner you start believing in yourself and building your self–confidence, the sooner you'll rise above your situation and move toward your dreams. If a one–legged bookworm can become a champion skier, and a one–time high school dropout can become a CEO, then you, too, can develop the confidence you need to dream big and achieve.

You've seen how confidence helps a dreamer repel discouragement. Now we'll look at how courage breeds the strength to overcome our fears as we journey toward our dreams.

Dream CPR Journal

In addition to the questions posed and exercises suggested in this and future chapters, use your *Dream CPR Journal* to uncover your forgotten dreams and develop new ones. Write down your answers to these questions:

When you were younger, what activities did you enjoy most?

What pursuits did you lose yourself in?

What drew you to these particular pastimes?

chapter 4

Courage: Conquer Your Fears

"COURAGE IS RESISTANCE TO FEAR, MASTERY OF FEAR, NOT ABSENCE OF FEAR." — LUCIUS ANNAEUS SENECA

We usually think of courage as the kind of bravery that leads to heroic acts. But courage is also what enables dreamers to face and conquer their fear of the unknown. It's scary to set off on an uncertain course, to leave the familiar behind, or to be the first to try something new. By accessing the Dream CPR essential element *courage*, you can conquer the fears that are keeping you from realizing your dreams.

College professor Marigold Linton, champion cyclist Lance Armstrong, and business owner Stephanie Ngo Pham all relied on their courage to reach their dreams. Marigold grew up in poverty on an American Indian reservation during the 1940s and 1950s — a time when the dreams of Native American girls were neither valued nor supported by most of society. An outstanding student, she dreamed of going to college and earning a degree. But nobody living on her reservation had gone to college, and Marigold was afraid that people were right when they told her that she would fail. Marigold had to summon courage to face her fears, leave the only home she'd ever known, and become a trailblazer.

Ever since he was a child athlete competing against bigger and older opponents, champion cyclist Lance Armstrong has been facing and conquering his fears. But his biggest test came when, at age 25, he was diagnosed with cancer. Would he ever race again? Would he even survive? Lance faced these terrifying unknowns and not only survived, but came back to claim victory at the brutal Tour de France a record seven times.

A Vietnamese refugee, Stephanie arrived in New York City with no money, no English skills, and two young children to care for. Confronted by homeless men begging for money at the airport as she arrived in her new country, Stephanie feared for her family's future: *How will I, a foreigner, be able to feed my children when these Americans have to beg to survive?* she wondered. But Stephanie faced her fears head—on, working hard to learn English and acquire a cosmetology license so that she could get a job at a nail salon. Just three years later, she opened her own nail salon; today, she's the proprietor of 25.

These three dream achievers reached their goals by finding the courage to overcome their fears and pursue their dreams. Their personal stories show how the Dream CPR essential element *courage* enables us to face challenges rather than run from them. Courage is about finding the strength within ourselves to move forward with our plans, despite our fear of the unknown.

MARIGOLD LINTON: BLAZING NEW TRAILS

Every time she turned around, Marigold heard someone predict that she was going to flunk out of college. It didn't matter to the naysayers that the American—Indian teenager was earning top marks in high school. A frightened Marigold had to call on courage to overcome her fears and pursue a college education. In the end, Marigold not only earned a bachelor's degree, she went on to become a college professor and renowned researcher who has helped secure educational opportunities for others growing up on

American Indian reservations. Marigold shows that courage can free our dreams from the stranglehold of prejudice.

The visit from her teacher caught the eighth–grader by surprise. Mrs. Adams came onto the reservation, marched straight to Marigold Linton's mother, and said: "Your daughter is very bright. You have to make sure she goes to college." Marigold had never heard these words before. At school she was always known as "the smart little Indian girl." But until that moment, nobody had ever mentioned the possibility of college; on the contrary, the message she had received time and again was that "Indian kids don't go to college."

People from the outside rarely came onto the Morongo Indian Reservation in Southern California where Marigold had lived since the day she was born. Life on the reservation was hard: Marigold's family of five lived in a tiny, two–room adobe house that they often shared with several relatives. There was no electricity or running water, and the family combed nearby fields for firewood on the weekends. Marigold and her brothers left the reservation every weekday to attend school, but none of the non–reservation kids or teachers ever ventured in. Except Mrs. Adams. Her visit was a sign to Marigold, who immediately began to save her pennies for college tuition. From that day forth, she dreamed of going to college.

Not that she knew what it was, exactly. When Marigold tried to picture college, what came to her mind was an official–looking building she had seen in nearby Riverside that was actually a citrus experiment station. What took place inside college was a complete mystery to Marigold. Her parents didn't have a formal education. Marigold's mother taught her how to play tennis and chess but did not know how to prepare her daughter for higher education other than to offer encouragement. No one on the reservation had gone to college. Marigold tried to get information from her friends at school, but got nowhere. She recalls, "I kept asking people what college was, you know, the great conversation opener: 'Say, what is college?' Typically I was told, 'Oh, you know what college is.' Period." Marigold needed courage to march forward and chart this unknown territory.

The excellent student was also a talented athlete; Marigold won the county tennis championships two years in a row. With her top grades, Marigold tied for valedictorian of her high school class, but prejudiced school officials arbitrarily moved her to second place. "I thought it was unfair," she says, "but being stoic, I did nothing about it. That was just the way things were. But I had begun to think that some day, people will realize how remarkable my performance is." Her high school achievements did gain Marigold acceptance for admission at the University of California in Riverside.

The summer after she graduated from high school, Marigold got a job at a shirt factory. Her employers were so pleased with her work that they wanted her to stay on permanently. "They told me: 'You're not going to make it through college, so why bother,'" she recalls. "They tried to entice me with pay. They said I would do very well for myself at the factory, earning more than what 90 percent of the people in my reservation were making." They weren't the only ones trying to change Marigold's mind. In school and on the reservation, people kept predicting that she wouldn't make it through the first semester. Even her own beloved father told her: "When you flunk out of school, you can come back. We will always be here."

Marigold worried that the naysayers might be right. She was afraid to leave her reservation, afraid of the mysteries of college life. But she didn't want to give up her dream. And so with just $900 in savings and a small scholarship, she enrolled at UC Riverside in the fall of 1954. "I told myself that I had to live an entire school year on this," she recalls. "I budgeted carefully and never spent more than $100 a month." She was the only American Indian on campus. (Many years later, a colleague discovered through research that Marigold had been the first California reservation Indian to have left the reservation to attend a university.)

In the beginning, the world of college was foreign and confusing to Marigold. "Everything was traumatic," she recalls. "First I couldn't figure out how to catch the bus and then, wanting to remain as unobtrusive as possible, I couldn't bring myself to pull the cord to get off. On campus, I was afraid to make a fool of myself so I never talked. When I was called on in class I would start crying and run out of the room. Fortunately, in comparison with other freshmen I wrote brilliantly so my professors graded me very high."

Frightened of flunking, Marigold spent almost every waking moment of her first semester studying. When she saw her report card, she thought there had to be a mistake. How could she have earned straight A's? Marigold recalls: "I literally went to the registrar and said, 'You have made a mistake and you must give these grades back to the person who earned them and give me my grades.' They thought I was crazy. It took a very long time before I believed that I might be successful."

But the next term, it was the same — she earned all A's. Marigold finally began to relax a little as it slowly sank in that the naysayers had been wrong. She started to go out and date, and obtained part–time jobs and bigger scholarships. And she kept studying diligently, continuing to get top grades while learning the ways of a world where she felt she didn't fit in.

She majored in experimental psychology, and after fulfilling her original dream of earning a college degree, Marigold kept going. Fascinated with her chosen field, Marigold completed graduate work at the University of Iowa and then earned a Ph.D. at UCLA. Marigold went on to have an illustrious academic career as a cognitive psychologist, making great research strides in the area of long–term memory and co–authoring *The Practical Statistician: Simplified Handbook of Statistics*, a bestseller. She has taught as a tenured full professor at both San Diego State University and the University of Utah. But achieving this tremendous success in her academic career did not dim Marigold's memories of her struggles as a college student. And so, Marigold began to dream of creating greater educational opportunities for other American Indians.

This dream led Marigold, at age 50, to accept a position with Arizona State University as the director of American Indian Programs. Among her many accomplishments, she secured grants from the National Science Foundation and NASA to bring quality math and science education programs to American Indians living on reservations in Arizona.

"People have different needs at different times," she points out. "Within the American–Indian community, those who want to leave the reservations should. Those who want to stay on the reservations should. But all need to be given the opportunity to develop skills."

Marigold co–founded the National Indian Education Association and has served on the board of the Society for the Advancement of Chicanos and Native Americans in Science. Today she is the director of American Indian Outreach at the University of Kansas at Lawrence, where she has secured $10.5 million in grants to fund programs, such as one that gives students at neighboring Haskell Indian Nations University science research opportunities working in laboratories with University of Kansas scientists. "This position is very fulfilling to me," she says. "I have just arranged special bioinformatics classes for Indian students, which will place them at the cutting edge of science — rather than years or decades behind."

Courage has helped Marigold not only reach her own dreams but encourage a new generation of American Indians to do the same. She recalls the moment she finally understood what college was: "It wasn't until I was getting out of graduate school that I had my epiphany: *College was someplace where you learned and explored.* Had someone ever said that to me? People can only hear what they are ready to understand."

Marigold's inspiring example shows that making a plan and sticking to it can help you develop courage and overcome your fears. Even before she knew what college was, Marigold began to plan and save money for it. And even before she realized she could succeed, she planned for success. "Plan early," she advises. "I have plans for every year of my life until I'm 95! Chart a course and follow it: You have to imagine your future."

LANCE ARMSTRONG: A TOUR DE FORCE

In the summer of 2005, he amazed fans and competitors by winning his seventh Tour de France in a row. But it was something Lance Armstrong said to reporters after winning his fourth Tour in 2002 that put it all into perspective: "Regardless of one victory, two victories, four victories, there's never been a victory by a cancer survivor. That's a fact that hopefully I'll be remembered for." It takes tremendous courage to compete in one of the most physically and mentally demanding cycling races in the world. But it takes greater courage to face and fight cancer.

At 25, Lance Armstrong was on top of the world. He'd twice won the 12–day Tour DuPont race in the United States and was the first American to win the grueling Fleche–Wallonne race in Belgium. Ranked as the number one cyclist in the world, Lance was a two–time Olympian who dreamed of winning the ultimate test in cycling endurance — the Tour de France. The "Golden Boy of American Cycling" had just signed a two–year, $2.5 million contract with French racing team Cofidis. Illness was the last thing on his mind.

Everything changed on October 2, 1996, when a urologist delivered the shocking diagnosis of testicular cancer.

Within 24 hours, Lance underwent surgery to remove the malignant testicle. Chemotherapy began four days later to fight the cancer that had already spread to his abdomen and lungs. Then, doctors made another devastating discovery: The cancer had spread to his brain.

Often throughout his budding career, the young athlete had called on courage to race against formidable opponents. Now Lance needed courage to fight the battle of his life. His first concern was: *Will I ever race again?* Then, the severity of the situation hit him. Doctors were giving Lance only a 50/50 chance of survival. Some of them privately thought his chances were closer to 20 percent. The real question was: *Will I live?*

In the midst of his fears, Lance found courage by reminding himself what he was made of. He was an endurance athlete, somebody trained to push himself to the limit. He was a fighter. Even as a fifth–grader, Lance had been a serious competitor when he took up running and swimming. He discovered that he was a natural at long–distance running but found swimming to be a challenge. Although he was 11, he was put in a class with seven–year–olds to learn basic strokes. He was embarrassed but didn't quit. His mother always said to turn every obstacle into an opportunity, so young Lance swallowed his pride and stuck with swimming. A year later, he placed fourth in the state in the 1,500–meter freestyle.

At 13, Lance combined his swimming, running, and cycling abilities and entered the Iron Kids Triathlon. He wasn't the biggest or the strongest competitor, but he won. By age 16, Lance was a professional triathlete, and he was gaining particular attention for his cycling abilities. As a high school senior, Lance accepted an invitation from the U.S. Cycling Federation to train with the junior national cycling team. He was thrilled to represent the United States in Moscow at the 1990 Junior World Championships. His high school's administrators, however, did not share his enthusiasm: Because his intensive training caused Lance to miss six weeks of school, they threatened to keep him from graduating. Furious, he and his mother found a private school that accepted Lance and enabled him to graduate on time.

After competing as an amateur cyclist in the 1992 Olympics in Barcelona, Lance turned professional. But at his first pro cycling race, the 1992 Clasica San Sebastian in Spain, his performance was so disappointing that he seriously considered quitting his sport. The last of 111 racers to cross the finish line, he felt the sting of humiliation as spectators laughed and mocked. It took tremendous courage for Lance to get back on his bike and face crowds again. He did, placing second at the Championships of Zurich that year. Despite his shaky debut into professional cycling, Lance came back to win the World Championships in 1993, took second at the prestigious Tour DuPont in 1994 and went on to win that race in both 1995 and 1996. And in the summer of

1996, Lance represented the United States at the Olympic Games in Atlanta.

But even Olympic athletes can get cancer, and as he faced brain surgery in late October 1996, Lance was frightened. Lying awake the night before his operation, he thought about life and death, fear and hope, what he had done in life and what he had left to do. He was comforted by the thought that cycling had given him so much already. If something went wrong during surgery and this was the end of the road, well, it had been a great run. Yet at only 25, he had just begun to live. There was so much more he wanted to experience: Things to do, places to see, people to meet, races to win. Lance did what he always did best — he fought his fears by clutching tightly to his dreams.

The following day, the delicate six–hour surgery went smoothly. Doctors, family, and friends — and of course Lance himself — were greatly relieved when he opened his eyes and spoke. The next morning, he was back on chemotherapy. Throughout the weeks of treatment that followed, Lance endured severe nausea and pain. But with courage he found strength in the knowledge that the toxic medicines were ridding his body of cancer. And he mustered the courage to get up on his bike between chemo cycles and ride, even if only for a few blocks, to keep alive his dream of competing again.

When his treatments were finished that December, his prognosis was good. Lance was thankful to be alive, thankful to his mom, his friends, and every doctor and nurse who had helped him get through the greatest battle of his life. Barely into remission, he wanted to do something for other cancer patients. He founded the international, nonprofit Lance Armstrong Foundation to raise money for cancer research, promote cancer awareness, and help cancer survivors. Helping others was cathartic for Lance.

By the spring of 1997, Lance was training in full force again. To the delight of his fans, he returned to professional cycling in 1998. He had lost the lucrative Cofidis contract, but had gained a new sponsor, the United States Postal Service, which sponsored Lance and his cycling team for six more years.

After Lance was diagnosed with cancer, no one would have been surprised if he had retired from competition. But having faced death and beating the cancer that had invaded his body, Lance reclaimed the dream that cancer had nearly extinguished. He wanted to win the Tour de France, cycling's ultimate test of endurance, strength, and speed.

In January 1999, Lance began to train for the Tour, which would take place the following summer. He practiced the course diligently, riding up to seven hours a day with his teammates across the rain–drenched Alps and Pyrenees. By the time the three–week race started in July, Lance was prepared. But he needed courage to face the crowds. Lance knew what people were thinking: *He almost died from cancer. What's he doing here?* He wanted neither sympathy nor skepticism. Lance was there to win.

At the end of the Tour's first day, Lance was wearing the coveted yellow jersey that sets the leader apart. As we all know, Lance went on to shock the world by winning the race. He went on to win the race a record seven years in a row until he retired from it after the 2005 contest, surpassing American Greg LeMond's three consecutive titles and Spain's Miguel Indurain five successive titles.

Watching him race today, it's hard to believe that Lance ever had cancer and underwent brain surgery, or that he was ever hairless, weak, and drained from chemotherapy. Now a proud father of three, Lance smiles easily these days. He's got a lot to live for. Courage saw him through cancer, the most harrowing ride of his life. As for the record seven consecutive Tour de France victories, those are just icing on the cake.

STEPHANIE NGO PHAM:
STRANGER IN A STRANGE LAND

The life of a refugee can be frightening and confusing, as "Stephanie" Ngo Pham knows firsthand. When she came to America from war–torn Vietnam, she didn't know how she would provide for her children. She couldn't speak a word of English and had no money or marketable skills. But Stephanie courageously faced her fears head–on to build a successful business and create a new life that's many times better than the one she was forced to flee.

Sometimes our circumstances shape our dreams. Growing up in Vietnam during the 1960s and 1970s, "Stephanie" Ngo Pham dreamed of a life of freedom and peace for herself and her family. In 1979, she got her chance. Cradling her three–month–old son in her arm and holding her two–year–old daughter by her side, the 21–year–old felt both excited and scared as she, her husband, and her mother–in–law arrived in New York City. They had left everything behind, bringing only a few items of clothing and the priceless documents that granted them entry into the United States. There was no direction to go except forward: Just as she had needed courage to escape the land of her birth, Stephanie would have to rely on her courage to start over in America.

As the newly arrived refugees made their way through the airport, Stephanie tripped and broke the strap on one of her thong sandals — her only pair of shoes. Unable to keep her balance with a broken strap, she removed her sandals, stuffed them into her bag, and continued barefoot through JFK airport on that cold October day. "As I was walking," she recalls, "people would look at my bare feet and laugh. They spoke in a language I could not understand. I was so humiliated. My feet were so cold but I managed to keep up with the others."

Once outside the airport, Stephanie was startled by the coldest wind she had ever felt. With no shoes and no coat, she held her baby close for warmth while the family tried to get to a nearby hotel. Snow began to fall, and Stephanie remembers how men wearing long, heavy coats came up to her with outstretched hands, begging for money. It was Stephanie's first encounter with America's homeless and she could not believe her eyes. She swelled with panic. "I had no money, not even a dollar," she says. "I was so cold, so thirsty. These men were asking us for money when we were poorer than them. I asked myself, 'Why did I come here? Why did I bring my kids here? How will I make money?'"

With help from American sponsors, Stephanie and her family settled in Virginia where she was reunited with her parents and siblings who had escaped Vietnam months earlier. But winters proved too difficult for Stephanie and the rest of the family. Unable to adapt to a climate so different from the warm tropics they'd always known, the family constantly got sick. The last straw was when Stephanie's father slipped on a patch of ice and injured his head so badly that he had to get stitches. So six months after Stephanie arrived in the United States, the entire extended family bade a tearful farewell to their sponsors and new friends and moved to sunny Southern California.

There Stephanie found the courage to enroll in Pasadena City College. While her parents and a friend looked after her two young children, Stephanie bussed tables at a restaurant to pay her tuition. "It was very difficult for me to learn English," she recalls, but restaurant patrons and coworkers alike helped her learn the language.

Stephanie knew she needed marketable skills and decided to study cosmetology. "I picked cosmetology because I love beauty," she explains. "I wanted to help make people beautiful." After earning her cosmetology license, she landed a job at a beauty salon, working as a nail technician by day while she continued to wait tables at night. Between her two jobs, Stephanie worked as many as 18 hours a day, saving as much money as she could.

That's because Stephanie had already formed a new dream: to run her own business. She could see that the demand for beauty services in Southern California was high. Working side–by–side with her manager, she watched carefully to see how a salon was run, and she saved diligently to open her own business. In 1982, just three years after immigrating to America, Stephanie had saved enough money to open her own modest 800–square–foot nail salon in the heart of Los Angeles. She took pride in the quality of her work and soon built up a loyal clientele. Many of her customers had trouble with her Vietnamese name, Ngo Hong Soa Thi, which she was using at the time. So she adopted the American name of "Stephanie," which she found pretty, to make it easier for clients to pronounce and remember her name.

From the beginning, Stephanie had the courage to tell her clients that she needed their help in order to succeed. She made an agreement with each customer: She would do her very best, and if they were happy with the results, would they please bring their family and friends to her salon? Her approach worked. "Within only five months, I was shocked to find how quickly my business had grown to become a success," she says. "Every morning before we even opened for business, people were already waiting in a long line to get in." Stephanie soon had to hire eight nail technicians to meet the demand.

With such good business, Stephanie wanted to expand. So she took some of her profits and invested in additional salons, opening them one at a time and sharing her good fortune with her family by hiring her 11 brothers and sisters to manage her shops. Within eight years, Stephanie was the proud proprietor of 15 salons stretching across Southern California and into Arizona. Today she owns 25, including three in Georgia and two in Canada.

Stephanie believes without a doubt that she and her family made the right choice by coming to the United States. "Before every family feast," Stephanie says, "we have a lengthy prayer to thank the good Lord for all he has done, for how he saved us and brought us here to this wonderful life." Among her many blessings is the courage that helped Stephanie get through those frightening first years, which propelled her to create the secure future of her dreams.

Courage to Move Forward With Your Dreams

Are you afraid of what might happen if you follow your dreams? You're not alone. Marigold Linton was afraid of flunking out of college, but courage helped her pursue her degree. She would have missed an incredible opportunity had she given in to her fears. That's why the Dream CPR element *courage* is so important. Too many people shortchange themselves by giving in to their fears and giving up on their dreams.

Courage is a matter of facing your fears and relying on your inner strength. Courage doesn't necessarily remove the fear, but it does foster the strength to overcome fear's paralyzing grip, freeing you to strive toward your dream.

Here are some ways you can develop your courage:

1   Acknowledge your fears. Whatever you are afraid of — failure, success, rejection, abandonment, public speaking — realize that countless other people on the planet have these same fears. Just don't allow these fears to rule you. Instead, set your mind on the goal you want to achieve.

2   Picture yourself doing something you'd love to do but have been afraid to try. *What's the worst thing that could possibly happen?* Whatever that awful thing is, it's probably something you can handle. Sometimes our fears take on life of their own. Understanding that an actual worst–case scenario is usually not as bad as we imagined can help us become more courageous. Lance Armstrong was afraid of losing a race and being laughed at. That's exactly what happened to him when he turned pro. Was that the end of the world for Lance? No. He felt hurt and embarrassed and he considered quitting — but he didn't. He got on his bike, trained hard, and became a champion. Have courage — you can survive most of your worst–case scenarios.

3 Once again, picture yourself doing what you'd like to do but have been afraid to attempt. Now ask: *What's the absolute best thing that can happen?* Wouldn't it be great to achieve that? By focusing on that fantastic end result, you'll develop the courage you'll need to get past obstacles.

Like everything else, courage takes practice and gets easier with practice. Where did Lance get the courage to fight and beat cancer? From years of practice. He began developing it as a child when he struggled to learn to swim. Resolve to practice courage regularly. How you practice is up to you, but here are some suggestions to get you started: Pick up the phone to talk to a difficult relative you've been avoiding. Visit a nursing home to confront a fear of aging. Try karaoke to ease your fear of speaking to an audience.

> ### Dream CPR Journal
>
> Continue to breathe life into your dreams by making a list of your favorite jobs or volunteer activities.
>
> What did you enjoy most about each one? Be specific.

Let courage work for you and your dreams:

1 Have you abandoned a dream because fear stopped you? If you had tapped into courage to follow and reach that dream, how would your life be different today? Would it be better? Don't beat yourself up over lost opportunities; rather, resolve to make the most of your current possibilities.

2 Make a list of the times that you reached a goal by calling on your courage to overcome fear. Didn't it feel great to achieve your goal?

Consider how you've stood at both ends of the spectrum: Fear has stopped you from reaching some goals, and courage has given you strength to reach others. Tap into your courage to gain control over your fears, until your ability to reach your dream becomes much more powerful than the fears that try to hold you back. Courage works in your favor.

It takes courage to dream. In some ways, we're all like Stephanie — starting over in a strange country, afraid of what we might encounter. Courage enables us to brave the uncertainties we meet as we traverse the path to our dreams. Courage helps us face challenges head—on and determine what our next step will be.

Confidence repels doubt and discouragement while courage breeds strength to overcome fear. Next you'll see how commitment enables a dreamer to go the distance.

chapter 5

Commitment: Devote Yourself

> " WE CAN DO ANYTHING WE WANT IF WE STICK TO IT LONG ENOUGH. "
> — HELEN KELLER

Somewhere along the way, you'll probably feel like you're working in a virtual vacuum, putting a lot of energy into your dream but seeing few, if any, results. Many people become so frustrated at this point that they quit. The Dream CPR essential element *commitment* helps us go the distance, bolstering us to continue toward our dreams even if we have little to show for our efforts.

The successful people profiled in this chapter know firsthand the importance of commitment. Abolitionist Barbara Vogel, golfing sensation Tiger Woods, and professional psychic Cynthia Hess devoted themselves completely to their dreams, focusing on what they needed to do to attain their goals.

Veteran teacher Barbara Vogel has always encouraged her students to become compassionate citizens of the world. In 1998, she and her fifth–grade class were appalled to learn that slavery isn't just something you read about in history books, that it thrives today in countries such as Sudan. When the children asked what they could do about this, Barbara was ready to teach her students that they can make a difference. Together, students and teacher became modern–day abolitionists, launching a campaign to free slaves and raise awareness about the ongoing cruel practice. At first, few took their efforts seriously. But after just two years, Barbara and her students testified before the U.S. Senate Foreign Relations Committee about the contemporary slave trade. Barbara's commitment to her students inspired their dedication to the campaign; to date, Barbara's students have helped free more than 2,000 slaves.

Barely in his thirties, Tiger Woods makes being the top golfer in the world look easy. But Tiger didn't become a golfing legend overnight: he's been perfecting his game ever since he followed his father around on the golf course as a precocious toddler. At the age of 11, Tiger dedicated himself to his dream of becoming the greatest golfer of all time. So strong was his commitment that years later he made the difficult decision to leave college to further his professional golfing career. Tiger shows that commitment to a dream means total devotion.

A sensitive child, Cynthia Hess knew intuitively that she had psychic abilities, but she kept this to herself so she wouldn't be laughed at. Trying to ignore her psychic side, Cynthia followed the conventional path of marriage and motherhood. But after her marriage ended in a messy divorce, she decided it was time to stop trying to appease others and start living her life on her own terms. Cynthia committed herself to developing her abilities more fully, to pursuing her dream of becoming a successful professional psychic. Today, she boasts a large clientele, a huge radio audience, and the satisfaction that comes with helping others.

Committing yourself to your dream means making your dream your top priority and dedicating the time and energy necessary to make it come true. Commitment requires focus; you must learn to block distractions, be it the television, the computer, the phone, or the fridge. Commitment means staying true to yourself and your dream, even if you have to go against the sta-

tus quo. Most of all, commitment means sticking with your
dream, no matter what.

BARBARA VOGEL:
ENCOURAGING STUDENTS TO STOP SLAVERY

> During her 30 years of teaching, Barbara Vogel has put this
> belief into practice: "If you can touch the heart of a child,
> you can reach the mind." When Barbara's fifth–grade class
> learned that there are people in Sudan, including children
> their age, who are enslaved by others, they wanted to start
> a campaign to free them. Despite critics, Barbara backed
> their efforts and cheered them on. Her unwavering com-
> mitment to her students enabled them to speak out and
> take action against the choking grip of modern–day slav-
> ery, learning to be responsible humanitarians in the pro-
> cess. Along the way, Barbara's students touched the hearts
> and reached the minds of countless adults.

It was February 1998 when suburban Denver schoolteacher
Barbara Vogel shared a disturbing newspaper article with her
fifth–grade class. The headline glared, "Slave Trading Thrives In
Sudan." As Barbara read aloud the account of 13–year–old
Akuac Malong, who had been forced into seven torturous years in
slavery, tears streamed down her students' faces. "We had just
finished a unit on American history about slavery," Barbara explains. "I had told the kids that slavery was over and conquered,
that it was a thing of the past. Then I saw the article. I was
shocked."

The article recounted atrocities perpetrated by northern Sudanese against the Dinka African tribe and other residents of
southern Sudan, victims of a brutal civil war that has claimed
more than two million lives and enslaved tens of thousands in the
last two decades. The students were horrified to learn that as a
six–year–old, Akuac was abducted by marauding horsemen
while fetching water with her mother. Sold into slavery, the
young girl was regularly beaten, physically mutilated, and nearly
starved to death. But the children also felt a glimmer of hope
when they heard that Akuac was reunited with her mother and

that, finally free, she danced with joy and burst into a song of praise. The Highline Community School fifth–graders were moved — deeply. Then they posed a weighty question: *What are we going to do about this?*

Barbara has devoted her life to helping her students soar, and not just academically. She strives to teach her pupils to become caring, conscientious world citizens. "Adults need to value children and model good citizenship by example," Barbara says. "Children need to be taught to think globally and act locally."

Powerful messages from great visionaries grace the walls of Barbara's classroom, such as Martin Luther King, Jr.'s proclamation that "The greatest sin of our time is not the few who have destroyed, but the vast majority who have sat idly by," and Mother Teresa's simple but powerful, "Do small things with great love." So when her students asked *What are we going to do about this?*, Barbara committed herself to supporting the children completely in their campaign against modern–day slavery and nurturing their shared dream of abolishing slavery, once and for all.

Through an Internet search, the students discovered Christian Solidarity International (CSI), a humanitarian group based in Switzerland that since 1995 has been purchasing freedom for Sudanese slaves and returning them to their villages. Barbara and her fifth–graders learned that $100 could free one person. Immediately they began raising money.

The kids called their campaign STOP to signify their mission to stop "Slavery That Oppresses People." Every day the children contributed coins and dollars — from their allowances, from selling lemonade, from doing extra chores around the house. When they had collected $200, they sent the funds to CSI, gratified to know that because of their efforts, two more people would be released from bondage and reunited with their families. "These are not children of means," Barbara notes. "They are in the lower socioeconomic class."

The fifth–graders also launched a letter–writing campaign to raise awareness about modern–day slavery and spur adults to action. Barbara's students sent impassioned, handwritten pleas to politicians, celebrities, and news reporters, asking them to use

their influence to help end the ongoing human rights violation. Most of the letter recipients never bothered to reply. And most of those who did reply didn't take the students seriously but merely sent form letters or silly stickers, or told the kids to keep up their grades and let adults handle world problems.

The community noticed what the kids were doing, however. And while the vast majority of teachers, administrators, and parents supported the campaign, there were some vocal skeptics who criticized Barbara's methods, saying that STOP was preventing the kids from getting a proper education by taking time away from regular course work. But Barbara stood her ground; she was committed to her students and refused to set a poor example by giving up. She managed to maintain rigorous academic standards while also encouraging the kids to continue their STOP campaign. "They are bright kids who work hard and earn the highest test scores in our school," she points out.

Then the students' letters started catching the attention of members of the media. Reporters visited the classroom to interview Barbara and her students, and articles started to spring up about the fifth–grade abolitionist movement. *Good Morning America* filmed a segment in Barbara's classroom and before long, *Time* magazine, *The New York Times*, the *CBS Evening News,* and National Public Radio had featured stories about Barbara and the STOP kids.

Even after Barbara's students moved up to sixth grade, they continued working on the STOP campaign. Meanwhile, Barbara's new group of students — this time fourth-graders — wanted to participate, and they, too, raised money and wrote letters. Word of the children's campaign spread across the nation and donations started pouring in. An anonymous Texas donor contributed $5,000. A Wisconsin truck driver was so touched that he became a frequent donor. An Alaskan homeless man scraped together $100. To date, the STOP campaign has raised enough money to free more than 2,000 slaves.

Barbara's commitment to her students did not waver. Even an intimidating phone call from a Sudanese official didn't daunt her. "We do not like the attention you are bringing to our country," said the voice at the other end of Barbara's cell phone. But his harsh tone softened after Barbara explained that she and the children have nothing against the country of Sudan. "We love your people," she said, reiterating the students' commitment to abolishing slavery and managing to end the call on a diplomatic note.

The following year, in 1999, Barbara took the bold action of accompanying CSI in a covert emancipation mission to Sudan, where she witnessed an incredible sight — the liberation of 4,300 slaves. She met leaders, teachers, health workers, villagers, and embraced former slaves who had been freed through the STOP campaign's efforts. After that life-changing trip, Barbara's commitment to her students and their cause was stronger than ever. "I've seen the results for myself, in person," she says. "I met a former slave who recently gave birth to her baby in freedom. So many people there said *thank you* for what the children are doing."

Then in 2000, Barbara and some of the STOP kids flew to Washington, D.C., to ask members of Congress and the Clinton administration to pressure the Sudanese government to end the slave trade. They met a dozen legislators, including Senator Jesse Helms who was so moved that he promised to hold special Senate hearings addressing slavery.

When the hearings were held later that year, three former slaves, five children representing the STOP campaign, and Barbara all testified before the Senate Foreign Relations Committee. Afterward, they met with then–Secretary of State Madeleine Albright, who issued a statement condemning slavery in Sudan and calling upon the government of Sudan to put an end to the practice.

In October 2002, Barbara and the STOP kids celebrated a major milestone in their campaign. During a historic meeting with an escaped Sudanese slave, President Bush signed into law the Sudan Peace Act, formally condemning the practice of slavery in Sudan and promising to help rebuild the areas that were destroyed during slave raids.

Within just four years of starting the STOP campaign, Barbara and her students had convinced people in power to take action against modern–day slavery. This amazing group of children and their dedicated teacher are the subject of a novel, *Dream Freedom*, and they've inspired students at more than a hundred schools across the nation to join the fight against slavery.

"Children's voices ring loudest and truest because they have no political or religious agenda," Barbara says. "I continue to dream that my students grow up to be humanitarians." Thanks to her commitment, they are well on their way.

TIGER WOODS: LEGEND IN HIS TIME

How does someone become a golfing legend by the time he's 25? Through commitment, focus, and hard work. Tiger Woods was born with a raw talent for golf, but it was his commitment to develop his talent to its full potential that propelled him to the upper echelons of the sport. Years of steadfast commitment and hours upon hours of focused practice have brought Tiger to the cusp of his dream of becoming the best golfer of all time.

The tall, slender young man with the engaging smile had hit a Grand Slam. In April 2001, Tiger Woods won the U.S. Open, the British Open, the PGA Championship, and the Masters, one right after the other. By winning all four major golf championships in a row, Tiger had achieved a nearly impossible feat, one that has eluded top professional players many years his senior. No one had ever before held all four titles at the same time. And in what has primarily been a white man's game, it's refreshing to see an American with copper skin and a multi–ethnic heritage (Thai, Chinese, African American, Caucasian, and American Indian) be the one to make the breakthrough.

Tiger worked his whole life — literally — to reach this phenomenal height. Born in Cypress, California, in 1975, Eldrick "Tiger" Woods was introduced to golf by his father, Earl, a retired U.S. Army colonel who died in 2006. Earl enjoyed practicing golf strokes by hitting balls into a net he'd set up in the garage, and he often let Tiger watch from a high chair. Although not yet a year old, Tiger was completely enthralled. Soon he was dragging a short, sawed–off putter behind him as he crawled through the house. He astonished his parents when he took his first swing at ten months. Even before he could walk, Tiger clearly had a gift for the game.

At 11 months, Tiger started joining his dad on the green. He demonstrated his rare discipline and coordination when he learned how to putt at just 18 months old. At age two, he appeared on *The Mike Douglas Show* putting with Bob Hope. By the time he was five, Tiger had been featured in *Golf Digest*.

Despite the youngster's early fame and accolades, Earl never forced his son to play. Tiger simply showed a natural fascination for the game, and it was evident that he loved to spend time with his dad on the golf course. Father and son turned golf into magical playtime, and they developed a very close, special relationship. Even today, Tiger cites his father as his greatest role model, while his mother, Kultida, remains Tiger's biggest fan.

The child prodigy quickly absorbed the basics of the game — even before he could read or count he showed an intuitive understanding of the scoring system, the distance of each shot, and the need to gauge the surrounding elements. When Tiger was three, his father taught him the pre–shot routine that he still relies on today, in which he visualizes each shot before executing it. This routine helped young Tiger learn how to stay completely focused on the game even in the midst of extreme pressure — or annoying distractions like Earl purposely jingling coins in his pocket or coughing loudly.

As a three–year–old, Tiger was winning competitions against 10– and 11–year–olds. At the age of six, his drive to become a champion had begun — he begged his parents for golf videos, and meticulously practiced and refined his swings after carefully studying footage of old Masters golf tournaments. By the time he was 11, he had formulated his dream. Tiger decided that he didn't just want to be a champion golfer; he wanted to become the greatest golfer of all time. And he knew it was possible because he had spent an afternoon charting Jack Nicklaus' statistics against his own. To his astonishment, Tiger discovered that he had achieved several golfing milestones at a younger age than his hero had. To reach his dream, Tiger committed himself to working hard and doing whatever it took to succeed.

It wasn't easy. Invariably the youngest on the course, Tiger sometimes felt intimidated by the older, bigger players. But his father helped him see that neither age nor size matter in golf, only scores. Since Tiger's scores usually equaled or surpassed those of his competitors, he soon stopped feeling intimidated.

But there were other obstacles. In the now–famous Nike commercial in which Tiger stated that there are still courses in the U.S. where he would not be allowed to play because of the color of his skin, he wasn't exaggerating. Up until the mid–1990s some private country clubs, like Shoal Creek in Alabama, excluded blacks. As a child, Tiger was not allowed on certain courses, not even a military golf course in his hometown. Earl and Kultida had to drive several miles to take their son to a course in Long Beach where he was welcome. Although it's hard to believe, Tiger —who is beloved and admired by so many — even received hate mail.

Nevertheless, Tiger was able to transcend racial bigotry to develop a positive attitude and focus on his passion for golf. Practicing every moment he could after school and on weekends, he had six Optimist International Junior World titles under his belt by the time he turned 15 in 1991. That year he also became the youngest person ever to win the U.S. Junior Amateur Championships. Three years later, in 1994, Tiger became the youngest man to win the U.S. Amateur title. These successes helped convince Tiger to turn pro in 1996 when he was just 20 years old. But his commitment to golf forced Tiger to make some difficult choices: He dropped out of Stanford University, putting his college education on hold to devote himself entirely to professional golf.

The decision to stick with golf paid off: The year after he turned pro, Tiger won the Masters, making him the youngest Masters champion ever and the first major championship winner of African or Asian heritage. In 1997, at the age of 21, Tiger became the youngest golfer ever to be ranked number one. And he continues to break records: Tiger is the career victories leader among active players on the PGA Tour.

Even though he continues to work on improving his skills, by many people's standards Tiger has reached his dream of being the greatest golfer of all time. And part of this success lies in his devotion to giving others the opportunities that he enjoyed. Tiger gives his time, talent, money, and compassion to the Tiger Woods Foundation. The philanthropy supports golf clinics nationwide for disadvantaged urban kids whose neighborhoods tend not to have golf courses — primarily children of color who normally wouldn't have any exposure to golf or any reason to believe that they could belong on the green. But the foundation's work is not so much about golf as it is about the self–esteem that comes with learning a new skill, especially one that a child might not have realized that he or she could learn. By helping children learn to believe in themselves, the foundation improves their chances for achieving success in life.

"Golf has been good to me, but the lessons I've learned transcend the game," Tiger explains. "Do your best. Play fairly. Embrace every activity with integrity, honesty, and discipline. Be responsible for your actions. And, above all, have fun."

Tiger's had a gift for the game almost from the moment he was born. He may look serious on the golf course, but he's been having the time of his life on his quest to be the best. History will be the judge, but Tiger has indeed staked a strong claim on the title of *Greatest Golf Player of All Time.*

CYNTHIA HESS:
CAREER PSYCHIC BY CHOICE

All her life, Cynthia Hess has put up with people thinking that she's strange. But though it's been misunderstood by many, Cynthia's psychic ability has been a part of her since childhood. For years, she tried to suppress her unique gift in order to fit in and be "normal." But when she finally made the commitment to pursue her dream of using her psychic ability to help others, Cynthia was on her way to living life on her own terms.

Having already fought her way through two rounds of chemotherapy for ovarian cancer, Claire Giovannielo worried about an enlarged lymph node. The doctors didn't know if it was cancerous, and Claire didn't know what to do. So she sought the advice of psychic Cynthia Hess.

"I felt it was cancerous," Cynthia recalls. "I saw the nodule deteriorating. I felt very strongly that it was hindering her recovery and that surgery would be needed."

At first, Claire wasn't convinced. "What Cynthia told me went against my own feelings," she says. "But Cynthia was very emphatic." In the end, Claire decided to have the surgery. After removing the lymph node, her oncologist determined that, indeed, it had been cancerous. Cynthia had helped Claire make a life–or–death decision.

"It's not always politically or socially correct to be a psychic," Cynthia says. "The pain I feel from being persecuted or misunderstood by others is real. But the joy I receive from helping people through this ability is far greater."

Born and raised in New York City, Cynthia knew even as a child that she was different from other people. "Being born psychic for me is like being born without sight for a blind person," she says. "It's not an unnatural thing, it's just a part of who you are." But young Cynthia was frustrated and confused when others couldn't perceive things that she saw clearly. "From the age of seven, I didn't understand why I was usually the only one who could tell that someone was hiding something, "she says. "The person might be smiling, and everybody would think he was terrific, but I could see the anger or jealousy behind his motives. Sometimes I felt like screaming, *Why don't the rest of you see this?*"

Growing up in the conservative 1950s, Cynthia quickly learned to keep her abilities to herself in order to avoid ridicule. But trying to suppress her psychic nature didn't stop her from receiving messages and seeing future events, and so she often felt lonely and misunderstood. Cynthia longed for normalcy, but she also knew intuitively that her psychic abilities were special. She wanted to use her gift to help people, to relieve their emotional pain. Yet she also yearned to just be a regular girl who would someday get married and have kids. And so Cynthia felt torn.

As an adolescent, Cynthia embarked on a personal quest to learn more about the supernatural. She studied the lives of Jesus Christ and the Catholic saints, focusing especially on their ability to heal others, perform miracles, and love unconditionally. She also studied the work of early 20th–century psychic Edgar Cayce, dubbed by many as "the father of holistic medicine." She even started to meet some psychics. "But the only [psychics] I knew personally who gave readings were at the beaches and in circuses," she says. "Although I felt a connection to these people, I had my reservations. I did not want to work at the circus!"

After graduating from high school, Cynthia started a success-ful career in advertising, got married, and gave birth to a son. Her childhood wish for a normal life had been fulfilled. But things went down-hill rapidly. "My husband got into drugs," she says. "He became abusive. I knew I couldn't let my son and myself be exposed to that." By the time she was 24, Cynthia was divorced and fighting a bitter custody battle. "My husband tried to convince the court that my psychic abilities would damage our son. But in the end I won full custody. Today, he's a college graduate and is doing well in marketing," she says proudly. "He's a good kid."

After her marriage fell apart, Cynthia realized that instead of trying to please others, she had to find her destiny by living on her own terms. She had dreamed about being a professional psy-chic, using her abilities to help people solve their problems. Now she made a commitment to pursue her dream.

"I decided that I would do this professionally and take it to the top, becoming one of the best psychics in the world," she recalls. "I decided I would use my gift to help people who are hurting. I wrote down my own roadmap to life. It said that I would be the best in this field. This meant I would need training and develop-ment. I wrote down that I would have my own practice, and that I would achieve certain credentials to boost my credibility. I also wrote down that in the future, I would teach others how to do this."

In 1977 Cynthia undertook a five–year apprenticeship with Robert Petro, a psychic and an expert on using the intuitive mind. She accompanied him on radio appearances; before long, she began making her own appearances on New York stations. She earned enough from private and public psychic readings to support herself and her son without any child support from her ex–husband. Her career progressed steadily, but it wasn't until after she moved to New Mexico in 1990 that things really began to take off.

While vacationing in the state known as "The Land of Enchantment," Cynthia had a vision that if she lived there, her career would grow by leaps and bounds. Cynthia relocated to Albuquerque, and doors began to open almost immediately. She launched a weekly radio show called *Psychic Love Lines* with veteran radio host Charlie Fox. She became a frequent guest on several other radio programs. This exposure gained Cynthia an invitation to make guest appearances on local television as a celebrity psychic, and from her television exposure came the opportunity to write newspaper horoscope columns.

These days, it's not unusual to find Cynthia sitting inside a cramped radio studio, headphones over her ears and a microphone in front of her. "New Mexico's Most Listened–To Psychic" concentrates intently on her callers' questions and takes their concerns seriously.

"I'm divorced. Will I be married again, and will I stay in Albuquerque?" a caller wants to know. Cynthia pauses, then replies: "Yes, I see you getting married again. But I don't see you staying in Albuquerque. Although good things have happened here for you, socially there may be some problems."

Another caller asks about her career. "I feel you're not living up to your potential," Cynthia responds. "I see you bored with your career. But there's a struggle, a conflict between your personal life and your career, that you need to resolve." The next caller asks about his love life. "You've had a tough time these last three years," Cynthia tells him. "I see that you've experienced a lot of loss and separation. Before you can have a satisfying relationship, I feel that you need to develop your emotions better. You are very intellectual, but you let your mind rationalize everything. You need to pay attention to your feelings more." The calls keep coming. And radio executives are elated.

"We have never had a guest that lights up the switchboard quite like you do," Sandy Horowitz, program director with Albuquerque's KTEG–FM radio station, testifies on Cynthia's web site. "I have been in radio a long time, and I have never seen anything like what [Cynthia] can do over the air."

Cynthia has given readings on radio waves in California, Arizona, Pennsylvania, and several other states. People call her from all over the nation, and she has developed a large private clientele in the Southwest. "One of my clients is a woman who came to me after losing her sight from juvenile diabetes," says Cynthia. "She was on disability and didn't think she had a future. During a reading I encouraged her to get into the field of helping people. Today she is a successful massage therapist. She has her own home, she's successful and independent."

Police departments and private investigators have enlisted her help in solving crimes, services Cynthia provides pro bono. Doctors and psychologists have also contacted her for insight into their patients. For example, a psychologist asked Cynthia for her opinion on a troubled teen boy whom the courts felt was a danger to society because he wouldn't stop stealing cars. Cynthia shared her impressions with the psychologist. She felt the young man was not stealing cars for money but that his behavior was connected to negative sexual experiences he'd been through. After investigating further, the psychologist discovered that the boy had, indeed, endured traumatic sexual abuse. In the end, the young man returned every car without a scratch, his sentence was reduced to one year, and he was able to get the therapy that he needed.

After 28 years as a professional psychic, Cynthia's primary goal is still to help people help themselves. "It really isn't about the prophecy so much," she says. "It's a matter of empowering people. We get stuck into certain patterns in life. But it doesn't have to be that way. We can use our minds to change these patterns and create a better life for ourselves. I try to use my gift to help people see that they really do have options."

Commit Yourself to Your Dream

"IF YOU ARE TENACIOUS WITHOUT BEING OVERLY AGGRESSIVE, IF YOU HAVE A COMMITMENT TO SOMETHING AND YOU FOLLOW THROUGH WITH IT, IT WILL ULTIMATELY WORK FOR YOU, OR SOME ASPECT OF IT WILL WORK FOR YOU. I BELIEVE THAT WHEN PEOPLE DO HAVE DREAMS, SOMEWHERE THEY KNOW THEY HAVE IT IN THEM TO REALIZE THEM. SOMEWHERE, THEY KNOW THEY CAN MAKE IT." — WENDY ISHII, ACTOR (CHAPTER 12)

Life is full of choices, with many different paths available. Some people wander from one path to another, never staying with anything long enough to discover if it's right for them. Commitment is the bond that allows us to stick with our choices long enough for one of two things to happen. Either we realize that the choice is wrong for us and we move on to something else, or we realize that we've found our dream and we keep going to make it come true.

Look at Cynthia Hess. For years she vacillated between developing her gift and pretending to be just like everyone one. After she committed herself to using her abilities to help others, she found the path that has led her to become a renowned professional psychic.

How can you develop commitment? Here are some pointers:

1 Practice. Pick something you've wanted to do for a long time but have been putting off, such as going on a trip, cleaning out your closet, or taking a class. Write down your goal, along with step–by–step instructions on how to reach it and an estimate of how long it will take. Then, commit yourself to following this roadmap. Take just one step at a time but keep going until you reach your goal.

2 Simplify your life so you can focus on what you really want. Many of us have very busy lives, but are we doing what we really want to do or are we just staying busy? Take a close look at how you spend your time during a typical week. Can you step down from a board or a committee? Can you get rid of stuff around your house that requires too much time to clean and maintain? Can you free up one of your evenings to enjoy some relaxing time at home?

By simplifying your weekly schedule, you'll gain the time you need to focus on what you really want. Rid yourself of commitments that you don't need and instead commit yourself to endeavors that bring you closer to your dream.

Use the Dream CPR essential element *commitment* to help you reach your dream. This will require you to:

1 Focus: It wasn't until Cynthia Hess began to focus on using her unique abilities to help others that she was truly on her way to making her dream a reality. Write down a roadmap for your dream, like Cynthia did, and focus on following it. Make a commitment to work on your dream every day.

2 Remove distractions and use your time wisely. Spend 15 minutes on a phone call instead of an hour. Rather than lose yourself while surfing the Internet, find what you need and turn off the computer. Why waste time watching television or reading junk mail when you can be working on your dream? Committing yourself to your dream means promising to give it your full attention. In some cases, it may even mean putting one goal on hold while pursuing another. Look at Tiger Woods: He couldn't give everything he had to professional golf and de-

> ### Dream CPR Journal
>
> Why spend your days on activities that really don't interest you? Why squander your life running around without a plan? In the long run it's much more fulfilling to commit to doing what matters most to you.
>
> Ask yourself: What do you see yourself doing a year from now? Five years from now? Twenty–five years from now? Write down your answers.

vote himself to his college studies at the same time. His commitment to golf meant that Tiger had to make a difficult choice.

3   Stick with it. Barbara Vogel made a commitment to her students, encouraging them to pursue their abolitionist campaign. At first, the kids wrote letters that went ignored and they raised only small amounts of money. Some of Barbara's fellow teachers criticized their efforts. A Sudanese government official even called to intimidate Barbara. Had her commitment not been firm, she might have given up. But she didn't. Barbara continued to support her students and help them pursue their dream.

You, too, need to understand that reaching your dream is a process that won't happen overnight. You have to nurture your dream, work at it, and give it the time and attention it needs. To reach your dream, make a plan and give it your heart and your sweat. You may not see results right away, but don't give up. You can depend on your commitment to help you go the distance.

You can make the choice to commit to your dream today or put it off. Once you've made a commitment to following your dream, you're ready to unleash the incredible creativity you possess inside. In the next chapter, you'll discover how.

chapter 6

Creativity: Create a New Reality

> "THE CREATIVE THINKER IS FLEXIBLE AND ADAPTABLE AND PREPARED TO REARRANGE HIS THINKING."
> — A. J. CROPLEY

If nobody was willing to try something new, nothing would ever be invented. Civilization would not advance and all of humanity would be stuck, as if frozen in time. What a boring world it would be. Thank goodness for creativity, which propels us to explore, question, dream, and discover. The Dream CPR essential element *creativity* enables us to imagine wonderful new possibilities that can become our realities.

Mohandas Gandhi said: "Every moment of your life is infinitely creative and the universe is endlessly bountiful." We were born to be creative, to dream dreams that can then become the foundation of a new reality. The more creative our dreams, the more innovative our reality.

Creative dreamers such as Bill Nye the "Science Guy," *VeggieTales* animator Phil Vischer, and personal chef pioneers

David MacKay and Susan Titcomb are open–minded and flexible. They think outside the box, play around with ideas, and enjoy trying things out. The most creative dreamers in our midst develop dreams that bring positive change to society.

Creative dreamers are not preoccupied with failing — where others see failure, they see an opportunity to learn. Instead of wallowing in defeat, creative dreamers apply the lesson learned to another, refined attempt. By constantly re–evaluating, improving, and changing their approach, creative dreamers ultimately reach their most heartfelt ambitions.

BILL NYE: EXPERIMENTING WITH FUN

This mechanical engineer pumped new life into science education by venturing into comedy. The critically acclaimed *Bill Nye the Science Guy* TV show has accomplished for science education what *Sesame Street* has done for literacy: it's made science fun, interesting, and accessible. Engineer, scientist, comedian, writer, producer, entertainer, educator — Bill lives the life of his dreams, fueling his diverse roles with abundant creativity and sharing his love for science along the way.

Donning his trademark lab coat and bow tie, Bill Nye explains stalactites, centripetal force, DNA, and a host of other science topics with both clarity and contagious enthusiasm. Emmy Award–winning *Bill Nye the Science Guy* blends comedy skits and music videos with lab experiments and a heavy but absorbable dose of scientific facts for a revolutionary, hip approach to teaching science. Kids are digging it. Bill is turning a whole generation on to the beauty of science, convincing today's children and teenagers — and their families — that science is cool.

Teenagers like 18–year–old Juliet Girard who, together with Roshan Prabhu, won a $100,000 scholarship in the prestigious Siemens Westinghouse Competition in Math, Science & Technology. Juliet and Roshan's science project, which involved doctorate–level research, identified the genes responsible for the early flowering of rice — a discovery that could increase worldwide production of this important food staple. When asked by National Public Radio what drew her to science, Juliet replied, "I think it started with *Bill Nye The Science Guy*, which I used to watch all the time when I was a kid. I used to run home and watch it at three o'clock every day."

Science and comedy have been central to William Sanford Nye from his earliest years. "I've always been fascinated by science, which is all about the world around you," Bill says. "I can't remember a time that I didn't love it." Born and raised in Washington, D.C., young Bill enjoyed taking apart his bike as much as he liked riding it — he inherited his father's penchant for tinkering with contraptions. He and his dad, who worked in advertising, often teamed up to create homespun inventions like their "friendly pedestrian horn" that let car drivers alert walkers without scaring them. In high school, Bill enjoyed tutoring classmates in both math and science.

His mother, who holds a doctorate degree, was the daughter of an organic chemist with a couple of patents to his credit. Understandably, both of Bill's parents stressed the importance of schooling and taught their three children to respect education. But Bill's parents also instilled in their children a great sense of humor.

"Being funny was expected of us in our household," Bill recalls. "My parents were always designing jokes. Humor was just a way of life in my family."

In 1977, Bill obtained a bachelor of science degree in mechanical engineering from Cornell University, studying under the likes of astronomer Carl Sagan, one of his favorite professors. After

graduation, Bill moved to Seattle to work in the aerospace industry for companies like Boeing and Sundstrand Data Control. As a
bright young engineer, his creative endeavors included designing
a hydraulic pressure resonance suppressor for airplanes, and
equipment to remove oil slicks from the sea.

Even so, Bill became disillusioned with his profession. Poor
decisions and political infighting doomed some engineering projects from the start, and Bill grew tired of hearing many fellow
engineers grumble about their jobs. He also was weary of the
general public's perception of science and engineering as something that was "boring," "dry," or understandable only to "nerds."
Bill wanted to change this negative perception but didn't know
how.

At the same time, he realized that something was missing
from his life: the comedic shenanigans he had grown up with. He
didn't quit his engineering day job (yet), but Bill did start writing
stand–up routines and performing at local comedy clubs. He
found that comedy restored his enthusiasm and positive outlook,
and that it was just plain fun. Over time, Bill developed a dream:
to use his comedic talents to improve people's understanding of
science and engineering.

So in 1986, he took the plunge and made a life–changing decision. Bill left his lucrative engineering position to concentrate on
writing and performing comedy, joining the cast of a Seattle television show, *Almost Live!*, sort of a local version of *Saturday
Night Live*.

"You just reach a point where if you don't do it, you'll regret it,"
he explains. "I did worry about money. But they were fun times."
During the late 1980s, Bill earned 13 local Emmy awards for his
work as a comedic writer and performer. Describing these years
as some of his most creative, Bill notes that this was when he developed his "science guy" character, who made his debut on Seattle's KJR radio station.

After Bill played his "science guy" role on a boating safety film
for the Washington State Parks Department, he got an idea: Why
not do a children's science show starring his science guy charac-

ter? After all, what better way to change society's perception of science than by starting with kids.

So Bill and a few of his colleagues set out to create the pilot "science guy" episode. By then Bill had hired an agent, who helped get the word out. Pretty soon, a call came in from the Walt Disney Company, and then the National Science Foundation offered support as well. That premier show led to the immensely popular *Bill Nye the Science Guy* TV series, the first program ever to be broadcast concurrently on both public and commercial television. In 1998, the 100th episode was taped to conclude a highly successful five–year run.

"My modest little goal," says Bill, "is to change the world." He is. "Science rules!" has become a household phrase, and a whole generation has grown enthusiastic about science. Bill and his show have won two Daytime Emmy awards and in 1998, Bill was honored as Outstanding Performer in a Children's Series. It's fitting that, 20 years after he graduated, Cornell University invited Bill as the guest of honor at a memorial dedication to Bill's former professor, the late Carl Sagan. As the creator of the *Cosmos* television program, Carl introduced "billions and billions" (well, almost) to the wonders of astrophysics.

Bill's legacy is changing the face of science education by proving that kids can have fun learning science. His popular textbooks and videos have become a staple of science education in classrooms across America. He also advocates for children in ways ranging from tutoring inner–city adolescents with the "I Have A Dream" program to speaking before the Congressional Committee on Science Education.

Bill has kept his foot in engineering as a consultant — but the recognition he's gained gives him the freedom to pick and choose from exciting projects at such places as NASA's Jet Propulsion Laboratory. He also continues to seek out ways to bring the beauty of science to new audiences: Bill's an on–air host on *The N* at Noggin Television, which airs reruns of his *Science Guy* shows, and he's working on developing a prime–time series for adults.

By doing what he enjoys and sharing his love for science with others, Bill has created the life of his dreams, revitalizing science education in the process. And as he continues to inspire and teach, he offers a few words of advice: "People don't regret what they do nearly as much as they regret what they don't do," he says. "So do it!"

SUSAN TITCOMB AND DAVID MACKAY: RECIPE FOR SUCCESS

This couple whipped up a new industry from scratch. Susan Titcomb, a gourmet chef with a demanding job at an upscale restaurant, longed for more time with her family. David MacKay, an entrepreneur with a half–dozen failed businesses to his credit, was looking for a business idea that would really take off. By creatively combining their talents, investigating new concepts, and analyzing possibilities, husband and wife teamed up to create a novel personal chef business that would inspire a whole new industry.

Working as a sous–chef at an elegant seaside restaurant north of San Diego was a dream come true for Susan Titcomb. Her life–long passion for cooking led her to this career. She enjoyed working with talented people in a creative field and even received culinary awards for her work. As a child, baking was her passion. "I loved getting up early on weekends to bake a coffeecake or cinnamon rolls for my parents," she recalls. While her parents ran a home–based business, teenage Susan eagerly took the responsibility of preparing family meals. When she turned 22, Susan entered culinary school, which opened doors to positions at some of Southern California's top restaurants.

Even so, it didn't take long for Susan to burn out from her dream job. "Weekends, evenings, and holidays — the times I wanted to be with my family the most — were spent working like mad at the restaurant," she says. After spending up to 70 hours a week creating gourmet fare for restaurant patrons, she lacked the time and energy to cook for her own family at home. Susan longed for a way to live her passion and have plenty of time to be with her husband and children, but it just didn't seem possible.

Meanwhile Susan's husband, David MacKay, had long dreamed of achieving success as an entrepreneur. At 12, he hired other boys for a lawn–mowing business he had started when he was 10 years old. So far in his adult career, he had launched six businesses, ranging from financial services to electronic test equipment, but none of these ventures had lasted. In fact, only two of his start–ups actually made money.

Nevertheless, David viewed his business attempts not as failures but as educational experiences. "Even when these non-successes came one right after another, and my parents and friends would tell me that maybe it was time to get a 'real job,' I wouldn't give up," says David. "I always looked for the reason that the business didn't make it. Sometimes the timing wasn't right. Or maybe under somewhat different circumstances, the business would have thrived. I learned to look at each situation creatively and analyze what worked, what didn't, and what I needed to do next time."

One evening in 1987, while David and Susan were dining with another couple, a golden opportunity materialized. The conversation turned to Susan's culinary talents, and one of their friends teased David: "It must be great having your own personal chef prepare wonderful meals for you every day." But cooking was the last thing Susan wanted to do when she came home from work. Instead, on days off she prepared and froze batches of several different dinners — like her chicken–and–apple curry — for her family to enjoy during the week.

As busy professionals with no time to cook either, Susan's and David's friends were intrigued. They asked Susan if she would consider cooking and freezing meals in their kitchen once or twice a month. After ironing out the business details with David, Susan agreed and prepared trial meals for the couple. They were such a huge hit that Susan was asked to come back again, and then again. She did, and the personal chef services concept was born.

Always the entrepreneur, David quickly realized that if one family could benefit from personal chef services, surely others would, too. He helped Susan develop and market their concept, and just three months after she had prepared those trial meals for her first customers, she and David launched Personally Yours, the first personal chef service in San Diego. As demand for Susan's services grew, she decided to leave the restaurant job to devote herself to her new venture. By November 1989, just two years after that pivotal dinner with friends, Susan was living the life of her dreams — working at her passion five days a week during regular business hours, leaving her free to enjoy evenings and weekends with family. And not only did Susan have a long waiting list of people wanting to hire her, she had another long list of people wanting to know how they could become personal chefs.

David had come to believe that the demand for personal chefs could become as great as the demand for housecleaning services. So he set out to create a personal chef service industry and envisioned himself training thousands of people to do what Susan was doing. First he spent months on his computer developing a detailed and comprehensive training system based on what he and Susan had learned from starting and running Personally Yours. He documented everything from getting a business license to finding clients, and he created an extensive database of Susan's recipes.

Then in September 1991, David founded the United States Personal Chef Association (USPCA) to train and support other personal chefs. For an annual fee, members received a training package consisting of manuals and videos highlighting step–by–step instructions on every aspect of launching, running, and growing a personal chef service business, as well as unlimited telephone support. From the start this has been David's favorite part of the business — talking directly with personal chefs to help them with their new ventures.

In the first two years, David had helped launch 158 personal chef service businesses in 36 states. But after Susan and David appeared on the CBS *Morning Show* in 1994, the USPCA began gaining as many as three new members a day. By 1996, David had helped launch a thousand personal chef businesses through his training programs, and today, membership stands at over five thousand personal chefs around the world.

"I'm having a great time!" says David, adding that in seven years, the business had become a debt–free, million–dollar company. "Today, I feel that my dreams have been realized. I've never been more fulfilled, satisfied, or happy."

Of course, there were surprises along the way. David thought the concept would catch on faster. In the early years of the USPCA, he expected to spend most of his time training and supporting new personal chefs, but he ended up devoting a great deal of time to marketing the concept. Now, the association has grown so large that David holds national and regional conferences to further support members and enable them to exchange ideas. "I never imagined such a phenomenal growth rate as we're experiencing today," David says.

Another surprise was that the people who gravitate to the personal chef industry don't necessarily have a background in cooking. "Originally I thought we'd be training people like Sue, people in the culinary field," says David. "But we end up with individuals from all backgrounds — dentists, marketing professionals, teachers, you name it. I know a lady who started doing this on a shoestring. She didn't have a car, so she attached a little trailer to her bike. She used this to cart around her pots, pans, and ingredients to clients' homes. She did this for about a year before she was able to buy a car. This woman built her business on sheer determination."

It's been quite a learning experience for David, who has spent the last 12 years revising and upgrading his training materials and adding new benefits for USPCA members. Today, membership benefits include e–commerce support, liability insurance, and a subscription to *Personal Chef* magazine. David strives to do everything he can to support both new and long–time members.

After 13 successful years, Susan retired from Personally Yours and joined David full–time in his efforts to train new personal chefs. The couple realized that many members wanted hands–on classroom instruction, so they founded the United States Personal Chef Institute, the educational division of the USPCA. Campuses are located in Arizona, Georgia, and New Jersey, and classes are taught by trained, certified personal chefs. The USPCA is so highly regarded that for the last four years, the federal government has contracted the USPCA to teach monthly courses to flight attendant crews of the U.S. Diplomatic Air Fleet, including Air Force One.

David and Susan have reached heights they never even imagined. Husband and wife helped each other reach their dreams. Their success resulted from a skillful combination of creativity and hard work, seasoned just right with flexibility, perseverance, and mutual support.

"If you want to realize your dream," says David, "never give up. Continue to persevere, even when you fail. It takes constant re–evaluating, constant analyzing of what's working and what's not in order to get something off the ground."

"Whatever you enjoy doing," Susan adds, "read and learn everything you can about it. Seek others who share your interests. And don't limit yourself to just one path, because you never know exactly what dreams you'll end up creating along the way."

PHIL VISCHER:
A HIGHER CALLING LEADS TO A BIG IDEA

A natural storyteller and expert computer animator, Phil Vischer didn't want to spend the rest of his life designing swirling pastries and other product logos for television commercials. He dreamed instead of using his talents to create something that would have a lasting positive effect. Sickened by the violence shown in so many children's cartoons, Phil set out to create an animated family series that would reinforce qualities like kindness and compassion, and that would deliver these messages with humor and wit. With the success of his VeggieTales videos, Phil has accomplished the *daunting task of getting kids to watch wholesome cartoons and love their, ahem, singing and dancing vegetables.*

"Everything we do starts with the assumption that there is a God, and that people have a spiritual side to their lives," says Phil Vischer, founder and chief creative officer of Big Idea Productions, best known for its *VeggieTales* computer–animated children's series. "What we're trying to do is bring lessons like thankfulness and kindness and loving your neighbors to kids. Much of pop culture is devoid of these biblical values."

For example, in the *VeggieTales* rendition of the Bible story, "Daniel and the Lion's Den," the message is "trust God." But the gags abound, with Daniel even thanking the lions for pizza as he climbs unharmed from the den. In "The Grapes of Wrath," a cranky bunch of sour grapes and Junior Asparagus learn about forgiveness and accountability. In "Madame Blueberry," a very blue berry learns that all the stuff in the world won't make her happy the way a thankful heart can. Props like flying slushies and sledding penguins, along with plenty of references to pizza, grab kids' attention. Top–notch writing and catchy tunes like "God Is Bigger Than the Boogie Man," convey the key messages.

Phil gets letters every day from parents who are grateful to have *VeggieTales* as a tool to help them instill values in their children. And the sales volume shows that children and their families are absorbing the values–based messages delivered by an eclectic cast of wacky, talking vegetables — and want more. Since the 1993 release of its first full–length computer–animated video, "Where's God When I'm S–Scared?" Phil's company has produced 30 *VeggieTales* episodes and sold more than 47 million copies. Not bad for somebody who started out with little money, no connections, a single computer, and one big idea: to create cartoons that nurture children.

Influenced by Dr. Seuss, Walt Disney, and Jim Henson, Phil grew up in a creative environment. "My passion for storytelling has deep roots," he says. "I was doing puppets at the age of six, and I made my first film at nine — filming my toy Batmobile moving across our basement floor in Muscatine, Iowa! I made it with my grandfather's 8mm camera, which I borrowed for ten years until it didn't work anymore." At 14, Phil decided he would some-day make movies. At about that time he also developed a keen in-terest in computers. "As I grew," he says, "I learned how to weave stories using whatever technology I could find."

Following in the foot-steps of his great–grand-father — the Reverend R. R. Brown, whose *Radio Chapel Services* broad-cast from Omaha, Ne-braska, drew a half–million listeners — Phil went to St. Paul Bi-ble College in Minne-sota. There he met Mike Nawrocki, a kindred spirit who shared Phil's gift for comedy. The two joined a pup-pet ministry team on campus and had a blast writing and per-forming silly scripts together.

After college, Phil wanted to go to California to make movies. Instead, the Midwesterner found himself going to Chicago to make a living. In 1986 he entered the fast–growing field of three–dimensional computer animation, working in Chicago produc-tion houses for advertising industry clients. He quickly mastered computer animation and enjoyed the work, but something was nagging at him. "In 1991," he says, "I felt the calling to produce 'nobler' things than flying breakfast pastries and swirling beer logos."

Now a parent, Phil had grown frustrated by children's televi-sion shows and videos, and he began to dream of creating some-thing that would counter the damaging effects of the violence, sarcasm, and destruction peddled at today's youth. Phil sought to raise kids' self–esteem and restore a sense of innocence and play-fulness. With help and creative input from Mike, Phil started to develop the *VeggieTales* concept in his spare time.

Then in 1993, he took a huge leap of faith. Phil quit his job to pursue his dream in earnest and founded Big Idea Productions. He wasn't surprised by the challenges he immediately faced. "Only my friends and family believed me when I said *Veggie-Tales* would work," he says. "Everyone else thought it was crazy. I finally decided the only way to convince everyone else was to just go do it. So I borrowed money from my friends and my family, and I made the first video with one computer and the help of a few friends."

"When my wife, Lisa, and I were struggling trying to get *VeggieTales* off the ground," he continues, "my family helped in any way they could — picking up the check for a meal or even quietly stuffing a wad of bills into my hand as we left after a visit." He remembers the time he reluctantly gave Lisa their last $10 to buy food for the dog. As his wife left for the store, Phil sat in their silent apartment, his two–year–old daughter sleeping soundly in the next room. Despair and doubt began to creep into his mind.

"For the first time," says Phil, "I really wondered if this vision I was pursuing wasn't what God wanted me to do after all. Maybe I had it all wrong. Maybe I should just give up." Absentmindedly, Phil flipped through the mail that had stacked up on the table and noticed a hand–addressed envelope with no return address. Inside was a cashier's check for $400 and an unsigned note that read: 'God laid it on my heart that you might need this.' That was just the encouragement Phil needed. "It couldn't have been more obvious than if God had sat down next to me and said, 'You're doing the right thing. Keep going,'" he says.

With limited resources, Phil couldn't exactly hire professional actors to provide the characters' voices. So Phil became Bob the Tomato, the helpful co–star of *VeggieTales* who sometimes takes things a little too seriously. Mike became Larry the Cucumber, the silly, fun–loving co–star who often lives in his own world. And Lisa took the part of Junior Asparagus, the sweet five–year–old that kids relate to best. (These key players still perform those voices.)

But that first video sold only 500 copies by mail order, which was "not even enough to pay for the ads," says Phil. In trying to market the series, he was met with resistance. "When we were first approached about making *VeggieTales* available in general market stores," recalls Phil, "we were told we would have to take out all references to God and the Bible verse at the end. We were starving at the time. It was very tempting. However, God 'showing up' in our stories is a very important part of our mission. There was no way to gut it, so we chose to pass on the proposal. A year later, we were approached by others who said, 'Okay, you can leave God in, but you have to get rid of the Bible verse.' Again, we said 'no.'"

Initially, it was the Christian market that embraced *Veggie-Tales*. Big Idea sold 130,000 copies, and saw steady increases each year after, hitting the three–million mark in 1998. Now they were ready for prime time. "Finally, we found folks who were so excited about *VeggieTales*, they wanted to take it just the way it was," says Phil. "We stuck to our convictions, and *VeggieTales* has proven to be extremely popular at the Wal–Marts and Kmarts of the world."

Indeed. By the end of 1998, sales had reached 6.3 million. Today, sales have topped 21 million, and the company has developed two other series: *3–2–1 Penguins!* and *Larry Boy*. In 2002, Big Idea released *Jonah*, its first feature film, which ranked sixth at the box office on its opening weekend and earned more than $6.2 million in its first three days.

And the company has garnered some pretty high praise. "In an era when much of kids' programming is littered with sexual innuendo and bloody violence, Big Idea's success shows that producing high quality works," the *Chicago Sun–Times* observed. *The Washington Post* described *VeggieTales* as having, "First–rate computer animation, inspired scripts, and an infectious, wacky sense of humor," while the *Detroit Free Press* proclaimed, "*VeggieTales* is the kind of amusement that appeals to entertainment–savvy kids."

Phil hopes to continue to grow his visionary company and return basic values to popular mainstream media. He wants to break into the Saturday morning television cartoon market, for example. And of course, *VeggieTales* remains his flagship cartoon. "We want people to fall in love with our characters and grow up with them," Phil says, noting that although *VeggieTales* is aimed at three- to eight-year olds, the series has a large following of high school and college students.

"The key to changing the world is picturing it differently in your head, and then thinking up ways to make your dreams real," Phil says. "Creativity is key. If you believe God has given you a dream, some way to make a difference in the world, don't give up, even if people tell you it can't possibly work."

Creativity Breeds Dreams

> "DREAMS CHANGE. EVEN THOUGH THERE MAY BE A THEME, THEY MIGHT CHANGE OR ALTER DUE TO CIRCUMSTANCES IN LIFE. SO AS THEY CHANGE, WE HAVE TO CHANGE WITH THEM."
> — CONNIE BRADY, SOCIAL WORKER (CHAPTER 11)

Our creative dreams come from imagination and original thinking. Every product we have today, from bagels to blue jeans and violas to vaccines, first existed in somebody's imagination. Each of us can create ideas, inventions, and innovations that could improve our lives.

To let creativity shape your dreams, don't be afraid of following "crazy" ideas. By some people's standards, leaving a secure engineering job to pursue a career in comedy is downright nuts, but if Bill Nye hadn't done just that, he never would have performed in his own television show or written those informative–but–fun science textbooks. Sometimes you have to follow ideas some consider crazy to reach your dream.

To develop creative dreams, take a look around — in your own life, community, society, and the world — and ask: "Is this the best it can be? How can I make it better?" Phil Vischer looked at children's entertainment and determined that he could improve the landscape of children's cartoons.

Nothing is cast in stone. Today, gasoline–powered cars are the norm. Tomorrow we might all drive electric cars, or something that hasn't even been invented yet. Someday, we all may power our homes with sunlight and wind. Everything constantly changes and evolves. As old industries die, new ones are born, the way Susan Titcomb and David MacKay created the personal chef services industry to meet the needs of busy two–income families. Creative dreamers develop new ideas for new realities, often solving current problems in the process.

> ☝ ···
>
> ### Dream CPR Journal
>
> Remember back when you played imaginary games as a child... Who did you pretend to be? What did you imagine yourself doing when you grew up?
>
> If you could do anything you wanted to, without any conditions imposed on you, what would you be doing this very moment?

To cultivate your creativity, try the following:

1 Practice creativity regularly. Phil Vischer tells kids to draw and write more, and this is excellent advice for teens and adults, too. There are many ways you can practice creativity. Make up new recipes. Improvise on a musical instrument. Put a puzzle together. Grow a flower garden. Decorate a room. Build a piece of furniture. Start a scrapbook. Sing. Dance.

2 Let yourself daydream. Some folks think daydreaming is a waste of time, but daydreams provide creative ideas we can apply to improve our lives. Take some time each day — on a nature walk, at lunch, right before bedtime — to daydream and explore your imagination.

3 Imagine something that's new or different, and then build it or put it into practice. For example, come up with a fun new way to help your kids learn the multiplication tables. Design a new holiday decoration and then put it together. Sketch a more efficient layout for your home office, then rearrange your office furniture to fit the new concept. Practice bringing your ideas out of the realm of imagination and incorporating them into reality.

As you boost your creativity, you can start applying this Dream CPR essential element to construct creative dreams and creative ways to reach them. The following exercises can help:

1 Imagine your future. Bill Nye imagined a future in which the beauty of science is appreciated. He created a character, the Science Guy, that led to a television show that got children interested in and enthusiastic about science. Similarly, Phil Vischer imagined what healthier entertainment options for children could look like, and then created *VeggieTales*, along with a company to produce and market the videos. Separately, Susan Titcomb and David MacKay imagined having more time for the family and running a successful business. Together, they made both dreams come true by supporting each other and pioneering the personal chef concept.

2 Let yourself dream big. Creativity enables us to break barriers to develop solutions, such as new systems, inventions, breakthroughs, or ways to express ourselves. Picture the best possible reality for yourself, your loved ones, and humanity as a whole.

3 Think about how you can get there. What different paths might you take? Write down your ideas, allowing your imagination and inborn creativity to help you develop your plans.

You, too, can create positive changes in your life and in the world. Creativity allows us to develop new ideas that, put into practice, bring about opportunities and solutions for ourselves and others.

You've seen how creativity spawns exciting new dreams that lead to exciting new realities. In the next chapter, you'll see how the Dream CPR essential element *purpose* elevates our creative dreams to even higher, nobler levels, propelling us to strive for something bigger than ourselves.

chapter 7

Purpose: Find Your Reason to Dream

"THE PURPOSE OF LIFE IS A LIFE OF PURPOSE." — ROBERT BYRNE

When we work for a cause that's larger than life — such as world peace or human rights — we elevate ourselves in the process. The Dream CPR essential element *purpose* awakens us to the needs in our world and to our power to effect positive changes. Purpose gives us a reason to go beyond our egos, our day–to–day routine, and our personal dramas and reach for our dreams.

The purposeful dream achievers profiled in this chapter — peacemakers Jimmy and Rosalynn Carter, 66–year–old new college graduate Beverley Berlin Mas, and Children of Peace founder Binh Nguyen Rybacki — each discovered a greater meaning in life. After Jimmy Carter lost his re–election attempt, he could have quietly slipped into oblivion. Instead, he and Rosalynn started the now internationally acclaimed Carter Center to actively pursue their humanitarian dreams. Even though they're private citizens now, the former President and First Lady continue to use their clout to promote social justice and mediate peace in hot spots rocked by civil unrest, from East Timor to Venezuela. Beverley Berlin Mas has lived a full life and could be enjoying a quiet retirement today. Yet her sense of purpose — to help people struggling with grief — propelled her to return to school at 59 and begin a new career in psychology. A Vietnam refugee, Binh Nguyen Rybacki had built a happy, successful life in the United States. But when she returned to her homeland 18 years after fleeing, she couldn't ignore the street children she encountered. Moved, Binh started Children of Peace International, a nonprofit organization that today helps more than 4,200 orphaned and abandoned children.

People who follow a greater purpose don't sit back and rest on their laurels. Instead, they use their past achievements as a springboard to dive into their next cause. They're risk–takers, unafraid of choosing unconventional paths or tackling huge problems. When we find a greater purpose for our lives, our dreams become more exciting to us, helping us grow as individuals as we help others. We begin to live with stronger resolve, and we eagerly wake up every morning to find greater meaning in each new day.

BEVERLEY BERLIN MAS:
TURNING TRAGEDY INTO TENDERNESS

She's led a fulfilling life, achieving her childhood dream of becoming a professional entertainer, and meeting and marrying the love of her life. But in her mid–50s, Beverley Berlin Mas was hit by one catastrophic loss after another, including the murder of her mother. From her own battle with debilitating grief, which required a five–week stay in a psychiatric hospital, Beverley found a new purpose for her life: to help others struggling with devastating tragedy and loss. To achieve that goal Beverley went back to college, along the way becoming a mentor to classmates young enough to be her grandchildren.

While many of her contemporaries are enjoying retirement, 66–year–old Beverley Berlin Mas is embarking on a new career. She recently finished her bachelor's degree in psychology and now interns as an academic advisor on campus. Beverley plans to enter graduate school next fall, with the goal of ultimately becoming a licensed psychologist specializing in bereavement counseling.

Enrolling in college at 59, Beverley knew she faced a long and challenging journey. But she is driven by a strong sense of purpose and the desire to help others transform the pain of personal tragedy into hope and overcome the stigma associated with mental illness; a process she has experienced firsthand. Along the way, she's unexpectedly won over friends who, age–wise, could be her grandchildren.

Beverley, a former professional entertainer, recounts one of her early community college experiences. "When I went into my first speech class, I was really nervous because I hadn't been in front of an audience for many, many years," she says. "To get us warmed up, our instructor asked what our pet peeves were. I would say that more than half of the students said their pet peeves were 'old people.'" So when it was Beverley's turn to stand at the podium and deliver her speech, she spoke of the many senior citizens who come to Florida not to die, but to live abundantly. She concluded with, "Some of us older people have had experiences that would stand your hair on end. And we are very interested in learning about what you think and how you feel. There is so much we can exchange." Afterward, she began to receive genuine appreciation and respect from her younger peers.

Certainly the plot of Beverley's life is full of twists and turns that could captivate any audience. She enjoyed a happy childhood growing up on a farm in Ohio with four generations — great–grandparents, grandparents, parents, and children — all living under one roof. "I was raised with a close–knit family and a strong Christian base," she says. "I think my childhood has really helped me to be as centered as I am right now." Her grandmother was especially influential, nurturing Beverley's love of reading, learning, and music.

In high school, Beverley was voted "best actress," excelled in sports, and belonged to the drama club, the student council, and the girls' quartet. She sang in school choir as well as in her church choir, and dreamed of singing and acting professionally. She married her high school sweetheart, but when her marriage ended in divorce, she decided it was time to pursue those youthful dreams.

So in 1969 Beverley, then 33, joined the United Service Organization, better known as the USO. As the lead singer of a group that performed at military bases and hospitals throughout the Pacific Rim, she entertained troops in Vietnam. When she completed her tour, Beverley moved to Hawaii where she sang in clubs and acted on television, once appearing on *Hawaii Five–O*. Then it was on to New York, where she connected with many top–notch entertainers. "I started doing opening acts for Lou Rawls, The Fifth Dimension, and many other wonderful performers," she says. "That was really a kick." Beverley entertained at elegant supper clubs and showrooms in Chicago, New York, and Toronto. She also worked as a singer aboard cruise ships where, as she says, "I'd sing one or two shows a week, get first–class accommodations, and they paid me for it!" Beverley had made her childhood dreams come true.

After meeting Oscar, a "tall, handsome, and sweet man from Peru," Beverley decided that nine years in show business was enough for her. Oscar and Beverley married and settled in California, where she obtained a middle management position at a prestigious L.A. law firm. She made a good living, and loved living with Oscar.

But in 1991, Beverley's world turned upside–down when she suffered a series of devastating personal tragedies. First, her uncle shot and killed himself. Then, her sister died from an overdose of prescription antidepressants. Beverley temporarily lost an important part of her support system when her husband was hospitalized after suffering a major nervous breakdown and being diagnosed with latent manic depression bipolar disorder. Worst of all, Beverley's stepfather shot and killed her sleeping mother, then killed himself. Beverley's close–knit family had unraveled at the seams.

Emotionally and spiritually, Beverley felt numb, then devastated. To cope, she tried throwing herself into work, but the demands of her job became increasingly difficult to handle. Beverley had no idea how to deal with her pain; she went through the motions of life but felt detached from everyone and everything. She wouldn't listen to her doctor, who urged Beverley to take time off from her high–pressure job — until she found herself confused about something as simple as getting the mail. She recalls: "I brought everything back to my husband and held the mail out for him to see. I asked him, 'Who is all this for?' He told me, 'Well, this is for us.' I stared at him, and thought, 'I am really losing it.'"

Beverley checked herself into a psychiatric hospital, where she remained for five weeks. She learned that she was dealing with post–traumatic stress and got the help she needed. During that time the law firm "released her from her duties," but Beverley doesn't regret her decision to stay at the psychiatric hospital for a minute. "Even though I lost my job," she says now, "it was the best thing I've ever done for myself." She also lost friends, who couldn't deal with Beverley's pain or her husband's diagnosis. During this challenging time, Beverley experienced firsthand the stigma society places on mental illness.

After the Northridge earthquake devastated their area, Beverley and Oscar decided to leave Los Angeles. They eventually moved to Palm Beach Gardens, Florida, where they found a cozy townhouse located near a wildlife preserve. To Beverley, the natural setting has had a healing effect. "There are birds, turtles, and lakes all around us," she says. "It's wonderful." She'd found a place to call home, but she didn't know where her life was headed. Losing her job and friends left her with low confidence, to the point where she viewed herself as unemployable. Beverley knew that to move forward she had to raise her self–confidence, so she searched her soul and every day prayed, "What am I supposed to do with my life now?"

The answer finally came: Having learned so much from her own experiences of loss and depression, Beverley realized she was in a unique position to help others recover from devastating losses. She developed a dream based on her newfound purpose: to go back to school and pursue a career in psychology. Her sense of purpose gave her the confidence to embark on this exciting but very uncertain new path.

Beverley enrolled in community college in 1996 and immediately wondered if she'd made a mistake. Going back to school at 59 was not easy. The workload was heavy and she sometimes felt that her younger peers were absorbing the material faster than she was. But Oscar rallied behind her, even taking on cooking and cleaning duties to give Beverley enough time to study. Oscar kept encouraging her, and Beverley's dedication to her purpose propelled her on. She earned straight A's and the distinction of being the valedictorian of her class — and as she concluded her two–year degree commencement speech to rousing applause, she realized her confidence was back in full measure. Her community college accomplishments won her scholarships that helped defray tuition costs at Florida Atlantic University, where Beverley completed her bachelor's degree with honors at the age of 65.

College has not only helped Beverley gain the skills she will need to become a professional therapist, it's also given her a forum for bridging the generation gap. Beverley became active in honor societies, which thrust her into volunteer work. A natural leader, she started a local chapter of the America–Reach Program, a literacy effort launched by former President Clinton. In recruiting and training volunteers for the program, Beverley was pleasantly surprised. "Young people today really want to serve. Students would come up to me and ask, 'What can I do?' They wanted to give of themselves to help someone read or help wherever needed," she says.

Beverley also received honors that she had never anticipated. In 1999, *USA Today* recognized Beverley's collegiate achievements with the All–USA Academic First Team award, an honor extended to only ten students each year. As a result, Beverley has been invited to speak to audiences in many organizations nationwide, including the National Collegiate Honors Council, Circle K International, and the Special Olympics.

Currently an intern advisor, Beverley offers academic guidance to as many as 25 students a day. But she finds that students often seek her out for emotional support as well, on issues ranging from feelings of loneliness to discord with parents to worries about finding a job in an unstable economy. "It is wonderful to be able to send them on their way with a smile on their faces and hope in their hearts," Beverley says. She's been the driving force launching Dream It Do It Clubs® for nontraditional students at several Florida college campuses.

If her past accomplishments and ongoing drive are any indication, Beverley will continue to help and inspire others. She's well on her way to reaching her dream, enjoying the journey while adding even loftier goals. And as she continues to advocate mental health through her purpose, her dreams, and her everyday interactions, Beverley holds on to what she feels is the most important lesson life has taught her: "I've learned that living through difficult, painful situations brings us to a point where we don't judge anybody in any way, anymore."

BINH NGUYEN RYBACKI:
REMEMBERING THE FORGOTTEN CHILDREN

She fled her war–torn country as a teenager, angry at being forced to give up her beautiful homeland and the way of life she'd always known. But 18 years later, Binh Nguyen Rybacki returned to Vietnam and was horrified at the sight of orphaned and abandoned children begging in the streets and prostituting themselves to survive. Binh resolved to help the displaced children of Vietnam, a compassionate dream fueled both by her sense of purpose and by the urgency of the need. Though she had never tried anything like this, Binh developed an international nonprofit organization that brings food, shelter, education, security, dignity, hope, and love to Vietnam's unwanted "children of the dust."

When Binh Nguyen fled Vietnam with her family, the 18–year–old university student didn't know if she'd ever see her homeland again. It was 1975, just two years after American forces had pulled out, and North Vietnam had just conquered South Vietnam, where Binh and her family lived. The new regime swiftly executed those seen as American sympathizers, including eight of Binh's college friends who were English majors, like her-self. Binh's older sister had worked for the U.S. embassy. Their father, a distinguished university professor in Saigon, had been an integral part of the anti–Communist movement. Their lives were in mortal danger: The family had to get out, and fast.

Binh and her family members were among thousands of South Vietnamese the United States helped evacuate during the early days of the Viet Cong takeover. Binh remembers hurrying through a secret tunnel to an underground room and then wait-ing for what felt like an eternity. They hid there for two days be-fore they were abruptly rushed to an airplane at two in the morning. Binh and her family flew to safety in the Philippines — in the movies this would have been a happy ending. But of course real life is much more complicated, and the question weighing on the minds of the refugees was: *Now what?* They had escaped un-harmed, but what about their loved ones who remained in Viet-nam? What about the way of life they had to leave behind? Binh didn't even have the chance to say goodbye to the man she was planning to marry.

During the months that followed, Binh and her family lived in one refugee camp after another. First they endured a mandatory quarantine period in the Philippines, which was followed by a brief stay in Guam. Then it was on to a military base in Hawaii be-fore spending several months in a refugee camp in Arkansas. "I felt I had no place to call home," Binh recalls. "We lived in bar-racks and ate in mess halls. I realized for the first time that I had no choice in the matter — I had to grow up." Binh's intense anger and pain tested her faith: She remembers spitting in disgust as she walked past the refugee camp's chapel in the Philippines.

Finally Binh and her family were given the opportunity to move to Northern Colorado with support from American sponsors. There, they began the slow and difficult process of building a new life in a foreign land. Binh went to college and became a computer specialist. She fell in love and married. Her anger dissipated and was replaced by laughter, love, and forgiveness, and she was able to make peace with her God.

Binh gave birth to three sons: Today, her oldest is a college student majoring in music while her youngest is a middle–school student with a passion for sports. But Garrett, her second child, died in infancy from an enzyme deficiency. Grieving the loss of her child, Binh inexplicably found herself thinking about the children of Vietnam, particularly her childhood friends and those in an orphanage where her mother had volunteered years earlier when the family had lived in Saigon. Binh wondered how these children were doing. Her thoughts made her homesick, and she realized that she dreamed of seeing Vietnam again. But it seemed ridiculous. What reason did she really have to return? It had been so many years since the family fled the country. How could Binh just show up on the doorstep of old friends and distant relatives and say, *Hi, I thought I'd come to see how you were after all these years...?*

But several years later, in 1991, her mother offered some sage words as she lay on her deathbed. Binh recalls: "My mother said to me, 'You have to go back to Vietnam one day. No matter what happens in the world, you have to go back. You cannot grow any further unless you go back and make amends with that part of your life.' So I needed to go to honor my mother's wish."

During that first trip back in 1993, Binh reunited with many relatives and friends including Sister Tan, who had worked with Binh's mother at the Saigon orphanage. Sister Tan and other nuns in her order were now caring for 27 orphans in a dilapidated old monastery, supporting themselves and the children by making and selling hand–embroidered clothing. Binh immediately offered $100 in U.S. currency to help the children. But afraid that American greenbacks would draw the unwanted attention of suspicious, unsympathetic government officials, Sister Tan refused the money. Instead she sent a little boy to Binh's hotel room the following morning under the guise of selling fresh bread.

With the door locked and curtains drawn, Binh cut several loaves and stuffed inside the Vietnamese bills for which she had exchanged her American currency. She hid the "money bread" at the bottom of the boy's basket, arranging uncut loaves on top. The child returned safely to Sister Tan with Binh's surreptitious donation. That was the start of Binh's dream to support Vietnamese orphans.

Binh was appalled at the number of children living on the streets in Vietnam, which contrasted sharply with her memories of growing up in Saigon. Despite the ongoing war, even despite seeing her family's house burn to the ground when she was just 11 years old, Binh had been blessed to grow up in a loving, supportive family, which gave her the security that every child needs. But there was no one to love and nurture these homeless children who had to resort to begging, stealing, and selling their bodies to survive.

Back in the states, Binh continued to send donations to Sister Tan. She returned to Vietnam many times, always seeking out ways that she could help. She held HIV–positive babies, hugged deformed children no one else would touch, taught blind kids to read Braille, even "purchased" a girl for $52 to save her from a life of prostitution. Binh was instrumental in relocating the growing orphanage to a larger facility, and soon the orphanage grew from 27 to almost 300 children.

Meanwhile, the Vietnamese government became suspicious. "Little by little, the government started watching me," says Binh. "I had to talk with government officials and explain to them what I was doing. They came to realize I was not dangerous. They saw that we were just helping a couple of nuns and their orphanage."

But that didn't stop government officials from throwing Binh in jail many times for going against societal norms. For example, Binh tried to enroll orphans who were ethnic minorities in public school and got into heated arguments with public school officials who would not accept these children — a "crime" that cost Binh four days in jail. But in time, Binh was able to persuade the Vietnamese government to let her open a school for orphans and ethnic minorities. And she hired Vietnamese attorneys to help her avoid getting into trouble with the government.

Binh's sense of purpose kept growing; she dreamed of helping not only the kids at Sister Tan's orphanage but every displaced child in Vietnam. Binh went to her original American sponsors, Bob and Fran Ausenhus, who have remained great friends over the years, and asked them, "How do I make this bigger?" Bob, a retired attorney, advised her to incorporate. "I said to him, 'I know beans about forming a corporation.' So he helped me through the process," she says. "And we prayed and prayed about it. I prayed for people to love me and love God enough to never allow any harm to fall on these kids." In 1996, she formed Children of Peace International, a name selected by some of the older orphans. The nonprofit organization serves as a powerful vehicle for raising funds for "her children," as Binh lovingly calls them.

In just seven years, the nonprofit organization has gone from supporting 300 children in one orphanage to more than 4,200 kids at five different facilities. The work has been overwhelming at times — especially with Binh active in her sons' lives and busy as a full–time computer expert at a high–tech firm. What many people don't know about Binh is that she donated her entire salary to Children of Peace. When she recently lost her job in a round of layoffs, she worried about the children in Vietnam. But with moral and financial support from her husband, Jack — who believes in her purpose just as much as she does — Binh focused her energy on full–time fund–raising for the orphans.

"He's the driving force behind this," Binh says of Jack. "He helps me whenever I'm ready to quit. He tells me, 'Sure, you can quit. Anytime you want to. They'll just starve.' He's got this dry sense of humor, you see."

Binh's efforts have garnered much deserved praise. In January 2002, Binh received the prestigious Kiwanis International World Service Medal, an award that comes with a $10,000 grant, which will fund a new pediatric HIV center in Vietnam. Then in the summer of 2002, an unprecedented honor caught Binh by surprise. The Vietnamese government, which had previously jailed her for humanitarian work, chose Binh as the recipient of a prestigious annual award honoring an individual who has improved the lives of Vietnamese people. She is the first woman and first non–Vietnamese citizen to win this award.

Binh shows us that with a strong sense of purpose, we can accomplish the seemingly impossible — in her case, bringing hope to thousands of orphaned children in a nation still healing the wounds of war.

JIMMY AND ROSALYNN CARTER: POST–PRESIDENTIAL PEACEMAKERS

When Jimmy Carter's term as 39th president of the United States ended with a disappointing election defeat, he and his wife, Rosalynn, wondered what would come next. Building a presidential library just wasn't enough for these humanitarians. The Carters' deep desire to advance world peace and improve global living conditions fueled them to start something bigger. They found their post–presidency purpose by creating The Carter Center, a nonpartisan, nonprofit organization that furthers peace and raises health standards around the world. Twenty years later, the international community formally recognized Jimmy as a peacemaker by awarding him the Nobel Peace Prize.

Jimmy and Rosalynn Carter moved into the White House in 1977 full of hope and ideals. Both had fought for social justice, equality, and peace for years; surely occupying the highest office in the country would help them make so many of their dreams for a better world come true. But the Carters met with resistance and criticism right from the start and were often cruelly portrayed as simple peanut farmers out of their league in sophisticated, fast–paced D.C.

It was a difficult four years. Even today, some have forgotten the long–term good that resulted from Carter administration initiatives: Over a hundred–million acres of Alaskan wilderness were preserved through the national park system. Relations with Latin America improved markedly. Diplomatic relations with China were restored. A U.S. Department of Energy was formed to focus on fossil fuel conservation and developing alternative sources of energy. Certainly the landmark of the Carter administration was the historic peace agreement reached between Egypt and Israel. Still, by 1980, many blamed the Carter administration for everything from the Iran hostage crisis to gas shortages, and from rampant inflation to the stagnant recession that had followed. On election night, American voters voiced their discontent by denying Jimmy a second term in the Oval Office.

As we all know by now, Jimmy and Rosalynn were not naive and uninformed as some critics had depicted. They were intelligent, compassionate, hardworking public servants, and they left Washington with many unfulfilled dreams. They could have settled into a quiet retirement, dwelling on the past and wondering what could have been. Instead, the Carters' deep desire to advance world peace and improve global health conditions fueled them to move on. So in 1982, Jimmy, then 58, and Rosalynn, 55, founded the nonprofit Carter Center in their home state of Georgia, and this would prove to be the Carters' greatest contribution to humankind.

Over the past two decades, the Carter Center has monitored elections in developing and struggling democracies, assisted nations torn by civil war, and taught more effective agricultural methods to alleviate hunger and famine. Electoral authorities from Nicaragua, Kenya, Mexico, and 20 other countries have invited the Carter Center to send, through its Democracy Program, impartial observers to ensure fair elections. The Carter Center's Conflict Resolution Program has been instrumental in restoring diplomatic relations between Sudan and Uganda, a key to achieving peace in these nations devastated by civil war. And the center's Agricultural Program helps farmers in sub–Saharan Africa significantly increase their crop yields. Through these and many other programs developed at the Carter Center, Jimmy and

Rosalynn have found a greater purpose for their lives, making great strides toward their dream of worldwide peace and social justice.

The Carters show the rest of us how to get from dreaming it to doing it. First, they dare to believe that it can be achieved, and then they roll up their sleeves and go to it. They've lived this way their entire lives.

Rosalynn's father, who owned an auto–repair shop in Plains, Georgia, died when she was 13. As the eldest child, Rosalynn took care of her four siblings, cooking and cleaning house while her mother worked for the post office and as a seamstress. Rosalynn first came face–to–face with social injustice when she was a ninth–grader typing a school paper as a favor for an African–American acquaintance. Reading the older student's paper, she was startled to discover that the education black children in her community received was of a significantly lower quality than the education of white children. She realized then that "separate but equal" was nothing but a myth.

Jimmy, the son of a registered nurse and a farmer, was no stranger to hard work. He was responsible for arduous farm chores, like pulling weeds and turning vines in sweltering heat. Jimmy was a humanitarian at heart who learned social justice by watching his open–minded mother believe in and practice racial equality, even in a heavily segregated South.

Somehow, both Rosalynn and Jimmy managed to make school a priority. Valedictorian of her high school class, Rosalynn went on to graduate from Georgia Southwestern College. Jimmy graduated seventh in his class from the United States Naval Academy.

The couple began dating in the summer of 1945 and married a year later. For seven years they lived the military life, moving from place to place while Jimmy served as an officer in the U.S. Navy. When his father died in 1953, Jimmy resigned his naval commission to return to Plains to manage the Carter farms. The Carters settled into the business of farming for several years, working full–time while raising their four children. Meanwhile, Jimmy became active in the community, serving on school, hos-

pital, and library boards. This taught him that politics could provide an avenue for putting his leadership and communications
skills to use on a large scale, enabling him to serve the public
beyond his immediate community.

As Jimmy saw the potential to do
good in public service, he set goals
for himself, achieving them one by
one. In 1962 he was elected to the
state senate. He ran for governor of
Georgia in 1966, lost that race,
then came back to win the
election in 1970. In his gu-
bernatorial inauguration
speech he said, "The time
for racial discrimination
is over," and he didn't
care if that made him un-
popular with segregationists. While Governor Carter focused on
racial equality, reorganizing the state government, and expanding the state parks system, Rosalynn dove into causes she believed in, especially improving services for the mentally and
emotionally disabled. After a successful term as governor,
Jimmy took an historic, monumental step — he announced his
candidacy for United States President.

For two years, Rosalynn traveled across the nation to tell people about Jimmy Carter. Meanwhile Jimmy also set out to talk to
people and garner support. The public, finding the couple's
openness and honesty refreshing and their desire to serve the
people genuine, elected Jimmy president in 1976.

After the discouraging re–election defeat in 1980, Jimmy and
Rosalynn picked themselves up, dusted themselves off, and
founded the Carter Center so they could continue their work for
social justice. Rosalynn created and chaired the center's Mental
Health Task Force and holds an annual symposium on mental
health policy. Meanwhile Jimmy uses the Carter Center as a vehicle for mediating between warring factions in some of the most
politically heated spots on the globe. In his efforts toward peace
and reconciliation, he has earned respect across borders and cul-

tures thanks to his integrity, honesty, and commitment to helping others.

These traits are his passports, granting him entry to face–to–face meetings with even the most inaccessible dignitaries, the most notorious dictators, the most elusive luminaries, and the most powerful leaders of the world — all for the sake of championing human rights. In 1994, Jimmy's talks with the president of North Korea resulted in a freeze of the nation's nuclear program and the first dialogue between the United States and North Korea in forty years. And in 2002, Jimmy became the first former or sitting U.S. president to visit Cuba since 1928, a trip where he urged both nations to mend relations.

Back home, Rosalynn and Jimmy also make time to volunteer outside the Carter Center. Every year they devote a week to building houses for Habitat for Humanity, a cause near and dear to their hearts. Undoubtedly they are Habitat's most celebrated volunteers.

But whether the Carters are sawing wood and painting walls, or meeting with foreign dignitaries to mediate peaceful resolutions, they remain humble in their success. At 82 and 79 years old in 2007, Jimmy and Rosalynn continue to captivate the public — not just in Georgia but around the entire world — with their honesty, simplicity, and grace. They are who and what they appear to be, with no pretenses and no disguises. Even when he won the Nobel Peace Prize in 2002 in recognition of decades of work to find peaceful solutions to international conflicts and advance human rights, Jimmy was quick to give credit back to the Carter Center.

"Much of the work we've done outside of politics is available to almost anyone," Jimmy says. "For most of us, learning about those who are in need, people who are often our immediate neighbors, can add a profound new dimension to our own lives."

"Our fast–changing world requires the talents, contributions, and leadership of every one of us to create the better life we seek for ourselves and our children," Rosalynn states. "Each of us has what it takes to succeed and make a positive difference in our own unique way."

She adds: "Set your goals high and work to achieve them. Never be afraid of failure. The tragedy comes not in failing, but in never having tried to succeed."

Purpose is the Reason Behind Our Dreams

> " IT'S REALLY IMPORTANT THAT WE RETAIN GOALS IN OUR LIVES, THAT THOSE GOALS ALSO BRING BENEFIT TO OTHERS AS WELL AS TO OURSELVES." — DENNIS WEAVER, ACTOR (CHAPTER 12)

Purposeful dreamers are the true movers and shakers of society, following a noble vision and making great things happen. They set trends, make policies, and build bridges between people with differing viewpoints. For example, by going back to school, 66–year–old Beverley Berlin Mas has not only followed her purpose to help people in grief, she's become a wise and hip surrogate grandmother for college students who are depressed, lonely, or confused about their career and life paths.

When our dreams are born of purpose, we can soar above limitations to accomplish the seemingly impossible. Despite a Vietnamese government that distrusted her intentions and a society that viewed street kids as "lost children of the dust," Binh Nguyen Rybacki broke social and political barriers to house, love, and educate these children.

To discover your purpose, try the following:

1   Ask yourself: *What do I believe in? What causes am I passionate about? What do I care most about?* Your answers might be broad, such as alleviating world hunger, or very specific, like starting a support group for cancer survivors in your community. Write your answers down in your *Dream CPR Journal.*

2   Now ask yourself: *What can I bring to this cause?* To answer this, you need to evaluate your abilities and strengths.

The Carters bring different strengths to advance the mission of the Carter Center: Jimmy uses his mediating skills and clout as a former U.S. president to negotiate international peace resolutions. Rosalynn applies her knowledge of mental health issues to raise awareness and propose policies in this arena. Both are veteran farmers who help developing communities around the world employ effective agricultural techniques.

3 Do some volunteer work on a trial basis in an area that addresses the cause that means the most to you. Volunteer work can help you learn about a specific area and even discover new skills. Volunteering also can help you determine if you want to work in this area — and whether you've truly discovered your purpose.

Once you know your purpose, you can develop dreams that align with your sense of purpose:

1 Start by asking: *How can I apply my gifts and talents to further the cause I believe in?* Look at what you can do and what you want to do, then take it from there. For example, say you have great organizational skills and you realize that your purpose is to share your love of reading. What can you do to further this cause in your community? Are there any reading programs in the public schools or libraries, or nonprofit organizations dedicated to fighting illiteracy? If not, can you launch a campaign to create such a program? Or can you expand existing programs somehow — by recruiting volunteers, donating books, becoming a tutor to an illiterate adult, or inviting children's authors to give readings? There are countless ways to further a cause you believe in. Develop a dream that will allow you to use

> ### Dream CPR Journal
>
> When you were younger, what causes were you drawn to? What did you believe in?
>
> Take the time to write your answers down. Then consider what is most important to you today and why.

your unique gifts to support your purpose, and you'll create positive results.

2 Ask yourself: *What do I want to be remembered for?* Binh Rybacki worked as a computer specialist for many years. But is that her legacy? No. Binh will be remembered as an advocate for children. And that's fine with her. Decide what you want to be remembered for, then start working toward that dream.

There's a song by two–man musical group Lost and Found that goes like this: "Everybody in the whole world matters. Everybody has a place." It's true: You have a place in this world, and you and your dreams matter. When you discover your purpose, you've found your place in our world. What an exciting discovery!

Knowing your purpose helps you develop dreams that are meaningful to you and helpful to others. In the next chapter, you'll see how uncovering your passion can add an exciting new dimension to your dreams.

chapter 8

Passion: Get Fired Up

> "FEELING AND LONGING ARE THE MOTIVE FORCES BEHIND ALL HUMAN ENDEAVOR AND HUMAN CREATIONS."
> — ALBERT EINSTEIN

When you're doing what you love to do, it shows — you feel it and others see it. Your energy level rises. Your eyes sparkle. You meld with the activity, lost in blissful satisfaction. The feeling you get is unmistakable: pure joy combined with the sense that, yes, this is exactly what you're meant to do. That's what the Dream CPR essential element *passion* does for us. When we build our dreams around the things that stir our passion, our lives become more joyful, meaningful, and exciting.

Passion drives people to achieve. It's the fire in your soul, the feeling of being completely absorbed, thoroughly enthralled, and profoundly energized about a vocation, activity, or cause. Without passion, even the best–laid plans may fail; with no feeling, thrill, or love driving our actions, we will achieve little. Having tremendous passion for our dream, an aching desire to do that one thing above all else, gives us the momentum to push forward in a maze of obstacles and tribulations.

When a 25–year–old Carl Karcher bought a hot–dog stand, he discovered his passion for running and growing a business. That passion drove him to build one of the largest fast–food chains from scratch. Young Gloria Estefan had deep–rooted shyness, but her passion for music enabled her to overcome her fear of singing in public and become an international pop star. Gloria's passion guided her spirit after a debilitating accident threatened to end her career, helping her endure grueling pain to rehabilitate her body and return to center stage.

Academy Award nominee Michael Clarke Duncan once dug ditches to support himself and his mom. But when he followed his passion — a deep, burning desire to become an actor — he broke into Hollywood against all odds. As a little girl, Eileen Collins was fascinated with space and flying. Even with no American female astronaut role models, she pursued her dreams and became the first woman pilot and commander of the NASA space shuttle.

Passion finds a way, sooner or later, to make itself known. Against the odds, the artist will paint, the writer will write, the scientist will discover, even though each may not always follow a prescribed path. Detours are not necessarily detrimental to our dreams; they can supply us with valuable life experiences that ultimately prepare us to live our dreams born of passion.

GLORIA ESTEFAN:
UNSTOPPABLE SINGING SENSATION

> She had planned to become a psychologist but her passion for music led her in a different direction. Quiet and shy, Gloria Estefan conquered her fear of singing in public by focusing on her passion, not her timidity. Overcoming that hurdle enabled Gloria to become one of the top entertainers of our time. Not even a life–threatening accident could keep this passionate performer from taking center stage.

Singer Gloria Estefan's performances are high–energy extravaganzas. But there is much more to the success of this Cuban–born entertainer than sheer talent. When Gloria sings and dances on–stage, whether in the U.S. or abroad, she connects warmly with her audiences. Fans love her, and the reason is simple: Gloria loves music and joyfully shares her passion through her performances. On stage, the petite five–foot–two woman generates enough energy to fill the largest stadiums in the world. Her "jump up and dance" rhythms make people want to celebrate life. Gloria does more than entertain people — she feeds their spirit. Watching this dynamic performer, it's hard to believe that she suffered a broken back in a devastating accident that threatened not only her career but her ability to walk. It's just as difficult to fathom that this self–confident woman once suffered from painful shyness.

Gloria Maria Fajardo was born in Cuba in 1957, the daughter of a military officer and a teacher. With turmoil permeating their homeland, the Fajardos immigrated to the United States when Gloria was only 16 months old, eventually settling in Miami, Florida. Young Gloria loved music. At home, her mother often played records from Cuba, introducing her daughters to Latin music. As she grew up, Gloria also enjoyed listening to popular American singers on radio — Barbra Streisand, Karen Carpenter, Diana Ross. "Music has always been a wonderful and beautiful form of escape," she says.

As a child, Gloria began writing poetry and songs. And for her ninth birthday, she received a guitar from her mother. At first, Gloria did not enjoy music lessons, but once she could imitate radio tunes, her love for the guitar blossomed. During the two years that Gloria's father served in South Vietnam, Gloria made homespun audiotapes of herself singing and sent these to her dad to lift his spirits. He returned safely from the war, but soon fell very ill. Eventually Gloria's father was diagnosed with multiple sclerosis, later attributed to Agent Orange.

Gloria grew up fast. From the time she was 11 until she turned 16, Gloria — a quiet, straight–A, honor–roll student — took care of her disabled father every day as soon as she got home from school. Gloria had to take on this responsibility because her mother worked full–time. Whenever she felt overwhelmed, discouraged, or sad, Gloria turned to music for comfort. "When my father was ill," she says, "music was my escape. It was my release from everything. I'd lock myself up in my room with my guitar. I would sing for hours by myself."

Music became her outlet and her greatest passion. Gloria's family, of course, saw her talent and encouraged her to perform. But she was private and reserved around strangers, and she was afraid of singing in public. Only after repeated coaxing from both her grandmother and her mother would Gloria sing even at family parties and weddings. The more she performed, the more she shed her shyness. She discovered that she enjoyed the applause, the accolades, and the thrill of singing her heart out before a crowd.

When 18–year–old Gloria met Emilio Estefan, Jr. in 1975, he was the leader of the nine–man band Miami Latin Boys, a popular local group. The 22–year–old Emilio, an experienced performer, was giving stage pointers to Gloria and other budding singers and musicians. Several weeks later, the two met again when the Miami Latin Boys played at a large wedding that Gloria and her mother attended as guests. Emilio recognized the reserved young lady with the beautiful voice and invited her to stand up and sing a song with the band. Gloria was reluctant, but with her mother's and Emilio's encouragement, she gave it her best — and the crowd responded with a standing ovation.

Soon afterward, Emilio asked Gloria to join his band. She declined. As a freshman at the University of Miami, Gloria was focused on getting a degree and becoming a psychologist. Only after Emilio assured Gloria and her family that she would sing with the band just on weekends and during school vacations did she agree. "I loved music so much that I couldn't let a great opportunity like this pass me by," she says. No longer all–male, the group changed its name to the Miami Sound Machine and quickly became one of the most sought−after bands in town.

Gloria fell in love with both show business and Emilio. In 1978, the same year that Gloria completed her college degree, the couple married. But Gloria chose not to pursue a career in psychology after all, dreaming instead of taking her musical career to greater and greater heights. Remnants of her shyness remained, and she knew that she needed to transform herself in order to reach her dream.

Gloria began an exercise program and improved her diet. Never a dancer before, she began incorporating simple moves into her performances with the band. As her confidence grew, Gloria became more assertive with her fellow musicians and engaging to her audiences. And, slowly, she transformed her role in the band from singing back−up and playing maracas to taking center stage. She learned to stand in the spotlight with confidence and joy, not fear.

Within a couple of years, the Miami Sound Machine recorded and released three albums, with songs in both Spanish and English. Each had been funded with money from the band members' own pockets. The albums received a measure of success in Miami, but Emilio wanted to go to the next level. He knew they needed to work with a record label, so he stepped back from performing to concentrate on the business side.

In 1980, the group got its first major break when Emilio cut a deal with CBS Discos International, a Miami−based division of CBS Records. The deal led to four Spanish−language albums aimed at markets in Central and South America. They were all huge successes, topping record charts in several countries including Venezuela and Honduras. Gloria and the band toured South America, playing to crowds as large as 30,000. Then in 1984, Gloria and the Miami Sound Machine hit No. 10 on U.S. pop charts, paving the way for the band's 1985 breakthrough album, *Primitive Love*. Featuring "Conga," "Bad Boy," and "Words Get In The Way," this album led to international fame. The Miami Sound Machine proved that their catchy rhythms could crossover to the mainstream and sell beyond the Latino markets.

During the latter half of the decade, Gloria and the Miami Sound Machine would release two more hit albums and go on several world tours. For Gloria, life was busy, exciting, and very, very good. Then, on a cold, snowy day in March 1990, her world turned upside–down.

With her husband, their son, and three staff members, Gloria was headed for a performance in Syracuse, New York, when their private tour bus stopped in heavy traffic on the Pennsylvania Turnpike due to an accident several miles ahead. Suddenly, a truck carrying 19 tons of pitted dates slammed into the back of the tour bus, hurling it into another truck in front. Sandwiched between two semitrailers, the tour bus was crushed and every passenger injured. But no one was hurt worse than Gloria. Laying on the floor of the bus, she knew immediately that her back was broken. X–rays showed two fractured vertebrae in her spine. Gloria had nearly been permanently paralyzed. Two days later, she underwent a risky surgery that involved a 14–inch incision, the insertion of two 8–inch metal rods, and more than 400 stitches.

The road to recovery was long and painful. For the next several months, Emilio and Gloria got up at 45–minute intervals every night and slowly walked around their home to keep her muscles from atrophying. She did not think about her singing career during this time; her only concern was getting her body and independence back. From having taken care of her father, Gloria knew what it was like to care for someone who was homebound, and she did not want her family to go through that with her. As she told Larry King in a 1999 interview, "Five months after the accident, I celebrated the day I was able to put my underwear on by myself. That's how long it took just to feel normal."

When her physical strength began to return, Gloria began writing *Into The Light* with Emilio's help, an album with songs inspired by her journey from tragedy to victory. It was this passion for music that brought Gloria back to the stage: Just one year after the accident, Gloria gave the performance of her life at the Miami Arena. By the end of her *Into The Light* tour, she had performed for more than five million people in nine countries.

"When I think of what could have happened," Gloria says, "I feel better — and luckier — every day." Her passion for music brought everything to this talented singer: laughter and pain, struggle and joy. But through good times and bad, Gloria continues to follow her passion, showing us how to hold on to hope and believe in your dreams.

MICHAEL CLARKE DUNCAN: DITCH–DIGGER NO MORE

He dug ditches for a living eight hours a day, five days a week. But on his time off, his eyes were glued to the TV set as he closely studied actors' words, motions, and expressions. "I can do that!" Michael Clarke Duncan told his work buddies, who laughed at his quixotic dream. But his passion took him to Hollywood, where Michael did indeed reach his impossible dream of becoming an acclaimed and successful actor.

Growing up in a poor neighborhood on Chicago's South Side, Michael Clarke Duncan listened to his mother. "You're going to be a star one day," she kept telling him, and he liked the sound of that. When Michael was in his 20s, his mother's words would echo through his mind during his long, eight–hour shifts digging ditches for the People's Gas Company in Chicago. After work he'd watch television, not to relax but to study the actors carefully, saying aloud, "I can do that!"

"Hollywood Mike," as his work buddies liked to call him, talked incessantly about his desire to act, giving his coworkers plenty of fodder for teasing him. "Bruce Willis is on the phone, he wants to talk to you about doing a movie," they'd joke. Michael took it all in stride, sometimes laughing along, other times assuring them that one day they'd have to pay $7.50 to see his face on the big screen. He was right. Only six years after Michael left the People's Gas Company, his old work buddies watched their former co–worker co–star alongside Bruce Willis in the blockbuster *Armageddon*. Back in Chicago to promote the movie, Michael was moved to tears when his former boss offered congratulations and a hug, telling the six–foot–five, 315–pound actor how proud the entire crew was.

It was a long, winding road from the South Side to Hollywood. Michael and his sister learned self–confidence and a strong measure of respect from their mother, a single parent. Theirs was a tight–knit, caring family. Although she worked long hours as a house–cleaner, Michael's mother made sure to teach her children to stay away from drugs and gangs and focus on doing well in school. When young Michael and his mom read storybooks together, she taught him how to read with feeling and flair, and he inherited his mother's soft heart and emotional streak. He fell in love with acting because it was a way to express himself and his feelings.

Michael attended Alcorn State University in Mississippi, but when his mother became ill with lupus, he dropped out of college to come home and help her. Michael found work digging ditches. By day, he dug ditches for the gas company, while at night he worked as a bouncer for local nightclubs. All the while, he dreamed of acting. He even found time to work out with weights at a gym, figuring that being toned and fit would boost his chances of breaking into movies.

Michael's experience as a bouncer helped him land a security job with a touring theater troop. He quit his day and night jobs to tour with the production of _Beauty Shop, Part 2_. When the show's 56–city run ended in Los Angeles in 1995, Michael decided to stay in Southern California to pursue his passion.

Without any formal training in drama, Michael began to audition for roles. He soon discovered that auditioning was about as grueling as ditch–digging! He was a newcomer from far away, with no friends or family nearby and no acting experience. Hollywood just didn't have any sensitive, serious roles for a large African–American man with no acting experience. Michael found himself living in a rundown motel, eating chicken nuggets from fast–food restaurants, and coming home to see roaches scurrying across his kitchen floor. He was unemployed, and his savings quickly dwindled down to his last $20.

Michael was about ready to throw in the towel. Every audition left him empty–handed. Hungry, lonely, a stranger in a strange land, he was ready to head back to Chicago. But in a phone conversation his mother cautioned that he might never get another opportunity to try. "You will never know for the rest of your life if you could have made it or not," she said. Michael didn't know how much more he could take, but he decided to stay in Hollywood and press forward. A week later, he got a $10–an–hour security job at a Hollywood studio lot. It wasn't an acting job, but at least he could support himself while he auditioned.

Michael finally got a part, playing a drill sergeant in a beer commercial. Through his security job, he boldly struck up a friendship with actor Will Smith, who acceded to Michael's continuing pleas to appear on *The Fresh Prince of Bel Air*. Other television roles came, as did small parts in movies. Michael was cast in the daytime soap opera, *The Bold and the Beautiful*, and appeared in single episodes of several TV shows.

His big physique proved to be his biggest ally when he was cast as oil driller Bear in *Armageddon*, appearing opposite Bruce Willis. The two became good friends during filming, and Bruce was impressed with Michael's determination, passion for acting, sensitivity, and raw talent. Bruce knew about a new movie, *The Green Mile*, that soon would be casting. A fan of Stephen King's novel, he felt Michael would be perfect for the part of John Coffey, the falsely accused convict with mystical powers. Bruce made a phone call and arranged for Michael to audition.

Director Frank Darabont watched in amazement as this newcomer brought the character to life, infusing the part with heart, soul, and feeling. Having read King's novel twice before auditioning, Michael identified completely with the character, and he knew no one could bring Coffey to life like he could. Coffey, too, was a misunderstood gentle giant in an often crazy, mixed-up world. Michael visualized himself as the character, feeling what it felt like to be him. He understood the character's sensitivity, ability to see inside a person's heart, and gentleness toward animals. Michael had walked into the audition ready to claim the role.

To his sheer delight and gratitude, he got the part and with it, the opportunity to show the world what he could do. The film co–starred Michael alongside Tom Hanks. Released in 1999 on Michael's 37th birthday, the film was a huge hit, and audiences embraced Michael's passionate, moving performance.

His dreams had come true. Michael was honored with an Oscar nomination for best supporting actor in *The Green Mile* and a nomination for the NAACP Image Award. He was overcome with emotion: These nominations had been beyond his wildest dreams. Just as his mother predicted, Michael has become a star, and he's ever thankful for listening to his mom and staying in Hollywood to give acting one more chance.

It wasn't the lure of money, power, or status that turned this former ditch–digger into a celebrated yet humble Hollywood star. It was passion. When entertainment reporter Christopher Brandon asked Michael what roles he'd consider, Michael responded: "I'm open to anything. I'm not leaving any doors shut. As long as it's something that I can really get into. I have to feel it. If I don't feel it, I can't do it."

EILEEN COLLINS:
WHERE NO WOMAN HAS GONE BEFORE

> She was the first woman to take the reins at the helm of NASA's space shuttle. Such an accomplishment doesn't happen overnight. Eileen Collins had to break gender barriers and work extremely hard to follow her passion for aircraft, science, and space in order to fly into history books.

"My father would take us to the Harris Hill glider port and the Elmira–Corning regional airport in New York," Eileen Collins recalls, "and we would have an A&W root beer while we sat on the hood of the car watching the airplanes take off and land." Eileen loved watching planes trace their paths across the sky on these family outings during the early 1960s. But little did Eileen know then that the passion she developed for airplanes would lead to a career flying military aircraft. Nor did the young girl imagine that she would grow up to become an astronaut — the first woman to pilot and command NASA's space shuttle. All she knew was that airplanes and space fascinated her.

When Eileen was in the fourth grade, a *Junior Scholastic* magazine article made a strong impression on her. "The Gemini program was in full swing," she says. "I remember seeing an article that argued pro versus con: Should the United States be spending money on the space program? I remember reading the pros, and reading the cons, and it was just totally obvious to me that we ought to be doing this. Even as a nine– or ten–year–old child it made total sense to me that we ought to go to space and explore. And I could not understand why anyone would say no."

By the time she reached high school, Eileen was dreaming of flying. She absorbed books about flight missions in World War II, the Korean War, and the Vietnam War, developing an appreciation for what military pilots do in wartime and peacetime. She became increasingly interested in flying for the military — not a typical dream for young women in the early 1970s. More than anyone else, her parents encouraged Eileen to follow her dreams.

She excelled in her favorite subjects, math and science — particularly geometry, biology, and physics. A bright student with good grades, Eileen won scholarships and grants for college, but also worked part–time and took out student loans to help pay her tuition. In 1978, she obtained a Bachelor of Arts degree in math and economics from Syracuse University in New York. In her senior year, she applied to the U.S. Air Force, and nearly was turned down when eyestrain hampered her normally perfect vision.

"I failed the eye exam," Eileen recalls. "My ROTC boss said, 'Hey, I'll give you a second chance to take that eye test.' Which was probably the biggest break in my career, because otherwise I never would have become a pilot. They let me take the test again two weeks later. So I rested my eyes and ate right. I slept a lot. I ate carrots. Actually, I ate so many carrots my fingertips turned orange! But when I went back to retake the eye test, I passed it."

In 1979 Eileen graduated from Air Force Undergraduate Pilot Training. She had reached her dream of flying. But she continued to have that passion for space exploration that had begun when she was a child. During Eileen's high school and undergraduate college years, there were no American women astronauts. Only one woman had flown in space — a cosmonaut from the Soviet Union who orbited Earth in 1963. But things had started to change. "In 1978, when NASA selected their first women astronauts, I really started thinking that this was something I wanted to do," Eileen says.

Eileen continued in the Air Force, working as commander and instructor pilot until 1985. In 1986, she completed a Master of Science degree in operations research at Stanford University and became an assistant professor in mathematics at the U.S. Air Force Academy in Colorado Springs. But still her dream of flying in space remained, and Eileen knew that if she was serious about becoming an astronaut, she would need even more training and education. So it was back to school again for a Master of Arts degree in space systems management, which she completed at Webster University in 1989. From there, she went on to the Air Force Test Pilot School at Edwards Air Force Base in California.

Finally, in February 1989, Eileen was ready to apply to NASA's astronaut program through the Air Force. That May, an Air Force board met to screen all applicants and forward selected names to NASA. Eileen made the first cut. Then in July, NASA's pre–screening board reviewed thousands of applications. Eileen was among the 120 people chosen to interview for the astronaut program.

Three months later, in October 1989, Eileen had her interview, and then had to wait another three months before she received the exciting phone call from NASA letting her know that she'd been accepted for the space program. It had been almost a year since Eileen started the application process.

With "permanent change of station" orders from the Air Force, Eileen and her husband — also a pilot — moved to Houston in July 1990. Eileen began the rigorous training program at Johnson Space Center. She was assigned to her first flight in September 1993, a mission she flew in February 1995. Years of training and preparation along with her passion for space and flying had finally resulted in this inaugural voyage. She made history by becoming the first woman ever to pilot the space shuttle. Eileen then flew her second space shuttle mission in May 1997. As with her first mission, the shuttle rendezvoused with Mir. But it was her third mission that made front–page news around the world.

In July 1999 — the same year she became an Air Force colonel — Eileen took a giant leap for womankind. Colonel Eileen Collins became the first woman to command the space shuttle, overseeing the entire mission and supervising the crew. Eileen oversaw the deployment of the Chandra X–Ray Observatory, which has brought scientists closer to quasars, black holes, and other phenomena of the universe. As commander, she successfully landed the shuttle to conclude her third mission. Eileen had logged a total of 537 hours in space.

After commanding one more successful shuttle mission in 2005, Eileen retired from NASA the next year. She has become a role model not only to her own two children, but to youngsters everywhere with big dreams. She remembers when her daughter was a preschooler and was just starting to grasp how rare it is for a person to go into space. She would pause for a moment, then ask, "Mommy, are you famous?"

Eileen frequently addresses young people across the country, encouraging them to reach for the stars in whatever field they have a passion. Young girls who dream of flying look up to her. She has become the role model that, as a young girl, she never had.

On a shuttle mission, astronauts have a packed schedule during their brief time in space. But during her second flight, Eileen did manage to spend 40 minutes gazing at Earth's beauty. "We were crossing New York City, above the Eastern U.S. seaboard," she says. "You could see all the way up and down the coast. It was nighttime, totally clear, and you could see all the city lights. It was just amazing. As the Earth turned below us, we crossed the Atlantic Ocean. We saw all of Europe, the Mediterranean Sea, Africa. It was still dark until we got to Greece. And then the terminator — the line around the Earth that separates night from day, I would say it's a very narrow band — was over Greece, so we saw the sunrise over Greece ... Just beautiful, thinking about all the history that took place down there. And then we came down across the Middle East, Israel, the Persian Gulf, the Sinai Peninsula, Egypt, the Nile River ... just absolutely gorgeous ... blue water, tan desert. Looking down again, thinking about all the history that took place down there was just tremendous. Then we came toward India, across the Himalayas, and toward Australia. ... I think that you get a different perspective on the planet.

"Being up that high, and being in space looking at these very historic areas and very large areas of the Earth at one time, makes you realize that we all share the same earth, the same air, the same water. It's a moment that will stay with me forever."

CARL NICHOLAS KARCHER:
FROM HOT–DOG STAND TO FAST–FOOD EMPIRE

Before you can get anywhere, you have to take that first step. That's what Carl Karcher did more than 60 years ago when he purchased a hot–dog stand and started selling lunch to factory workers. Soon he fell in love with being in business for himself. He passionately grew the business, creating Carl's Jr. restaurants, building a fast–food empire, and having a great time along the way.

When the friendly farm boy from Ohio and his bride bought a hot–dog cart in Los Angeles, little did they know that their modest business would grow into one of the largest fast–food chains in the nation. The year was 1941 and the term "fast food" hadn't even been coined yet. But Carl Nicholas Karcher and his wife, Margaret, had a dream: to own a self–supporting business that would provide well for themselves and the family they envisioned. With this dream and the single small hot dog cart that they purchased for $326 (with $15 cash and $311 borrowed against their car), the young couple embarked on their American dream adventure.

Carl grew up in a close–knit family that stressed self–sufficiency and strong values. His parents instilled in him and his brothers and sisters an unswerving faith, impressing upon each child the importance of honesty and integrity. Everyone worked hard on the family farm, rising early each day to tend to a host of chores. Carl didn't attend school beyond the eighth grade, choosing instead to help with the farm where he felt he could contribute the most. But at the age of 20, the young man decided to go west. So Carl, a brother, and a buddy all piled into a 1935 Ford and headed to the land of orange groves and sunshine. In Anaheim, Carl met and fell in love with Margaret Magdalen Heinz, and the two married in November 1939.

Carl got a job delivering bread for Armstrong Bakery, and while on his 75–mile daily delivery route, he noticed hot–dog stands set up on street corners all throughout Los Angeles. One day he saw a cart for sale. He and his wife dreamed of being self–employed, of owning and running a successful business. Why not try this?

As soon as Carl and Margaret bought the hot–dog stand, they discovered that business truly was booming. Its prime location across the street from the Goodyear plant meant that the business catered not only to assembly line workers but also to the weekend visitors who came to see the Goodyear Blimp. They did so well that the following year the couple purchased a second cart and hired two employees to help out. Just a few months later, 25–year–old Carl bought a third cart.

Carl soon discovered that he had a passion for running a business. He loved talking with his customers and finding out what they liked. He enjoyed experimenting with new menu items and creating special sauces. He liked being his own boss and making business decisions. By 1945, Carl was ready to open his first full–service restaurant, Carl's Drive–in Barbecue, birthplace of the now–famous Carl's Jr. star logo.

Business at Carl's Drive–in Barbecue was good from the start. People liked Carl's food and his friendly rapport with customers. Meanwhile, in 1946, Carl added hamburgers to the menu at his hot–dog stands. A decade later, he opened the first Carl's Jr. — a smaller version of the full–service restaurant. The business, and Carl's family, continued to grow in the decades that followed: By 1974, Carl and Margaret had 12 children and 100 restaurants.

One of the character traits that enabled Carl to succeed was that he always saw a setback as an opportunity in disguise. For example, when property owners failed to renew Carl's lease to his highly successful full–service restaurant in 1955, he was devastated. But he quickly developed and carried out a new plan. Carl purchased a building across the street from his restaurant and managed to obtain the necessary city and county approvals to convert it into a restaurant. Carpenters were hired to do the transformation. Equipment and furnishings were moved from the existing restaurant to the new one. Finally, the prominent star sign was given a new home across the street. Carl did all this in just 30 days. In the end, Carl's Drive–in Barbecue not only survived, it flourished, doing even better business than before.

Throughout his career, Carl has enjoyed experimenting and taking risks. His restaurant menus have changed again and again, at one time including shrimp baskets and pizza, at another time boasting complete steak dinners. Some of these experiments did not pass the test of time, while others revolutionized the industry. Carl's Jr. was the first of the fast–food hamburger giants to introduce a salad bar, chicken sandwiches, and "all–you–can–drink" self–serve beverages.

The menu isn't the only thing Carl experimented with. He and his fast–growing team constantly tried new building designs, different decor, and additional locations, whatever was necessary to grow the business. Soon Carl's Jr. establishments could be seen up and down California. Expansion continued into other states and even to Japan.

Carl made sure to hire only competent people who had integrity and heart. A hands–on leader, Carl has always done whatever it takes to keep operations going smoothly: preparing food, pulling weeds, or chatting with the customers. To this day, customer service is paramount to Carl, and he's always enjoyed mingling with the customers, joking good–naturedly with them, and making sure they're satisfied. He often dropped in at each of his establishments to offer the manager constructive criticism. Along with giving praise and encouragement, Carl noted such things as a smudge on the wall or a waiter who should have been treating customers better. Carl was consistently fair and kind, but he was also a perfectionist.

But with growing competition in the fast–food market, and with greater options for consumers, Carl found that by the early 1990s, his business was struggling. Carl faced one of the biggest hurdles ever. In 1993, the 76–year–old Carl was ousted from the very enterprise he had built from the ground up. His board disagreed with his business plans and removed him from the position of chairman. It was a hard blow for Carl, who remained passionate about the business. But in 1994 a new chairman was named who brought Carl back as chairman emeritus.

His troubles, though, were still not over. In 1995, advisers urged Carl to file bankruptcy. Deeply in debt with stock value dropping, there seemed to be no viable alternative. But filing bankruptcy went against Carl's belief system. As he had done countless times throughout his career as a businessman, Carl trusted his instincts. He told his advisers, "From a moral point of view, it touches my heart, and I'm not going to do it." It proved to be the right choice: During the next three years, the company's stock rose tenfold.

Through it all, Carl has never lost his sense of adventure, his faith, or his passion for running a business. "I couldn't be happier," he says. "I've been in business 62 years, been married to a wonderful woman 63 years. We've been blessed with nine daughters, three sons, 48 grandchildren, and 30 great-grandchildren. God, family, principles, and basic spiritual values have always been very important to me."

Today Carl continues to serve as chairman emeritus of CKE Restaurants, Inc., which operates more than 3,000 Carl's Jr., Hardee's, and La Salsa restaurants.

"Never, never give up," Carl says as he approaches 90. "I don't want to retire. I'm having too much fun with the business." And that's the key. Carl's passion for running the business makes his job fun, giving him the energy and enthusiasm he needs to succeed. "Work has to be fun," Carl adds. "If it isn't, you're in the wrong business."

Passion Fuels Your Dreams

> "WHATEVER YOU'RE INTERESTED IN, READ AND LEARN EVERYTHING YOU CAN ABOUT IT. CONSTANTLY GATHER INFORMATION TO FEED YOUR INTEREST. SEEK OTHERS INVOLVED IN THE SAME FIELD. AND DON'T LIMIT YOURSELF TO JUST ONE PATH, BECAUSE YOU DON'T KNOW EXACTLY WHERE YOU'LL END UP." — SUSAN TITCOMB, PERSONAL CHEF (CHAPTER 6)

The Dream CPR essential element *passion* engages the heart and soul. When our heart is involved in making our dream come true, and our feelings are invested in the project, the dream has a tremendous chance of coming to fruition. When we're doing what we love and we're deeply longing for a specific goal, we fuel our dreams.

Eileen Collins felt a passion — an excitement, a strong pull — for flying and space. But she had no role models: There were no women astronauts when she was a kid. She pursued her passion anyway, becoming a military pilot. When NASA began to accept women into the space program, Eileen realized she could be an astronaut, too. To have the best chance possible to be accepted for space shuttle missions, she went back to school to boost her already impressive credentials. It was a long, challenging path to become an astronaut, but Eileen didn't mind. She loved studying, learning, and flying, and she deeply longed to experience being in space.

When we are following our passion, we lose track of time. We forget to take breaks. We become so absorbed in the task at hand that everything else fades away, and when we're interrupted, it takes a few moments to "come back." Passionate dreams are a great escape from the mundane into a world of excitement and joy. Gloria Estefan escaped the pain of her life through her passion for music, which made her feel good when she was lonely and sad. Her passion ultimately shaped her life, leading to an exciting, successful career as an international entertainer.

To spark your passion, try the following:

1 Make a list of activities that make you feel good, bringing you a sense of happiness, joy, excitement, aliveness, and belonging. Be honest with yourself, and write down everything that comes to mind. Your list might include activities as varied as playing the piano, walking in the woods, eating out, woodworking, taking the dog for a walk, going to the movies, riding your bike, remodeling your home, helping a friend, throwing a party, playing basketball, building contraptions in your garage. When you're done, read the list back to yourself, saying aloud for each item, "I have a passion for..." Feel how your body reacts to each statement. If you feel a burst of energy or excitement, then that truly is a passion of yours. If you don't feel anything or you're not sure, then it's probably not your passion. Cross it off the list.

2 Ask yourself: *If money were not an issue, what would you be doing right now? What do you want to do more than anything else in the world?*

3 Look over your list of what makes you feel good, and ask yourself: *Is there a way to turn this passion into a dream?* For example, the person who likes to walk his dog might dream of starting a dog–walking service. The person who loves going to the movies might consider becoming a movie reviewer or critic. Someone with a passion for basketball might dream of becoming a basketball coach. Opportunities exist — or can be created — to fit your passion.

Many people jump into jobs or careers that will reward them financially. But, do they have a passion for their work? Sadly, the answer too often is no. A consumer survey report completed in 2002 by The Conference Board, a New York–based nonprofit business group, shows an alarming trend: More Americans are less satisfied with their jobs today compared to seven years ago. Only half of those surveyed say they are happy in their jobs. And the other half, what would they rather be doing? What dreams are they sacrificing for the sake of financial security? What dreams have you sacrificed because "there's just no money in it" or "it's too unconventional" or "too unrealistic"?

> ### Dream CPR Journal
>
> What do you enjoy doing most today?
>
> What activities and pastimes can you lose yourself in completely?
>
> What can you do to take that first step to get closer to your passion?

Follow your passion and discover where it leads you. A passion for acting took Michael Clarke Duncan from ditch–digging to Hollywood. Passion helped Carl Karcher turn a single hot–dog stand into one of the largest fast–food empires in the nation. Take that first step closer to your passion and see where you go from there. Passion can lead us to surprisingly successful and enjoyable careers.

In the next chapter, we'll discuss a quality that everybody profiled in our book knows well — persistence. Also known as tenacity, persistence enables us to keep moving and continue pushing despite ongoing trials and tribulations.

chapter 9

Persistence: Try and Try Again

> " I HAVE LEARNED THAT SUCCESS IS TO BE MEASURED NOT SO MUCH BY THE POSITION THAT ONE HAS REACHED IN LIFE AS BY THE OBSTACLES WHICH HE HAS OVERCOME WHILE TRYING TO SUCCEED."
> — BOOKER T. WASHINGTON

The dream achievers featured in this book didn't realize their dreams overnight. Reaching a dream is a process that takes time — a month, a year, a decade, sometimes even a quarter–century or longer. Since we encounter obstacles and are tempted to give up along the way, the Dream CPR essential element *persistence* is vital to achieving dreams. Having persistence means trying again and again, until you succeed. As Carl Jr.'s founder Carl Karcher, profiled in the previous chapter, advises: "Never, never give up."

In this chapter you'll read about journalist Barbara Walters, AIDS researcher Edward A. Berger, and safety advocate Janette Fennell. Against the odds they persisted, reaching milestones many thought impossible. By following her dreams, Barbara landed many "firsts" — she was the youngest television producer ever at New York's WNBC, the first female co–host on the *Today Show*, and the first woman to co–anchor network evening news. Her persistence led to opportunities for herself and other women journalists — opportunities once available only to men.

Edward A. Berger knows that scientific research rarely offers quick payoffs. It's time–consuming, slow–moving, and loaded with dead–ends. In Ed's case, it took ten years just to develop an experimental process. But his meticulous, persistent problem–solving led to a breakthrough that's helped scientists better understand the intricacies of HIV, bringing us closer to developing an effective vaccine, or maybe a cure, for AIDS.

A marketer turned at–home mom, Janette Fennell single–handedly took on the powerful automobile industry. For five years she lobbied for release latches in car trunks so that a person trapped inside could get out. Others called her a dreamer, but her persistence paid off when the federal government finally set a new, mandatory safety standard.

Do you remember the classic children's book *The Little Engine That Could*? In it, a tiny engine with a ridiculously heavy load faced a steep, treacherous road. Its task seemed impossible, but the little engine had an important mission and knew it had to try. As the little engine struggled uphill, it chanted "I think I can, I think I can." It kept trying, and once over that daunting hurdle its chant turned to a triumphant "I thought I could, I thought I could!" Because it kept encouraging itself to keep trying and not give up, the little engine succeeded.

That's persistence. When we learn to master this Dream CPR essential element, we learn the secret to reaching life's rewards.

BARBARA WALTERS: BREAKING BROADCAST BARRIERS

When young Barbara Walters dreamed of becoming an on–air reporter, men dominated the field of broadcast television. And as an introspective writer with a speech impediment, her chances of breaking into broadcast news seemed slim at best. But through dogged persistence, Barbara not only became a respected broadcast journalist, she helped open the field of television news to women.

She has attained celebrity status for her riveting interviews with the world's most influential people, but Barbara Walters considers herself a journalist first and foremost, not a star. Chatting in front of cameras with the likes of Katharine Hepburn, Colin Powell, Gloria Steinem, and Christopher Reeve, Barbara poses the questions that most people would love to ask, given the chance. She has one of the most interesting jobs on television, but her high–profile career didn't just land on her lap. It took tremendous persistence: Barbara has toiled her entire life to break gender barriers and overcome obstacles while creating the job of her dreams.

Born in 1929 in Boston, Massachusetts, Barbara was a lonely child. Her sister, Jackie, was diagnosed with borderline mental retardation. Barbara dearly loved Jackie and suffered silently when others made fun of her sister. Because Jackie required so much of their mother's attention, Barbara was left seeking companionship from books and schoolwork. Meanwhile, their father focused his energy on building and running glamorous nightclubs in three states, which meant the family moved frequently. In a 1999 interview with *McCall's* magazine, Barbara recollected, "I went to three different high schools in four years."

But her childhood did help prepare her for television. Barbara's ease with celebrities and dignitaries stems from having grown up around the rich and famous. Her father's nightclubs, each called The Latin Quarter, were frequented by the likes of billionaire Howard Hughes and actor Maurice Chevalier, and club acts featured such talented performers as Frank Sinatra and Patti Page. Ironically, Barbara didn't appreciate this exposure to celebrities at the time, and often wished her father was in a more conventional profession, like dentistry. But being the daughter of a club impresario meant that Barbara instinctively remained composed as a reporter interviewing the stars. And thanks to her compassion for Jackie, Barbara genuinely empathizes with people subjected to ridicule, abuse and tragedy.

A quiet, introspective teenager, Barbara was a serious student who earned good grades and enjoyed writing for her high school's literary magazine. As a student at Sarah Lawrence College in New York, she joined the campus newspaper staff as drama editor and movie critic. After graduating in 1951 with a Bachelor of Arts degree in English she obtained part–time secretarial jobs, but within a year Barbara landed a job writing press releases at New York television station WNBC, where she fell in love with the burgeoning field of television production. Her strong desire to learn everything about the field impressed her employers, who liked that she worked diligently and paid meticulous attention to detail. After spending a year in the promotions department, the 24–year–old was assigned to produce a live, 15–minute daily segment for children called *Ask the Camera*, an opportunity that afforded a degree of creative freedom. Barbara became the youngest television producer hired by WNBC, and one of the youngest producers anywhere.

She thrived in the television studio environment, so when her children's segment was suddenly cancelled and she found herself unemployed, Barbara quickly searched for another television job. She found it at CBS's *The Morning Show*, where she became a staff writer in 1955. Barbara's strength was her knack for generating unique story ideas — especially those that appealed to women viewers — and locating unusual, fascinating guests. Although she was good at researching stories, writing copy, and booking guests, she dreamed of working in front of the cameras, not just backstage. She got a taste of that dream when she modeled an outfit for a fashion show segment. Barbara discovered that she had a natural poise and ease in front of the cameras.

While Barbara enjoyed developing fashion and cooking segments, she longed to cover the political arena. Her dream was to interview the movers and shakers of the world, and to do so in front of the cameras. But major obstacles loomed ahead. In the 1950s and 1960s, most women journalists were relegated to covering soft "women's interest" stories, while matters of politics and world events were handled by men. In addition, Barbara had a noticeable speech impediment and a strong Boston accent. It took determination, hard work, and persistence for Barbara to break into the male–dominated world of television news.

In 1957, CBS cancelled *The Morning Show* and Barbara was again out of a job. This time, she couldn't find work in television: The few openings available were quickly filled by men. Barbara settled for a lower–paying job writing client profiles and press releases for a public relations firm. This kept her employed for four years while she supported herself and helped her parents financially after they were forced to declare bankruptcy when their nightclub empire collapsed. It was a difficult time for Barbara, but she still didn't give up on her dream.

In 1961, a window of opportunity opened. Barbara finally returned to television, landing a position at NBC's *Today* show as a writer. She was thrilled to be back in broadcast journalism. But again, although she loved collaborating with others behind the scenes, she still hungered to work in front of the camera. Barbara tenaciously worked her way to becoming an on–camera reporter and on–the–scene interviewer, starting out by reporting on fashion. She covered the New York fashion scene and won her first overseas assignment reporting on the Paris fashion season. During these early assignments she had to learn everything about television reporting on her own, from editing her work to talking to the camera. But she did her job well, and these fashion segments led to Barbara's first high–profile assignment: *Today* sent her overseas to join the press corps covering first lady Jacqueline Kennedy's 1962 goodwill trip to India and Pakistan. With this assignment, Barbara crossed over to political reporting.

Barbara stayed with *Today* for 15 years, getting up at 4:30 in the morning every day and regularly working long hours. After getting her foot in the door with Jackie Kennedy's goodwill trip, Barbara moved from covering soft stories about fashion and entertainment to reporting hard news stories of major political significance, including President Kennedy's assassination. Because her colleagues had little or no experience working with women reporters, and many political figures were not used to being interviewed by a woman, she often had to work harder than her male counterparts to prove she could do the job as well, or better, than they. And Barbara battled stereotypes and sexism — not to mention inflated egos — every step of the way.

For example, *Today* co–host Frank McGee actually negotiated into his contract that he was to ask guests at least three questions before Barbara could pose even one. She also had to overcome producers' concerns about her speech impediment, working for a time with a speech therapist to improve her diction. Through these and other trials, she persisted. She knew she had to make her mark in order to keep doing her dream job.

"What I had to do was get my own interviews — the Henry Kissingers, the Dean Rusks [the U.S. Secretary of State during Kennedy and Johnson administrations]," she explained to *McCall's* in 1999. "I had to win them. I would call. I would write. I was very persistent."

Barbara's persistence landed her interviews with top political figures of the day, including Israeli Prime Minister Golda Meir, Britain's Prince Philip, even communist leader Fidel Castro of Cuba. Just as important, Barbara added a new dimension to interviewing; with tact and diplomacy, she asked direct questions to get answers that revealed the human being behind the public figure. Barbara's interviews were too good for any producer to pass on — even if they came from a woman with a distinct accent. Barbara's tenacity and drive led to more coveted assignments, including traveling to the People's Republic of China to cover the visits of President Richard Nixon in 1972 and President Gerald Ford in 1975.

By the early 1970s, Barbara had become very popular with *Today* viewers, and she leveraged her hard–won clout to negotiate an unheard–of stipulation into her contract: Should Frank

McGee ever leave the show, she would replace him. When Frank died unexpectedly of bone cancer in 1974, Barbara made history by becoming the first woman to co–host the *Today* show, and the only female co–host on any television news or public affairs program at the time. It was a giant step not only for her but for all women journalists.

And even bigger gigs would follow. In 1976, Barbara moved to ABC where she made the difficult switch from morning show to nightly news and became the first woman to co–anchor a national network news broadcast in the highly coveted evening time slot. She also negotiated a record–breaking salary of $1 million a year for five years. Once again, Barbara had opened doors not only for herself, but also for female colleagues around the world.

From there, Barbara's career has continued to skyrocket and shows no signs of slowing down any time soon. In 1976, ABC started airing *The Barbara Walters Specials*, a popular showcase of her trademark exclusive interviews. In 1977, she brought together Egypt's Anwar Sadat and Israel's Menachem Begin for a historical first joint interview with these powerful heads of state. In 1984, Barbara joined long–time friend and colleague Hugh Downs as co–host of the popular television news magazine *20/20*. In 1995, her moving interview with paralyzed actor Christopher Reeve netted Barbara the highly prized George Foster Peabody Award. In 1997, Barbara became co–owner, co–executive producer, and co–host of Emmy–winning daytime talk show *The View*.

It's been an incredible ride to the top for Barbara, built on hard work, character, and persistence. Her amazing professional accomplishments have not gone unrecognized. Barbara has received the Lifetime Achievement Award from the International Women's Media Foundation, the President's Award from the Overseas Press Club, and she has been inducted into the Academy of Television Arts and Science Hall of Fame, among many other honors. Over time, she won the respect of male colleagues and the appreciation of women by helping close the gender gap in broadcast journalism. Most of all, Barbara has won the admiration of the public for overcoming great obstacles to bring her own blend of compassion and straightforwardness to television news reporting.

EDWARD A. BERGER:
REVOLUTIONARY AIDS RESEARCHER

In 1996, Dr. Edward Berger and his team of researchers were lauded by Science magazine for making the "Scientific Breakthrough of the Year," a discovery that's revolutionized AIDS research worldwide by shedding new light on HIV. It took him nearly a decade of persistence to develop and implement the method that ultimately led to this critical finding. Ed's meticulous approach has brought the scientific community closer to developing an effective AIDS vaccine.

A good scientist needs to master persistence because results often take so much time to materialize. Dr. Edward Berger is that kind of scientist. A methodical, exhaustive approach to unraveling the mechanism by which the human immunodeficiency virus (HIV) enters a human cell led him and his team to discover the first HIV coreceptor, and later to identify additional coreceptors. Prior to that, nobody knew about the key role that coreceptors play in HIV transmission and infection, which can lead to Acquired Immunodeficiency Syndrome (AIDS). This vital missing link was not easy to uncover — Ed compares it to finding a needle in a haystack.

Ed has been studying the intricacies of HIV in all of its strains and mutations for 14 years at the National Institutes of Health in Washington, D.C., where for the past six years he has run the Molecular Structure Section of the Laboratory of Viral Diseases within the National Institute of Allergy and Infectious Diseases. Ed and his team study the complex behavior of HIV, as well as other viruses, at the molecular level. It's Ed's dream that this research ultimately will lead to new drugs and vaccines to treat and prevent HIV infection and AIDS.

Ed studies how the protein on the surface of a virus enables it to bind and fuse with a cell, ultimately entering and infecting it. With HIV, it's been known for many years that the virus' surface has a specific protein that hooks up with a protein molecule, called CD4, found on the surface of certain T–cells, the cells that make up an indispensable part of a person's immune system. Each T–cell's CD4 protein is thus a receptor for HIV, just like a lock and key mechanism. But scientists, including Ed, observed that there had to be more to it; there had to be another protein molecule — or maybe several others — on the cell's surface that enabled the virus to fuse with and actually enter the T–cell. But what was this molecule? This is what Ed and his team set off to answer, leading ultimately to the discovery of coreceptors.

Finding these was a daunting task. "Basically, we decided to not make assumptions about what kind of molecule we were looking for," Ed says. "We took an unbiased approach and set out to check the whole library of human genes. We asked, 'Can we develop a method that will pick out the right genes for us?'" Through genetic engineering, Ed and his group devised an ingenious way of testing the entire library of genes in the human genome to find just the right protein that enables fusion to occur between HIV and T–cells. Much thought and experimentation went into creating this tricky process of elimination — in fact, it took nearly ten years to develop. Once they got the method working, though, it took only a couple of months to pinpoint the first HIV coreceptor, which they named fusin. Persistence paid off.

"I think it's fair to say that the discovery has revolutionized AIDS research," Ed says. "It's changed the whole way that we're looking at the AIDS virus from the standpoint of understanding how the virus gets into the body to begin with, how the virus causes disease, and why some people are resistant to the virus but most people are susceptible. It's generated whole new avenues to discover new treatments and new vaccines for AIDS, based on what we know about how the virus uses these coreceptors." For their achievement, Ed and his research team received the prestigious Newcomb–Cleveland Prize from the American Association for the Advancement of Science.

According to Ed, who is in his mid–fifties, making such a significant scientific discovery takes tremendous patience and persistence. "It's a very slow process," he says. "That's the thing about science, it's really mini–step by mini–step, and you have to be satisfied with the day–to–day solving of little problems that ultimately come together. And occasionally you solve a major problem."

Born and raised in the Bronx, Ed attended Bronx High School of Science and then went on to City College of New York, where he obtained his Bachelor of Science degree. "I was basically good at math and analytical stuff," he says. He started out with a math major, but found that the subject didn't satiate his curiosity. He began to explore psychology, then biology, finally settling into a chemistry major.

After college, he moved upstate to attend Cornell University, where he spent five years earning his Ph.D. in biochemistry. He attributes his meticulous approach to research partly to a thesis advisor who "applied an absolute insistence on getting things right." From Cornell, he went to Stanford University in California to work on the nervous system. After four years, Ed joined the staff of the Worcester Foundation for Experimental Biology in Massachusetts, where he began to study molecular developmental biology. He spent ten years there, researching how a single cell develops into different cell types that form different organs and, ultimately, a complete living organism. His molecular–level work there lay a solid foundation for his AIDS research at the National Institutes of Health that he began 14 years ago.

"I'm a very methodical kind of scientist," Ed says. "I think in a very focused way, and I try to answer each next little question. There's always a roadblock in our understanding of getting from start to finish. I'll focus on that little roadblock until I get past it, and then I'll go to the next part." Ed thrives on asking questions that have never been asked before, tracking down answers, and solving problems.

Nobody knows for sure how soon we will have a readily available, effective vaccine against HIV. But the work that Ed and his team are doing is bringing the scientific world much closer to developing such a vaccine. Meanwhile, Ed's team is creating new methods of treatment and prevention.

"We are developing drugs to prevent the transmission of HIV," Ed explains, "and other drugs to eliminate the virus from a person who has it. We should be able to do clinical trials in the next year or two." Used in conjunction with treatments available today, these future drugs could effectively ward off AIDS. Time will tell. Ed continues forward, knowing that as scientists uncover more and more about HIV, better treatments will follow — and that's a dream for which he's willing to devote a lifetime.

He offers this piece of advice to others seeking to follow their dreams: "Listen to what your own voice is telling you. Don't get frustrated if it takes a while to find your calling in life. Don't be afraid to try different things. If you take a wrong step, well, life is long. You'll have the opportunity to reorient yourself. Sometimes it's not obvious what direction you should take. But keep trying things, and you'll figure it out."

JANETTE FENNELL:
SAFETY STANDARDS THAT SAVE LIVES

After surviving the nightmarish ordeal of being kidnaped at gunpoint and trapped in her car's trunk, Janette Fennell began to advocate for escapable trunks. She founded the nonprofit organization TRUNC (Trunk Releases Urgently Needed Coalition) to stop the preventable tragedy of trunk–entrapment deaths. Her persistence paid off: Janette's five years of tireless lobbying and research led to a new federal mandate requiring cars to be outfitted with internal trunk releases so that children and adults can escape unharmed.

It began late one night in October 1995 when Janette Fennell and her husband, Greig, came home after an evening out with friends. As they pulled into their garage in their quiet San Francisco neighborhood, their nine–month–old son sleeping soundly in his car seat in the back, they were shocked to see a masked gunman roll in deftly as the garage door closed. The intruder shoved a gun in the couple's faces, grabbed their car keys, and shouted at them to get into the trunk of their car.

"It was a very frightening, surreal scene," recalls Janette. "We had no idea what was going on. We tried to talk and negotiate with him, but he wasn't interested. He just kept yelling, 'Get in the trunk!'"

The gunman let an accomplice into the garage, and the two forced Janette and Greig into the trunk, then slammed the door shut over them. Statistics ran through Janette's mind, statistics showing that the chances of survival are greatest when an escape takes place within the first five minutes of being abducted. "I knew that you never want to be taken to a secondary location if you can avoid it," she says. But there was no way she and her husband could have made a run for it with their baby still in the car. His well–being was all that mattered. Trapped inside the trunk, husband and wife uttered prayers for their baby while they strained to hear him. They heard the abductors say, "There's a baby." After a brief pause the engine started and the gunmen raced the car through the streets of San Francisco.

When the car stopped, Janette heard another engine running nearby. The gunmen shouted at the couple still trapped in the trunk: "How much money do you have? Take off all your jewelry!" The men opened the trunk, and Janette felt a hard blow to the back of her head when she tried to straighten up. They took the couple's jewelry, money, and credit cards, locked them back in the trunk, and drove away in the waiting getaway car.

Alone in complete darkness in an unknown part of town, husband and wife prayed for a way out when, miraculously, Janette noticed a tiny light she hadn't seen before. "It was very specific and it shone directly on this little silver piece of metal," she recalls. "I said to my husband, 'I think I've found the trunk release.' I don't know where those words came from. They just left my mouth." Her husband saw nothing in the darkness so Janette took his hand and placed it where she saw the light. His fingers ran over the spot, and as he felt around he pulled a cable and the trunk popped open. They had found the release mechanism.

They climbed out and ran to see their baby in the backseat. Janette's heart sank — he wasn't there. "We went from a little bit of a high to lower than you can ever imagine," she says. Janette retrieved a hidden car key and they drove off, stopping at a well–lit phone booth to call 911. Soon the police arrived with the best news possible: their baby was alive and well. A police officer found the child still strapped in his car seat in front of the Fennells' house, tucked under an archway decorated with angels. The abductors had left him behind.

Another officer looked at Janette and said, "You are very lucky. It never ends like this." Janette asked, "What do you mean?" The officer replied, "You're okay, the baby's found, and you're all relatively unharmed. It just doesn't end this way."

Those words haunted Janette. *Just how does it end for others locked in trunks?* She began to investigate but became frustrated by the lack of re-corded information on trunk en-trapment cases. She contacted police departments, fire departments, the Bureau of Criminal Statis-tics, hospitals, the highway patrol, everybody she could think of who might have information, but nobody could help her. So she turned to the Internet where she began to uncover real–life ac-counts of people trapped in trunks.

Since nobody had statistics about trunk entrapment cases, Janette started to compile her own based on the number of inci-dents she discovered through Internet research and her conver-sations with many of the victims. Gradually, she developed the most comprehensive database available on the issue. And what she learned was chilling. She uncovered more than 1,300 in-stances in the last three decades in which children or adults had been stuck inside a car trunk with no way out. She discovered that at least 300 people have died trapped in trunks. Some were victims of crimes while others — including children playing an innocent game of hide–and–seek — were trapped accidentally.

For at least three decades, people had written to auto manufacturers asking for internal trunk release mechanisms, to no avail. The more Janette learned, the more incensed she became that nothing was being done to remedy the problem, and the more determined she became to enact change.

In 1996, just a few months after her frightening ordeal, Janette launched the Trunk Releases Urgently Needed Coalition, or TRUNC, and began to advocate for the installation of a release mechanism inside every car trunk. "I feel that God was telling me I had to be the voice for the people who couldn't get out," she says. Her dream was to put an end to these needless tragedies.

Arming herself with statistics and a hundred case histories that she and fellow TRUNC volunteers compiled, Janette began to write and lobby representatives from federal and state government and auto manufacturers. Her extensive research, which continued to uncover more and more case histories, shot down the frequent argument that trunk entrapments "simply don't happen very often."

Even so, few people took Janette seriously. Most of the responses she received were lukewarm, laughable, or downright discouraging. "I got ridiculous answers and excuses," Janette says. "I was told that if release mechanisms were placed in trunks, criminals would become more violent. Or [that] it would encourage children to play in trunks. None of these arguments made any kind of sense to me. People are dying in trunks from hyperthermia. A simple release latch would easily prevent these tragedies from continuing to happen."

Janette persisted and wrote even more letters to government officials and car manufacturers, citing additional real–life cases of people suffering and dying while trapped in car trunks. Again, most of her letters were disregarded. Janette continued to network and gather information, knowing she had to get more people involved in her cause before anything would change.

She reached a major milestone in 1999 when, after three years of dialogue and correspondence with Janette, the Ford Motor Company took the monumental step of voluntarily installing trunk releases in its new vehicles. It was a major victory. But

Janette knew that to enact change on a large scale, she had to convince the federal government to set a mandate.

As the founder of TRUNC, Janette had been named to a federal panel formed in November 1998 to study the issue of trunk entrapment. The panel was convened at the request of the National Highway Traffic Safety Administration in response to the horrific summer of 1998, when 11 young children died accidentally trapped in trunks — five girls in Utah, four cousins in New Mexico, and two brothers in Pennsylvania — all of them age six or younger.

Janette shared her extensive knowledge of car trunk entrapment cases with this multi–disciplinary panel of experts, bringing volumes of data that her research had uncovered. It proved crucial in convincing the rest of the panel to recommend that internal trunk release mechanisms become required standard equipment.

All of Janette's tireless work finally paid off on a national scale on October 17, 2000, when the U.S. Department of Transportation announced that effective September 1, 2001, all passenger cars with trunks must have an internal trunk escape release. All car makes and models from 2002 forward come equipped with a trunk release mechanism, and older models can be retrofitted with a release latch.

Janette is elated. She worked tenaciously for five years to see this happen, spending her money, time, and tremendous energy on her cause. In the end, her persistence paid off.

"I'm sure that some people looked at what I was doing and said, 'Boy, she's a dreamer. She's never going to be able to do this,'" Janette says. "But I knew in my heart and in my soul that this was going to be done. When I started researching cases of people locked in trunks, I didn't know if it was going to take me six months or six years to change things around.

"But I knew I had to do it. God gave me this mission. And God opened a lot of doors for me to be able to get this done."

Persistence in an Instant Gratification Society

> "THERE'S AN OLD VIETNAMESE SAYING MY
> PARENTS WOULD ALWAYS SAY, WHICH
> TRANSLATES TO THIS: IF YOU ARE WILLING
> AND ABLE ENOUGH TO TAKE ON THE TASK
> OF RESHAPING A LARGE PIECE OF METAL
> AND TRANSFORM IT INTO A SMALL,
> SHAPELY NEEDLE, YOU ARE THEN ABLE TO
> CONQUER EVERY ASPECT OF LIFE."
> — STEPHANIE NGO PHAM, ENTREPRENEUR
> (CHAPTER 4)

Perhaps life's rewards seem to escape so many because our society has forgotten how to wait. Expecting immediate gratification, we give up too soon, aborting the process prematurely and sabotaging any chance of success. Learning persistence is key to staying with our dreams long enough to enjoy results.

As we follow our dreams we traverse new territory, and we can't expect immediate success while we grapple with the unfamiliar. Barbara Walters had to keep persisting to land interviews with leading political figures, a daunting and intimidating task. Barbara just kept at it and, over time, her exclusive interviews became her trademark and her ticket to her dream job.

Most people who are recognized for their remarkable accomplishments started out stumbling and struggling just like anyone else. Each time we try, we learn something new that we can use next time. In the process, we build a reserve of knowledge that serves us along the road to reaching our dream. Each new attempt becomes a little easier, and brings us closer and closer to achieving our goal until we finally succeed.

You can develop your persistence by:

1 Setting up a simple routine and sticking with it until you succeed. Set a small goal for yourself. If your goal is to type faster, for example, practice typing several times a week and time yourself each week until you've reached your desired speed. Keep at it, no matter how long it takes.

2 Take a short break if you become frustrated. Stop pursuing your goal for a few days to clear your mind. When you return to working toward your goal, you'll find yourself refreshed and able to approach it from a new angle. Allowing yourself to take breaks helps you to persist over time, rather than just give up.

Once you have a better grasp on persistence, you can use this Dream CPR element to boost your dreams:

1 When you feel stuck along the road to your dream, step back and take a good look at the big picture. *What haven't you tried yet? What are you missing? What would improve your attempts?* By taking the time to analyze and alter your approach as often as needed, you learn to persist with your dream. Researchers like Ed Berger already know the importance of persistence — they live this Dream CPR essential element every day at the lab. Scientific experiments require patience, discipline, and repeated attempts — attributes that define persistence.

2 Understand that you will encounter the unfamiliar as you work toward your dream, and that many tasks will be challenging at first. But the more we practice, the easier it gets. Janette Fennell had to learn how to lobby in order to reach her dream, and it wasn't easy — her letters garnered lukewarm response in the beginning. But eventually, Janette found herself so recognized as an expert that she was appointed to a federal panel where she was able to influence public policy. We all

Dream CPR Journal

Persistence keeps us trying in a society that expects instant results but forgets that success is a process, not a one-time event. Our dreams require persistence so that we can enjoy the fruits of our labor.

What is your definition of success?

can learn from our mistakes and apply our newfound knowledge to future attempts. Persistence helps us keep trying when we've not yet mastered the tasks that will enable us to reach our dreams.

As we continue to breathe life into our dreams, we'll venture next into the R's of Dream CPR. We'll begin by studying resilience. Related to persistence, resilience is the ability to bounce back from failure and deep disappointments — a quality that every dream achiever must cultivate and that every survivor masters.

chapter 10

Resilience: Rise Up With Hope

We know that persistence is the ability to keep trying until we succeed, but sometimes it's difficult to muster the strength to do that. That's when we need to call on the Dream CPR essential element *resilience*, the quality that enables us to recover from adversity and try again, even when life repeatedly knocks us down. With resilience, we can reclaim dreams that have been snatched away. Resilience enables us to hope, dream, and work toward a greater purpose.

Author Maya Angelou has overcome adversity at every stage of her life. As a child, she experienced cruelty in the segregated South and abuse in her home by her mother's boyfriend. Maya struggled as a young African–American woman looking for work to support herself and her son. She endured the pain of marriages that did not last. Such experiences could have left her bitter and distrustful. Instead, Maya learned to survive and, in the process, she learned to focus on her dreams and concentrate on what connects people, not what separates us. Even after suffering deep losses, Maya has learned to rely on resilience to maintain an outlook of hope and compassion.

Doug West tried to make it as an artist, but he kept running into dead-ends. Then when doctors told him he had lymphoma and only six months to live, he went from shock to grief to acceptance, ultimately making peace with himself. When the diagnosis proved wrong and Doug recovered from what most likely was a lymph node infection, he discovered a resilience that later helped him hold on to his dreams despite struggles and frustrations. Ultimately, Doug became a successful, accomplished artist.

Resilience helped author and speaker Susanne Blake find new meaning in life after her husband died at age 40. Resilience enabled H&R Block co-founder Richard Bloch to win his grueling battle against cancer and then reach out to others struggling with the disease.

Life can knock us down flat. It's our measure of resilience that determines whether or not we'll keep dreaming and reaching for our dreams.

RICHARD BLOCH:
SHARING A WEALTH OF HOPE

In 1955, 29-year-old Richard Bloch and his older brother, Henry, founded the tax preparation company H & R Block. Five decades later, their company is a household name, filing more than 19.5 million tax returns a year from than 11,000 offices nationwide. Richard had everything he could have hoped for when, at the age of 52, he was diagnosed with terminal lung cancer. One doctor gave him only three months to live. But Richard far surpassed that prognosis, living another 26 healthy and cancer-free years. His resilience has given newly-diagnosed cancer patients hope for battling the disease. Here's his story, written before he passed away in July 2004 at age 78.

Born in Kansas City, Missouri, in 1926, Richard Bloch caught the entrepreneurial bug in childhood. "I liked to work," he remembers. "I was a serious child." At the age of nine, he started his own printing business, with local high schools as his primary clients. Richard began by purchasing a hand-printing press; three years later, he used his profits to buy three automatic presses that allowed him to work faster. At the age of 16, he sold his business and used the proceeds to go to college. At only 19, he earned a bachelor's degree in economics from the prestigious Wharton School at the University of Pennsylvania in Philadelphia. He soon went into business with his brother, Henry, who shared his entrepreneurial spirit. "We started in the bookkeeping business in 1947," he recalls. "Then we went into the tax business on January 25, 1955. We saw the need for providing such a service. We opened one office to begin with, and over time we expanded."

Things went well for the co–founder of H&R Block, both in business and in his personal life. He married a lovely woman named Annette, and they were blessed with three daughters. Richard continued to grow the business he shared with his brother, poring himself into work he enjoyed immensely. Tax preparation services quickly became highly sought by the public and by 1978, the business had grown to 8,000 offices nationwide. Richard and Annette continued to enjoy a close, loving relationship after more than 30 years of marriage. Their daughters were doing very well with their own adult lives, and the couple delighted in their four beautiful grandchildren. Things couldn't be better — until that fateful day in March when Richard received the most shocking news of his life.

His nagging stiff neck and shoulder pain, first misdiagnosed as a muscular problem, later misdiagnosed as arthritis, turned out to be symptoms of lung cancer. A large tumor was found in his right lung; a biopsy revealed it was malignant. His prospects were exceedingly grim; doctors deemed his tumor inoperable and expected Richard to die within three months. To Richard and his family, his prognosis was completely unexpected and mind–numbing.

With support from family and friends, Richard summoned the courage to fight the disease. Annette told Richard: "We are going to lick this thing together," and she asked friends and family for prayers and any other help they could offer. One friend referred Richard to a physician at the M.D. Anderson Tumor Clinic in Houston, Texas, one of the premier cancer research and treatment centers in the world. After undergoing an exhausting battery of tests, Richard heard a different story from his new doctor.

"At the end of March," he recalls, "I was told I was terminal. Five days later, my new doctor said, 'Dick, you're a very sick boy. We're going to make you a lot sicker, but we're going to cure you. We're going to cure you so that you can work for cancer.'" As ominous as the doctor's words were, Richard and his family were elated to have been given this glimmer of hope. Here was a doctor who hadn't given up and was willing to treat Richard.

So Richard underwent two weeks of radiation therapy followed by a week of chemotherapy. After a three–week respite, he underwent surgery to remove the tumor. Immunization therapy followed. And then Richard had to endure a full year of chemotherapy. It was grueling, to say the least. He became progressively weaker. The chemicals in his body distorted his sense of smell and taste; certain ordinary odors, like dried flowers and cooking aromas, became intolerable. Food tasted terrible. Richard lost all of his hair and a great deal of weight, and he always felt extremely cold. But even at his physically weakest, his resilience helped focus his mind on the bright side. If the drugs were doing this to him, Richard told himself, think of the power with which they must be attacking his cancerous cells. This positive outlook gave him the strength to continue to fight.

In the end, the treatments worked. On May 1, 1980, his Houston doctor delivered unbelievably good news: Richard was cured! He had survived the crucial two–year period for monitoring lung cancer; it had been 25 months since his first diagnosis without a recurrence. His doctor informed him that his chances of getting cancer at that point were no greater than anyone else's. Richard and his family thanked God and the expert team of doctors for giving him a second chance at life.

"My doctor was as good as his word," says Richard. "He cured me. My wife and I felt we had a big debt to pay. We've devoted our lives ever since then to helping the next person who gets cancer have a chance of beating it." After he and Annette developed a dream to help newly diagnosed cancer patients connect with former cancer patients for support and encouragement, Richard sprang into action. Using the business skills that made H&R Block such a smashing success, Richard started a cancer hotline, still operating today, with dedicated volunteers sharing their personal stories of surviving cancer so that each new cancer patient may find hope.

In 1982, Richard retired from H&R Block to dedicate himself completely to raising cancer awareness and helping cancer patients. At the University of Missouri, he and Annette founded the R.A. Bloch Cancer Management Center, which offers free second opinions by an expert staff of more than 100 physicians. In 1988, the couple opened the R.A. Bloch Cancer Support Center to provide patients, their friends, family members, volunteers, medical staff, and other supporters a tranquil place to talk about the disease. Every Bloch program is free to the public.

Richard came up with the idea of having a computerized system to track and disseminate information about the latest cancer treatments available, which he shared with the National Cancer Institute. NCI listened and implemented this system in Bethesda, Maryland, naming it the R.A. Bloch International Cancer Information Center. The Blochs have written three books to give cancer patients hope. These, too, are available for free through their web site.

Richard and Annette have received numerous awards for their efforts to help cancer patients. But of course, recognition is not the reason they are doing this. Recalling the fear and uncertainty they felt when they were first told Richard had lung cancer, they want to alleviate these fears in other cancer patients. They want to empower each cancer patient to have the best chance possible of surviving. Richard speaks with thousands of cancer patients every year, helping them build the same resilience that helped him battle the disease.

"I have seen a lot of miracles," he says. "I was just having lunch this week at the club, and a fellow came over to say hello. The last time I visited with him in person, he was terminal with pancreatic cancer. I said, 'Don't give up. I don't know that you're gonna make it, but I know you've got every chance if you fight.' He's out there on a golf tournament now, playing golf. He's in complete remission, finished with all his treatments." This is what it's all about for Richard — helping the next cancer patient develop the resilience to keep fighting the battle for life.

MAYA ANGELOU: WRITING THE WRONGS

In her roles as author, poet, playwright, actress, and professor, the talented, remarkable Maya Angelou can't help but impart her hard-earned wisdom. She's a resilient survivor who keeps dreaming despite the pain and hardship she's known since childhood. Maya's outlook of hope and her compassion for all people demonstrate beautifully the power of resilience.

Standing on the west steps of the Capitol on a cold but sunny Inauguration Day, Maya Angelou stirred hearts and minds as she eloquently read "On the Pulse of Morning." President Clinton had asked his fellow Arkansan to pen a poem for the occasion — Robert Frost, who read at Kennedy's inauguration in 1961, is the only other poet to receive this honor. On that brisk January morning in 1993, Maya's dignified, steady voice read hauntingly beautiful words that created powerful images in the minds of millions of listeners: Images of hope ever rising from the ashes of injustice, images of unity and cooperation among people of every race and creed. Maya challenged every American by ending her poem with an entreaty to look straight into a sister's eyes or a brother's face and greet one another with hope.

It was a crowning but poignant moment for the author, for "On the Pulse of Morning" reflects not only the growing pains of a great nation but also of her personal life. Maya has experienced more adversity than anyone ever should have to endure, but her resilience propels her to dream regardless of what life brings. And long before she dreamed of becoming a successful writer,

Maya lived a bittersweet life that would later provide fodder for her acclaimed autobiographies and works of poetry.

Born Marguerite Annie Johnson in 1928 in St. Louis, Missouri, she was nicknamed "Maya" by her older brother, Bailey. Shortly after her birth, the family of four moved to California, but when Maya was three her parents divorced. So Maya and four–year–old Bailey were sent to live indefinitely with their paternal grandmother, "Momma" Henderson, in Stamps, Arkansas.

Stamps was a rural, heavily segregated town, with the black community living in stark poverty, many of its residents earning paltry wages as farmhands. Believing that they must have done something terrible for their parents to "abandon" them, Maya and Bailey developed a strong attachment to their grandmother, who owned a general store and was well–respected in black Stamps. In a climate of terror perpetuated by mobs of cruel, angry whites during the pre–Civil Rights era, Momma was a pillar of strength and source of abiding love for the children, and a special role model for Maya. Witnessing her grandmother's strength in the face of discrimination, her enduring faith, and her compassion for downtrodden cotton pickers worn out at the end of each day, Maya learned about resilience and mercy.

In her first in a series of autobiographical books, *I Know Why the Caged Bird Sings*, Maya recounts how, at age 12, her jaw throbbed with excruciating pain because advanced cavities had decayed two of her teeth. The nearest black dentist was a meandering 25–mile bus ride away. With Maya in such agony, Momma Henderson rushed her to a local white dentist who owed her a favor — she had lent him money during the Great Depression. But he wouldn't even look at the child because of his stubborn, arrogant refusal to treat black patients, even in an emergency. Maya had to endure a slow, bumpy bus ride before she finally got medical attention.

Maya didn't spend her whole childhood in Stamps. When she was seven, her mother abruptly and unexpectedly sent for Maya and Bailey to come live with her in St. Louis. The children were elated to be welcomed back, but they found city life strange and confusing. Maya was mesmerized by her mother's beauty and spontaneity and intrigued by her fast–paced lifestyle; a nurse by training, she made a living running illegal card games in saloons. Maya was happy to be reunited with her mother, until a terrible thing happened.

Young Maya was repeatedly molested by her mother's live–in boyfriend. He scared Maya into silence by threatening to kill her brother if she told anyone what had happened. Then he raped her, injuring the eight–year–old child so badly that her family discovered the abuse. Charges were pressed and a frightened and confused young Maya testified in court against her attacker, who was convicted but released. Later he was found beaten to death in an alley — allegedly by Maya's uncles, who were never charged with murder.

All this left young Maya in deep turmoil. Trying to make sense of what had happened, she concluded that her testimony had killed the man. Her words had done it. So to avoid hurting any-body else, she went into a self–imposed silence. She would talk only to her brother — Maya loved Bailey so much that she knew she could never harm him — and she spoke with him only when they were alone. Not knowing what else to do, their mother sent the two children back to Momma Henderson in Stamps.

Back in Arkansas, Maya poured her pent–up feelings onto pa-per, writing poems to heal her broken spirit. Her self–imposed silence lasted six years. But a friend of Momma's intervened to help bring Maya out of silence. Bertha Flowers, who was highly regarded for her beauty and sophistication, invited Maya for lemonade and cookies. As they sat together she took out a copy of Charles Dickens' *A Tale of Two Cities* and began reading aloud eloquently. Knowing that Maya was a voracious reader, Bertha told her she would lend her books under one condition: Maya had to read the words aloud and pay close attention to the sounds and inflections. Bertha — Maya's first mentor — not only broke the girl's silence, she validated her literary predilection.

As teenagers, Bailey and Maya once again bid farewell to Momma Henderson and went to live with their mother, this time in California. By now, Maya was coming into her own, trying many different paths before deciding to focus on a singing and dancing career. During this uncertain time of discovery, Maya's strength and determination earned her a job as a San Francisco streetcar conductor when she was only 16 — the first black female to hold this job. But her emotional vulnerability led to a teen pregnancy that produced her son, Clyde (who later changed his name to Guy) and an early marriage that dissolved within a few years. To support herself and her son, Maya held whatever jobs she could find — diner cook, cocktail waitress, exotic dancer.

Maya's search for identity led her to become a popular nightclub entertainer, first in San Francisco and then in New York City. She adopted the stage name of Maya Angelou and began writing songs. Talent scouts spotted her, and Maya landed a dancing role in a year–long international tour of George Gershwin's opera *Porgy and Bess*. When the tour ended, Maya returned to singing in popular upscale nightclubs.

Even though she wrote her own song lyrics, as well as poems and short stories, Maya wanted to write more and have her writings recognized by the public. This became her dream. She joined the Harlem Writers Guild — which from its humble beginnings in 1950 has enjoyed an impressive membership, including author Alice Childress and songwriter Irving Burgie. Through the guild, Maya received honest, constructive criticism that helped her reach new heights as a writer. Then inspired by Dr. Martin Luther King, Jr., and his civil rights organization, the Southern Christian Leadership Conference (SCLC), Maya wrote the musical review *Cabaret for Freedom* in 1960, and helped produce a benefit performance for the SCLC. She went on to become SCLC's northern coordinator for a year.

While active in the civil rights movement, Maya fell in love and married a South African lawyer and freedom fighter. With her son, Guy, Maya and her new husband moved to Africa where his work was based. Although the marriage did not last, living in Egypt and Ghana gave Maya a broader perspective on the world and a chance to get to know her African heritage. Maya continued to develop her writing abilities working for the English–language *Arab Observer* and later as an instructor, administrator, freelance writer, and editor at the University of Ghana, where her son attended school.

At times feeling very homesick, Maya knew she wanted to return to the United States, but something kept telling her to remain in Africa longer. Then one day, quite unexpectedly, she learned why her intuition had been urging her to stay: Maya discovered a village where the people closely resemble both her and her grandmother, and she had a joyful, tearful "reunion" with the villagers who were convinced that her ancestors were born there. At peace with having found her roots, Maya was ready to return to America in 1966.

Urged by peers to artistically record the story of her incredible life, Maya set off to write her first autobiography. Published in 1970, *I Know Why the Caged Bird Sings* received tremendous critical acclaim and spent two years on *The New York Times* bestseller list. In 1972, Maya received a Pulitzer Prize nomination for *Just Give Me a Cool Drink of Water 'Fore I Die*. To date, Maya has written six autobiographical volumes, culminating with *A Song Flung Up to Heaven*, published in 2002. She also has five poetry collections to her credit, including *Oh Pray My Wings Are Gonna Fit Me Well* (1975) and *I Shall Not Be Moved* (1990). In reaching her own dreams, Maya has also preserved moving accounts of African–American life in the 20th century, and she has inspired countless people.

Maya's achievements have garnered many accolades, including the Horatio Alger Award in 1992 and several honorary university degrees. She has held visiting professorship posts at several universities and serves as the Reynolds Professor of American Studies at Wake Forest University in Winston–Salem, North Carolina.

Maya continues to write and create, her mind ever productive, her heart ever open, her soul ever longing to share stories with the world. Wherever she goes, Maya imparts her hard–earned wisdom with younger generations, sending the message that people are more alike than different, and that our similarities connect us all. Maya's ability not only to survive pain and injustice but to build the resilience to keep pursuing dreams has brought her to great heights. By maintaining an outlook of hope and compassion despite deep hurts and disappointments, Maya is a model for overcoming adversity and letting our spirits soar.

DOUG WEST: THE POWER OF CALM

When Doug West was misdiagnosed with terminal cancer, he ultimately found within himself a place of peace and acceptance. That empowering sense of calm is what he tries to convey through his art today. The resilience he formed while enduring painful symptoms and experiencing a roller coaster ride of emotions helped the aspiring young artist reach his dreams in the long run.

For the past 24 years, Doug West has been living his dream by working as a full–time, professional artist. He uses serigraphy — a silk–screen technique for producing original, limited–edition prints — to beautifully express his deep love of nature. Doug has created more than 200 evocative landscape scenes, handcrafting 100 prints for each. His work takes him to wide, open spaces where sky and earth merge in almost surreal desert beauty. Whether he's outdoors creating a preliminary sketch or back at his art studio absorbed in the meticulous process of making stencils and preparing inks, Doug recreates the vibrancy and majesty of the natural world while adding a dreamy, fantasy–like quality.

"My landscape images focus primarily on the beauty and vast terrain of the great Southwest," he says. "On a more subtle level, I'm trying to convey the meditative state of mind I feel while at one with a moment in time. I feel that this reality is just as significant, and perhaps much more profound than the technology that surrounds our lives, or the daily events and tasks that absorb our waking minds."

Doug's art exudes soothing tranquillity. Perhaps that's why so many of his prints are displayed in hospitals and doctors' waiting rooms, as well as in high–stress offices of banks and corporations. Many prints also grace private collections. "My dreams truly have come true," Doug says. "I've enjoyed a wide audience for my work. Moreover, I really love my work. I appreciate the quality of life that art affords, and the time it gives me to be introspective about life."

But it wasn't always this way. Doug's road to recognition as an artist has been long and rocky. Now 56, he struggled for years to find his place in the art world. He even left art behind for a while to focus on a more financially secure career, which proved frustrating. So Doug ultimately returned to his greatest passion — expressing himself through his creativity.

Born in Riverside, California, in 1947, Doug enjoyed a happy childhood with his parents and older sister. "My childhood was very nurturing," he says. "I had a great deal of freedom to explore and to enjoy time by myself." He was always drawn to creative pursuits, such as building things out of wood. As early as kindergarten, Doug often skipped recess to stay in class working on art projects. His father, who enjoyed landscaping and home remodeling, was a wonderful role model for Doug. His mother also supported his artistic interests, giving him a set of oil paints for Christmas when he was 16. Doug was immediately smitten with his new paints and stayed up until three in the morning creating a vivid seascape that took his parents by surprise. They had always known about his interest in art, but until then, nobody had fully recognized his tremendous talent. It was an awakening for Doug and his family.

After graduating from high school, Doug spent a year studying scenic design at California Western University before transferring to the University of Southern California in Los Angeles, where he earned his Bachelor of Fine Arts degree. But finding work as an artist, his chosen profession, was difficult at first. To pay the bills, he drove taxis and delivered pizzas all over Los Angeles.

Then came the scare of his life. He fell extremely sick. Doctors diagnosed his illness as lymphoma and gave him only six months to live. The diagnosis stunned Doug. Over the course of three weeks, his emotions went from shock to grief to acceptance and, finally, to a heightened sense of peace. Then came unexpected, incredible news: the original diagnosis had been wrong. Doug did not have a terminal disease. Doctors concluded that his fevers, persistent bodily pain, and tennis ball–size lump under his arm were most likely caused by an infection.

With antibiotics, the symptoms disappeared. But something profoundly spiritual took place during the three weeks that Doug faced death. "During this time, I struggled with accepting my fate and trying to understand how it all could be over when I was newly married with a small child, had just finished my undergraduate degree in art, and was just on the doorstep of emerging into the adult phase of my life," he recalls. "Slowly I came to a knowing that whatever was spiritually intended for me was a reality I had to release myself to. I certainly had always turned inward and trusted in prayer since childhood, but there was a huge power I found in releasing my struggle into acceptance in the will of the Divine." The place of peace he reached during this challenging time has bred a strong resilience in Doug.

In the early 1970s, when Doug was in his mid–20s, he and his family moved to Hawaii so he could pursue graduate studies at BYU–Hawaii and obtain teaching credentials to become an art teacher. There he finally obtained an art–related job teaching ceramics at an Army base. In his spare time he created art through a variety of mediums, and was excited and honored when one of his scenic serigraphs was juried into an art show at the Honolulu Art Museum. But it would be another five years before his work would be publicly presented again.

Moving to Santa Fe, New Mexico, to live closer to extended family, Doug took a job as a vocational trainer in order to make a living. He worked with developmentally disabled adults, training them for janitorial and woodworking jobs. Only once in a while did he get the chance to teach arts and crafts. Largely removed from his art, he became utterly frustrated. He couldn't stand to feel his creativity stagnate. Doug became more determined than ever to make art his life's focus, regardless of the obstacles.

Doug tried his hand at jewelry–making because of his love for "any craft that involves detailed handwork." He consigned several pieces of jewelry with a gallery in Oklahoma but gave up on the venture when none of it sold. Then in 1977, Doug took another leap of faith when, recalling the joy he felt creating a print in Hawaii, he decided to invest in his own silk–screening supplies. Using his income tax refund, he purchased a silk screen, squeegees, and paint. With this modest amount of equipment, he began creating what would become his trademark Southwest landscape prints. Within a year, his work had appeared in several shows and galleries in New Mexico and Texas. His prints received high praise, and many of them sold. Doug was elated. After struggling for 12 years, he had finally found a way to work as a professional artist. His inspiring serigraphs have since been featured in art galleries from Miami to New York, and Aspen to Osaka.

"Through my prints," says Doug, "I try to help people get in touch with the beauty and simplicity of nature. My experiences with nature are sacred and profound. I try to share some of that through my work."

An illness that he thought was terminal instead taught Doug a life–affirming lesson about how to attain a place of peace that allows him to face the worst. With that inner peace and trust in a higher power, Doug has bounced back from the frustration of unsuccessful art projects, unfulfilling jobs, and an art career that at first met one dead–end after another. Resilience enabled him to rise up after every disappointment and ultimately succeed as a professional artist.

SUSANNE BLAKE:
FINDING SPIRITUAL SUSTENANCE

As she looks back on her 61 years, Susanne Blake divides her life into three phases: parenting and career–building, a spiritual quest, and giving back to the community. Through the ups and downs of her life, she has learned to trust God and herself for answers. Her resilience has helped Susanne learn from her struggles, and then share her lessons with others as a public speaker and seminar leader, and as the author of When Spirit Speaks.

As a high school student during the late 1950s, Susanne Blake believed what society at large told young women back then, that she was limited to basically three career options: teaching, nursing, or working as a secretary. Choosing the secretarial path, the Oklahoma native completed two years at a business college, worked as a secretary for several firms, married, and had children before landing a secretarial position with American College Testing in Iowa City. When a family illness forced her supervisor there to take a month–long leave of absence, Susanne ran the office so efficiently that upon his return, her boss told her: "When you leave here, don't get another secretarial job. You have to apply for a higher–level position."

It was the first time anyone had encouraged Susanne to reach beyond the limitations of her era and strive for bigger dreams, and the words stayed with her. In 1971, when her husband's work as a speech pathologist took the family to Portales, New Mexico, Susanne decided to take a risk on herself and pursue her dream of finding work that would challenge and fulfill her, and give her a sense of purpose.

She approached the local university to ask for a job in the academic arena, figuring she could build on her experience with college testing. "I went to the dean of student affairs at Eastern New Mexico University and told him I wanted to work there," she said. "When he offered me a 20–hour–a–week, minimum–wage job, I told him I was worth more than that. You see, I had already begun to realize that when we believe in ourselves and in what we can do, the doors will open." The dean kept calling her back with other low-paying, clerical positions, and each time Susanne would reply, "I can do more than that."

Impressed by her drive and determination, the dean called Susanne in to interview for the position of assistant director of the campus drug abuse prevention center. Susanne was excited about this position, but when the dean looked at her resume he realized that she didn't meet the qualifications. "I'm sorry," he told her. "Even though I'm very impressed with you, I can't give you this position. It requires a master's degree, and you only have two years of college." Susanne's heart sank. But unwilling to take no for an answer, she offered to volunteer at the center and work her way up.

A week later, Susanne was working in her garden when she received a phone call from the university. The assistant to the president of the university wanted to talk to her immediately about a position at the drug abuse prevention center, so she went over in her yard clothes without taking the time to change into a business suit. "After all," she thought, "it's just a volunteer position." Relaxed during the interview, Susanne answered questions easily and asked quite a few of her own. She even stated that she would require the freedom to occasionally bring her kids with her to the center. Finally, she was asked, "How much money do you need?"

Susanne was taken by surprise. She had no idea she was interviewing for a paid job — in fact, for the position of assistant director she'd previously discussed with the dean. The president's assistant knew Susanne didn't have the required master's degree, but she made her an offer anyway. Without hesitation, Susanne took the job.

The day after Susanne started, the center's director, a qualified counselor, resigned. This left Susanne with a caseload of 21 people and no counselor on staff. But instead of panicking, she sprang into action. Susanne called each client, one by one, and introduced herself. "I told them that I had no theory, no background," she says, "but that I liked people, I had common sense, and I was willing to listen to them until another counselor arrived, if they wanted to continue coming. And each one said they'd keep coming, and they did." When a new counselor was finally hired months later to become the center's director, he was impressed by what Susanne had accomplished without a counseling background. Their mutual respect enabled them to work well together and expand the center. Susanne's skills in networking and fund-raising helped them add mental health programs to assist people dealing with life issues. That's how Susanne began a successful career in the mental health field.

To come up to speed in the field, Susanne went through several intensive training sessions. She also learned as she went along and applied her newfound knowledge to developing additional programs, primarily those focused on improving self–worth and coping with major life changes. In her ten years at the center, Susanne helped expand and transform it from a university–associated drug abuse prevention center to a full–fledged comprehensive mental health center serving seven counties.

By the mid–1970s Susanne had become one of the first women elected president of the New Mexico Mental Health, Drug Abuse, and Alcoholism Association. She held training seminars for volunteers who worked with the growing center's clients and their families, and she became a popular public speaker, addressing such topics as regaining self–esteem and moving through loss and change. Susanne also gave talks to directors of other community mental health centers, explaining how to raise funds more effectively and develop new programs. She was instrumental in educating state legislators on mental health issues so that New Mexico would pass a Mental Health Act, and she spoke at the local school of psychiatry about how the new law would affect them. Susanne had reached dreams she could not even have imagined back in high school. But her joy sharply turned to despair when her husband, Don, fell ill.

A high–energy director of the Speech and Hearing Department at Eastern New Mexico University, Don began to experience severe stomach pain that often required hospitalization. He was diagnosed with ulcers, yet despite many surgeries the pain persisted. Together, Susanne and Don searched for the underlying reason for his symptoms but found few answers until analyses at the Mayo Clinic in Minnesota revealed cancer. The doctors said Don had only six months to live. Suddenly, Don's and Susanne's worlds turned upside-down. And Susanne came to realize that, despite all the talks and seminars she'd given on the subject, she knew precious little about grief.

"Even though I had two beautiful children who were fine, I was doing a great job co–running a mental health center, and I had built up a successful speaking career, I felt like everything had been stripped out from underneath me," she says. "I was raised in an age where the wife did nothing but support the man. Now my husband was dying. Everything suddenly lost meaning for me."

Susanne devoted herself to caring for her dying husband. They continued to see more specialists, hoping for a cure or a change in diagnosis. None came. Susanne watched Don's weight drop from 185 pounds to barely 55. Holding on to their final moments together, Susanne and Don spoke of life and death and what happens to the spirit when the body dies. "I asked that when he died and got to the other side, if he had the opportunity, could he ask God and Jesus to give me answers while I'm here on this earth? I told my husband that I wanted to understand life more fully while I was still living." Don gave Susanne a puzzled look. "That's not the way it works," he said. "Well," Susanne replied, "God can do anything God wants to do. Even answer my questions." Susanne so desperately wanted to understand the meaning of life that Don, in his love for her, agreed to her request.

Don died in 1979 at the age of 40. After 14 years of marriage, Susanne found herself suddenly alone. She met her children's practical needs but felt too depressed to help them deal with grief over the loss of their father. Feeling lost in her new role as a single mother, Susanne impulsively married the first man she met who brought her some joy.

During that second, ill–fated marriage, Susanne says her first husband kept his deathbed promise by appearing to her in a vivid dream that would transform her life. In her dream, Susanne recalls, she spoke directly with Don and felt overcome by a sense of peace and beauty. When she awoke, her second husband was awake, and he told Susanne that he had just seen Don standing by the bed, looking at her before fading away.

Susanne was amazed. Had this been the spirit of her beloved first husband, bringing her the answers she sought? Regardless, the mystical event changed her outlook on life and gave Susanne a renewed sense of purpose. Instead of feeling sorry for herself and depending on others, Susanne began to adopt an outlook of hope, resilience, and responsibility. She developed a new dream: to understand life more fully and to live joyfully. Susanne had always believed in a loving God, and after this experience she began to foster a closer relationship with her creator. Her new resilience carried her through her difficult second marriage, which ended in a messy divorce and left her in debt. Susanne's faith enabled her to reach out to her children and help them deal with their feelings. She came to accept, even enjoy, being single.

After a chance encounter at a crowded restaurant with a wise Lakota teacher, Susanne became immersed in Native American spiritual traditions, which ultimately gave Susanne an understanding of herself that she never before had known. By praying regularly and looking for the synchronicities in life, as is the Lakota tradition, Susanne says she has reached a point of feeling so secure in herself that she could finally stop searching for security from the outside.

"I thought being married would bring me security," she says. "Then the man I loved died and left me with a big, empty house. I remarried to try to regain that elusive security. Then we divorced and I was left with bills to pay. I had to sell my house and move into a tiny apartment. But it was there that I began to discover that security does not come from a spouse or partner, a big house, a good job, or any of those things." Rather, she realized, security comes from the strength, balance, and self–esteem found within.

Susanne's 12–year spiritual quest culminated in her 1997 book, *When Spirit Speaks*. Susanne continues to be a sought–after speaker and also raises funds for cultural and historical projects in her community of Pauls Valley, Oklahoma, where the local chamber of commerce named her "Citizen of the Year" in 2003. But she feels that the spiritual insights she developed as she recovered from adversity have given her words deeper meaning. These days, Susanne incorporates the wisdom she gained from her Lakota friends, who weave prayer and spirituality into everyday life, into her talks and seminars. With help from what she describes as "earth angels" — such as the counselor she saw during her second marriage, the support group she joined before her divorce, her wise Lakota teachers, her children, and her new husband, John — Susanne feels certain that she has received many of the answers she sought.

Of all the counsel she shares during her speaking engagements today, Susanne emphasizes this one the most: "We've come to earth with lessons we need to learn and overcome. We bring the answers with us. And when we finally ask for help, we'll start hearing those answers. Help is only a prayer away. There is always hope and help. Do not give up hope."

Learn Resilience to Recover from Blows

> **"BE YOURSELF. LEARN TO TRUST YOUR JUDGMENT. LEARN TO LISTEN TO YOUR INTUITION. NO MATTER WHO TELLS YOU THAT YOU'RE NOT GOOD ENOUGH, JUST KEEP TELLING YOURSELF 'I CAN DO IT.' YOU KNOW, LIKE THE LITTLE ENGINE THAT COULD. TELL YOURSELF, 'I CAN DO IT. I CAN MAKE IT.' AND THAT BECOMES A SELF–FULFILLING PROPHECY." — NANCY ARCHULETA, CEO (CHAPTER 3)**

You can't practice resilience the way you can other Dream CPR essential elements. But you can prepare yourself beforehand so that resilience can carry you through when adversity strikes. Here are some ways you can prepare today for whatever trials may come tomorrow:

1 Develop and maintain a positive outlook. When chemotherapy made Richard Bloch feel sicker, weaker, and more depressed than ever, he held on to this thought: the chemicals that were making him sick were also ridding his body of disease. By focusing on the desired outcome rather than the painful side effects, Richard was able to get through the treatment and defeat cancer. Don't wait for a catastrophe to happen before you start practicing positive thinking. Begin today, regardless of where you are in life. Whenever you find yourself thinking negative, dooming thoughts, stop and purposely replace them with a positive mantra. For example, instead of thinking, "I'll never get this done," tell yourself, "Every day I'm closer to completing this project."

2 Understand that on the other side of struggle lies personal growth. When Doug West thought he was dying, he first felt fear before he reached peace. Struggles are hard but once we overcome them, we gain something — maturity, wisdom, confidence, balance, tranquility, and of course, resilience.

Resilience can help us continue to reach for dreams, even after tragedy and adversity, by protecting us at some level:

1 Resilience prevents you from sinking into bitterness, self–pity, and hate. At many points in her life, Maya could have given in to lower emotions and given up on her dreams. Instead she survived the hurts — by temporarily shielding herself from the outside world through a self–imposed silence, by immersing herself in books, by pouring out her feelings on paper. Resilience helped Maya find safe outlets for her confusion and

> **Dream CPR Journal**
>
> What are your greatest personal strengths?
>
> What inspires you?
>
> What do you value most?

rage so that she could heal her spirit and continue dreaming.

2   Resilience helps you get back on your feet and steady yourself after a major blow. Susanne Blake's life changed dramatically when her first husband became terminally ill. The first blow came with his death; the second blow was the pain of jumping too quickly into a second marriage that would only end in divorce. But with guidance from the spirit of her first husband and after a long personal spiritual quest, Susanne was able to use her resilience to change her life, strengthen herself, and dream again.

Although we cannot control the struggles we unexpectedly face, we do possess a quality — resilience — that helps us overcome the pain and maintain hope. Resilience brings us back to our dreams when the storm is over.

In the next chapter, we'll take a close look at the adage "Nothing ventured, nothing gained," and learn why we often need to take a risk to reach our dreams.

chapter 11

Risk: Take a chance

> " Twenty years from now, you will be more disappointed by the things that you didn't do than by the ones you did do. So throw off the bowlines. Sail away from the safe harbor. Catch the trade winds in your sails. Explore. Dream. Discover."
> — Mark Twain

Following your dreams is a chancy proposition. When you launch your dream, you don't know where it will take you, when it will be fulfilled, or even whether you will succeed. But if you don't try, you'll always wonder how high you could have soared. That's where the Dream CPR essential element *risk* comes in. Risk is inherent in following dreams: You don't know where your dreams will take you, but you can't afford not to find out.

In this chapter, you'll read about master cellist Yo–Yo Ma, social worker Connie Brady, electric guitar co–inventor George Fullerton, and computer start–up founder David Howard. Each one knows about risk — and each is well aware that risk and dreams go hand–in–hand. Yo–Yo Ma learned long ago that artistic risks lead to artistic growth. Time and again he has explored new musical territory, which ultimately led to creative growth and unconventional albums like *Appalachian Journey* and *Soul of the Tango*. Connie Brady faces risk regularly; her job with the Child Protective Services Agency in California requires her to venture into unpredictable, possibly dangerous, situations. Yet this grandmother of four knows that risk is necessary to protect abused and neglected children.

In the 1940s, George Fullerton was a young man with a passion for music and a predilection for electronics. Happily employed in radio repair, he nonetheless took a risk by leaving his reliable line of work to help develop what would become the renowned Fender guitar. David Howard always wanted to start his own business, but with a stable engineering job, a mortgage to pay, and a family to support, it seemed too risky. But his dream kept calling until David took a calculated risk and became an engineering consultant. His new career path led him to ultimately start his own businesses.

These dream achievers all had something significant to lose. Yo–Yo risked losing his reputation as a classical musician. Connie risks her own safety to ensure the safety of children. Both George and David risked losing steady income for ventures that came with no financial guarantee. Yet despite the risks involved and the lack of certainty, each one chose to take a chance rather than play it safe.

Yo–Yo Ma:
Exploring Artistic Frontiers

One of the most accomplished and celebrated classical musicians of our era, Yo–Yo Ma constantly pushes the envelope of musical interpretation by pairing his cello with the Argentine tango, Asian martial arts, and American bluegrass, among other artistic collaborations. The soft–spoken musician with the winning smile learned long ago that artistic growth requires taking risks.

At the start of each performance, master cellist Yo–Yo Ma greets his audience warmly, like a gracious host making his guests feel at home. But the moment the music begins, he becomes locked in concentration, simultaneously focusing on the orchestra's pace, the audience's response, the vibrato of his cello strings, the arc of his bow strokes. As he gauges the unfolding symphony experience, Yo–Yo becomes the conduit between composer and audience, masterfully releasing the angst or ecstasy inherent in every note. Yo–Yo uses music to bridge past and present, connecting people from different cultures.

He's built a successful career based on his two–fold dream: To bring classical music to higher levels of expression and to bring people together through music. Perhaps none of his creative endeavors reflects his dream better than the Silk Road Project. Yo–Yo started this nonprofit organization in 1998 to illuminate the artistic, educational, historical, and cultural connections made along the ancient trade route that linked East and West and facilitated the exchange not only of goods but of ideas and traditions. Through this innovative project, Yo–Yo addresses his deep desire to understand, by means of musical interpretation, how diverse cultural perspectives evolve from a common humanity. This desire was shaped by Yo–Yo's own multi–ethnic upbringing, a mixture of Chinese, French, and American influences.

When he embarked on his ambitious project, Yo–Yo knew he was taking a big risk. He needed to find the right mix of international musicians who would come together to successfully recreate forgotten musical styles. There was no certainty that sponsors would support the project. Yo–Yo didn't know if he could accurately transcribe pieces like obscure Renaissance dances and ancient Chinese folk tunes that follow now–obsolete musical notation. But true to his passion, he took a risk and jumped in — and his gamble paid off.

Sponsors came forward, from the Aga Khan Trust for Culture to the Ford Motor Company. Yo–Yo's first collection of folk traditions from Silk Road regions, *Solo*, was released in 1999. A Silk Road Ensemble soon formed, made up of gifted musicians from India, Iran, China, Japan, Kazakhstan, and other countries and ethnic regions along the ancient route. To date, the ensemble has produced two albums, *Silk Road Journeys: When Strangers Meet*, and *The Silk Road: A Musical Caravan*. They've also toured across the United States and around the world to share history and culture through music.

It's not the first time Yo–Yo has taken a risk to grow as a musician and, in the process, expand the scope of classical music. The now–seasoned 50–year–old cellist first realized the necessity of risk as a budding 19–year–old playing a concert at the 92nd Street Y in New York City. "While sitting there at the concert," he stated in a 1989 interview, "playing all the notes correctly, I started to wonder, 'Why am I here? I'm doing everything as planned. So what's at stake? Nothing. Not only is the audience bored but I myself am bored.' Perfection is not very communicative. However, when you subordinate your technique to the musical message, you get really involved. Then you can take risks. It doesn't matter if you fail. What does matter is that you tried."

Born in Paris to Chinese parents, Yo–Yo first held a cello at the tender age of four. Taught to play both piano and cello by his father, a violinist and former professor at Nanjing University in China, Yo–Yo awed audiences at the University of Paris when he gave his first concert there at the age of five. When Yo–Yo was almost seven, his family moved to New York. There the young boy studied with accomplished cellist Janos Scholz before going to the Juilliard School of Music to study under Leonard Rose, a mentor who helped the young, timid Yo–Yo gain confidence and bloom musically. At age 12, Yo–Yo began playing concertos with the Doctors' Orchestra of New York.

Ever since that insightful moment at age 19, Yo–Yo has dreamed not of perfection but of understanding and interpreting what music conveys on a higher, emotional level. His liberal arts education at Harvard, which included studies in Chinese and Japanese history and modern Chinese literature, whet Yo–Yo's appetite for music outside the Western classical canon. Even as he built a career as a classical cellist, he studied the music of Africa, Asia, and South America.

As a result, along with recording sonatas and symphonies by Beethoven, Brahms, and Rachmaninoff, Yo–Yo performs and plays Japanese melodies, Vietnamese songs, Appalachian folk tunes, Argentine tangos, and music with ties to Ireland, Turkey, Scandinavia and Africa, among other regions. He frequently collaborates with other creative forces, including vocalist Bobby McFerrin and pianist Emanuel Ax, to generate new sounds. Yo–Yo performed the original score by composer Tan Dun for the 2000 martial arts film *Crouching Tiger, Hidden Dragon*, winner of an Academy Award for best original score and two Golden Globe awards for soundtrack. Time and again, he's taken a risk by tackling projects outside the realm of traditional classical repertoire. And each time that risk has paid off with a new collection of hauntingly beautiful musical renditions. In the process, he's recorded more than 50 albums, won 15 Grammys, and was even named Artist of the Year in 1997 by Gramophone Awards.

What drives Yo–Yo to go where no classical cellist has gone before? "I think, first of all, that music describes something that is so grand that you can never get to the end limit; it has limitless ways to get us to express this," he stated in a live Internet chat on barnesandnoble.com in February 2000. "In some ways, the easiest way to deal with our work is to feel that the work is never finished. There are just temporary markers in performance, but the subject matter is limitless, and we are lucky to be able to participate in this grand scheme of things — because music is something much greater than ourselves."

Although he now suffers from painful tendinitis, Yo–Yo continues to maintain a rigorous schedule, giving concerts all over the world while also sharing his knowledge and passion for music with talented young musicians. In his constant quest for new ways to interpret music, Yo–Yo willingly takes a risk every time he performs. "I feel that when a composer writes a piece of music," he stated in 1989, "he's translating a human experience into sound. I know that some people see music as merely sound for sound's sake. I disagree. There can be moments when you are in contact with the experience from which the music came. ... When that happens, the ritual of concert–giving is at its highest. And a composer's ideas from 200 years ago find absolute contact in their purest form with people living now. That's quite amazing."

CONNIE BRADY:
PUTTING CHILDREN'S NEEDS FIRST

> As a child, she dreamed of having a stable home life. Although that dream never came true, social worker and grandmother Connie Brady now helps abused and neglected children find the security and protection that every child deserves and needs.

Hers is a risky job, but she does it gladly for the children. Connie Brady has been through the types of frightening experiences that most of us only see on TV. As an emergency response team member with the Child Protective Services Agency in Riverside County, California, Connie intervenes on behalf of children who are abused or neglected by their caretakers. She has been called upon to accompany police officers on drug busts: Her mission in these dangerous and unpredictable situations is to take children away to safety. Connie and the police have to move in quickly; guns abound, and she doesn't even get to wear a bullet–proof vest. It's one of the most frightening duties of her job, but she risks her own safety for the sake of abused and neglected children.

This compassionate grandmother of four knows what it's like to grow up in an unstable environment. Born in 1941, young Connie, not quite understanding that her father was a soldier fighting in World War II, always wondered where he was. Without her dad around, Connie felt tremendous uncertainty. Her sense of instability grew when her father returned after six years and, trying to provide for his wife and three children, uprooted the family frequently in search of construction jobs, none of which provided enough income for the family.

"Mom often said that she and Dad were always struggling for us to have enough food to eat," Connie recalls. When she started high school, Connie's parents divorced. Her only dream during her entire childhood and adolescence was to have a happy, secure family life. Today as a social worker, Connie's dream is to give at–risk children a chance at a normal, stable life, the dream that eluded her.

When a call comes in to the Child Protective Services Agency alleging abuse, Connie goes out to interview the child, sometimes with a police escort and frequently accompanied by one of the child's teachers or school counselor to help the child feel at ease. What happens next depends on what Connie uncovers. She may interview parents, grandparents, neighbors, doctors, siblings, guardians, teachers, or others close to the child. Or, she may begin the emergency response procedure immediately to take the child to a safe place.

"I try to keep the family together if at all possible," Connie explains. "Sometimes it's a matter of arranging counseling for the parents on something like anger management or alcohol management." But certain scenarios put the child in so much risk that he has to be taken to safety right away. "Every case is different," says Connie. "Let's say a child is being abused by one parent. I have to determine — is the other parent willing to protect the child? In some cases, yes; in others, no. If no, then the child needs to be removed from the household and put into foster care. Then I have to determine, does the child need to see a counselor, a doctor, a nurse? I get the necessary referrals and place the child where she needs to go for help."

It's a demanding job where just her day–to–day tasks can thrust her into difficult, heartbreaking situations. Connie encounters dysfunctional families and negligent parents on a regular basis. She sees babies born with cocaine and heroine in their systems, causing irrevocable developmental, mental, or physical problems. She sees innocent children suffer silently, and hurt teens lash out angrily. Connie interviews from four to ten kids every day, and she strives to ensure the safety of each one.

Connie completely empathizes with many of these kids. She not only understands what it's like to have an unstable home life, she also knows what it's like to suffer from low self–esteem: During high school, Connie didn't take college–prep courses because, in her own mind, she wasn't college material. But at age 20, after having worked several odd jobs, she took a risk by enrolling in a college course. Connie married, gave birth to a daughter, and worked outside the home, but she continued to take evening classes, one or two per semester, at the University of Nebraska in both Lincoln and Omaha. "My husband helped raise our daughter while I was going to college at night," she recalls. "I just had this insatiable thirst for knowledge. College was opening doors for me that I never thought could be opened."

Over time, Connie developed a dream: to help others. Connie began to work with the disabled through Goodwill Industries, and later became a probation officer with a program that rehabilitated drunk drivers. She then worked as a counselor, first at a recovery center for alcoholics and then at a halfway house for female criminal offenders. In 1978, 17 years after taking her first college course, Connie proudly received a bachelor's degree in criminal justice and social work from the University of Nebraska, Omaha.

The family moved to California where Connie became a drug and alcohol counselor at a hospital and began to take graduate courses part–time. Taking four years to complete the two–year graduate program, she obtained her master's degree in social work from California State University, Long Beach, and then transferred to the hospital's psychiatric unit where she remained for many years conducting group and individual counseling. Then in 1998, she went to work for the state's child protective agency. While her dream of helping people has remained with her, the way in which she's doing that has shifted. "Dreams change, even though there may be a theme," Connie says. "So as they change, we have to change with them."

Connie continues to take personal risks for the sake of at–risk children, knowing that her compassionate work today will yield positive reverberations for years to come. "People have to be responsible and committed to kids for the long term," she states emphatically. "Kids need to be taken care of. They need to feel safe. They need to be protected."

GEORGE FULLERTON: DEVELOPING A NEWFANGLED GUITAR

Following our dreams can sometimes reveal hidden opportunities we had never before imagined. That's what happened to George Fullerton. His passion for electronics and music put him in a unique position to help develop a new instrument, the modern electric guitar. He quit his job to devote himself to this endeavor, with absolutely no guarantee that the new instrument would catch on, or even work very well.

Eric Clapton's 1956 Sunburst Fender Stratocaster guitar set a record in 1999 when it sold at auction for an astronomical $497,500. A half–century earlier, that half–million–dollar instrument had been the brainchild of the late Leo Fender and George Fullerton, who together developed the solid–body electric guitar and invented the electric bass. More than 50 years after the first Fender made its debut, the Fender line remains the standard by which other electric guitars and basses are measured. And while the instruments may carry the Fender name, George's technical and musical talents proved essential to their development.

George was born in 1923 into a musical family in Arkansas. His parents entertained at square dances on weekends, playing the piano, guitar, violin, and mandolin. George soon learned to play several instruments as well, but his favorite has always been the guitar. "Even when I was too tiny to hold the guitar," he recalls, "Mother would lay it down on something flat and let me strum the strings. I learned to play the guitar early on and got quite good at it. I had a dream of making it to the Grand Ol' Opry and standing on that stage one day."

George's love of music matched his fascination for electronics. From the age of seven, he enjoyed tinkering with radios and other electronic equipment. And as a young man in the 1940s, George moved to Southern California and followed his childhood passions. He played with a band on the weekends and got a part-time job fixing radios. Soon he met Leo Fender, who ran a radio repair and record shop where George liked to hang out. Leo was 14 years older than George, but the two quickly became great friends, working together on weekends setting up speakers and amplifiers for local concerts.

When Leo decided to leave the radio repair business to concentrate on designing, customizing, and manufacturing amplifiers, he invited George to work at his new shop. At first George didn't want to take a risk; he was happy with his radio repair job and the electronics classes he was taking at community college. But Leo was persistent. He invited his friend to join him for a cup of coffee at a small café down the street from his shop, where he shared his dream: Leo wanted to build and produce the world's first practical solid-body electric guitar, and he asked if George would join him in this venture. The young man lit up. "Join you? I'd love it! When do we start?" he replied.

In the 1940s, electric guitars were actually modified hollow-body acoustic guitars with custom electric pickups mounted inside. They were cumbersome instruments and had nasty feedback problems. Even worse, repairs on a hollow-body, customized electric guitar could take months, and musicians couldn't afford to wait that long. Leo and George knew that musicians had a real need for a better electric guitar.

George immediately recognized the chance of a lifetime. It was a risk, no doubt: The collaboration might not produce anything, and after leaving his radio repair job and college classes — which George enjoyed immensely — he might soon find himself pounding the pavement in search of a job. But George was willing to take that chance. The opportunity to help develop something as exciting as the world's first practical solid–body electric guitar wouldn't come twice. And George knew that, regardless of what might happen, he would still be living the life of his dreams, immersed in music and electronics.

So George took the risk and came aboard Leo's business full–time. The two of them, along with a few employees, designed and manufactured amplifiers for the shop by day. But after closing time, George and Leo stayed at the shop to develop ideas for a solid–body electric guitar, sometimes until two or three in the morning. Leo — who did not play the guitar — relied on George's experience as a musician and his expertise in electronics.

The two spent hours discussing their new guitar. They wrote down every feature they thought it should have. Both agreed that the guitar had to be affordable, easy–to–repair, strong, light-weight, and able to produce a top–quality sound that was out of this world. After an entire year of working on the design evenings, nights, and weekends, their prototype was ready. In 1949, the pair christened their creation the Fender Telecaster. They chose "Tele" because television was a major phenomenon just coming into its own.

"We started taking the guitar to beer joints and smoke–filled ballrooms," says George. "We got wonderful response to it." Pleased that their guitar made such a favorable impression, George and Leo took another risk — they set up a production line, moving into a larger facility, fabricating tool dyes to produce the instrument, and hiring more employees. In 1950, they took one of their guitars to a popular dance hall in Los Angeles. A young man walked into the hall and noticed the new guitar.

"He wanted to try it out," George recalls. "We told him, 'Sure, that's why we brought it.' He played it for a while, unplugged. When the band took a break, they let him plug the guitar into one of their amplifiers. He played beautifully. No one at the dance hall had ever heard anything like it. Everybody, including the band members, crowded around that young man to listen to him play for the rest of the evening." That night proved to be a major turning point for the creators of this "newfangled" guitar — the young man happened to be the popular musician Jimmy Bryant.

"Of course, we furnished him with two or three Fender guitars immediately, and that opened the thing up like wildfire," George recalls. "Everybody wanted a Fender guitar so they could play and sound like Jimmy Bryant." Sales and productions picked up as the Fender name spread quickly. Within a year, they'd gone from making 40 guitars a week to building 40 a day, with 50 employees to help with production. By the time Leo and George sold their company in 1965, they had 750 employees making 350 guitars a day.

Even though their guitars have enjoyed a solid reputation, George and Leo did run into criticism. "Some people said to us, 'All you guys did is put some strings on chunks of wood.' But that's not the case at all," George says. "We could take any of our guitars and, regardless of what was wrong, repair them and have them working again in 20 minutes. Everything on the guitar was removable and replaceable. We could fix it right there at the shop while the musician waited. It was unheard of in those days."

George helped Leo invent, design, and produce the world's first electric bass, which they began marketing in 1951. Over the years, George and Leo came up with several new models of electric instruments, including the Stratocaster electric guitar, which was introduced in 1954. Both spent countless hours talking with musicians, learning their likes, dislikes, and wishes for specific features. Both George and Leo strove to develop the most user-friendly instrument possible. In doing so, they weren't afraid to take chances with new looks and features. Even the attractive contoured shape they developed for guitars had a functional purpose: The smooth, rounded body prevented sharp edges from cutting into a guitarist's arms or ribs.

Today George works as a consultant for G&L Musical Products, which owns more than 50 patents developed by George and Leo. Together with his wife, Lucille, George preserves the Fender guitar history. He has written two books detailing the work he, Leo and many others did to bring the Fender guitar to the world. Leo Fender died in 1991 at the age of 81, working up to the day before he passed on. "There aren't too many of us left to record this story," 83-year-old George points out.

By taking a risk, leaving his reliable job in radio repair for something as chancy as building a newfangled guitar, George helped transform the music industry. Every popular musician from Tennessee Ernie Ford to Speedy West, and George Harrison to Bruce Springsteen, has played a Fender guitar.

Interestingly, George's childhood dream came true after all. A few years ago, he got his chance to stand on the stage of the Grand Ol' Opry. He wasn't performing, though. George was there to be honored by hundreds of musicians whose careers have flourished with the help of the Fender guitar. Life certainly can fulfill dreams in the most unexpected ways.

DAVID HOWARD:
FACING HIGH STAKES IN HIGH-TECH

Giving up a good salary and the relative security of an engineering job with industry giant Hewlett-Packard, David Howard took a chance to follow his dream of running his own business — even though he had a family to support, a mortgage to pay, and two kids nearing college age. Taking a calculated risk, he became an independent engineering consultant, a move that helped him launch two computer start-ups and become his own boss.

When an industry changes as quickly as the personal computer industry does, there are bound to be growing pains. Most people just try to keep up, catch up, or make do with the technology. But a few visionaries step back, take a look at the bigger picture, and find solutions. David Howard is one of these visionaries. Founder of two startups, Colorado Software Architects and 1Vision Software, David created a software technology to help computer users simplify their lives. His patented persistent file system, or PFS, keeps track of every file that enters the computer and tells you where to find it — even when the file is saved not on the computer but on a disk or tape that's sitting on the shelf.

"'Persistent' means that it remembers," David explains. "With any other file system, if you take out the CD or the floppy, the file system forgets it ever existed. With PFS, you can find anything on any disk that was ever in your system. From a single drive letter, locate the file you want, and we tell you what disk it is on." To the PC user, this centralized file system turns the task of file management into a simple, user–friendly reality.

David's brainchild has been lauded by such publications as *PC World* and *Laptop Buyer's Guide & Handbook*, which praise not only its functionality but also its ease of use. David has designed his PFS into several software products he sells, including 1Disk, which tracks and manages files, and 1Safe, which adds backup functions. A June 1999 *PC World* article asserted that 1Disk is "indispensable," while a November 2000 article in *Small Business Computing* described 1Safe as "effective and intuitive." Proud of his products, David says, "We've shipped half a million copies of our software. Our system comes in a form that people can easily understand, and excellent support starts with the software working the way people need it to work."

None of this would have ever happened if David hadn't taken a risk, leaving a secure job with benefits behind to first consult and then start his own business. "I began thinking about running a computer software business back in 1981," he says. "That era was still the infancy of the personal computer. I had many ideas about products that could be produced and wanted to explore them." But it wasn't until the mid–1990s that he actually pursued this path.

He realizes today that in a sense, his business training began during his childhood in Wisconsin. The second child of two educators, David had excellent role models: His father was the director of guidance at a high school while his mother ran a church's kindergarten program and taught elementary school. "My dad always fixed things around the house," David recalls. "Instead of calling the plumber or the carpenter, Dad would take care of it himself. From watching him, I learned to later on do whatever had to be done to keep my business going. I've hauled trash, installed cubicles, photographed products for press releases, written marketing documents, and created logos, even though I have no such training." From his mother, David says, he learned that sometimes you just "have to get busy and do it yourself."

David went to the University of Wisconsin at Madison to study civil engineering, but halfway through the program he realized that he was more interested in computers. So he transferred to the university's electrical engineering program, which offered computer training, even though switching majors meant it would take him longer to finish his degree.

After graduating in 1980, David went to work for Johnson Controls as a digital engineer, writing firmware and software for computer applications such as climate control and security systems in commercial buildings. He also purchased a TRS–80 computer for home use — primitive by 21st century standards, as the video card alone in today's personal computer has 4,000 times the memory and performance that the entire TRS–80 had — but it served him well. Even with two preschool–age daughters and a full–time job, David found time to develop software for the schools his parents worked at; with his TRS–80, he developed a program that allowed teachers to create interactive lessons and tests, and track student results.

In 1987, the family moved to Northern Colorado where David's wife, Ellen, had grown up. There, 32–year–old David got a job as software manager for a small startup company called Colorado Memory Systems in Loveland. He oversaw a group of four engineers who developed tape drives. It was David's first management position and his entry into the field of data storage. Working for a startup that employed only ten people in the engineering department was risky — startups do not have the financial solvency or the resources that larger companies generally do — but he found it very exciting.

"It was a fast–paced environment that I really enjoyed," David says. "I learned a lot about running a small business while working there. In less than five years, my group went from four to 90 engineers, so I learned about growth dynamics. I learned how to launch products in the computer industry, and how to survive cash–flow problems." His group was on the brink of a promising new product for networked backups when Hewlett–Packard purchased the company in 1992 and made cutbacks to the software side of CMS. The new network product was placed on the back burner, and David transferred into the company's advanced research group, moving away from management and into practical research of products that HP wanted to develop.

In his new position, David came into regular contact with managers, engineers, technicians, marketers, and vendors from other divisions and companies. The more he talked with computer users worldwide, the more he saw a need to reduce the complexity of storing, protecting, and retrieving data. Unable to convince his managers of the viability of his ideas for storage management, David looked elsewhere. When he heard that the Dutch electronics company Philips was developing a new tape drive, he figured his expertise just might appeal to them.

David contacted Philips and arranged to fly to the Netherlands to present a comprehensive proposal to develop backup software and a file management system for the new Philips tape drive. While waiting for a response, David shared his ideas with several trusted colleagues that he wanted to bring aboard, who became excited by the prospect of joining his new venture. After waiting several months and still not getting any response from Philips, David decided to contact the company himself and make an offer. "I called them up and basically said that if they gave me a contract to fund me for two months, I would quit my job and develop this software for them," he says. The company agreed, and David left steady work and company benefits to become a consultant engineer.

"With a house to pay for and two growing daughters quickly approaching college age, giving up a good, steady job with benefits seemed unreasonable," he recalls. But his wife supported his dreams, and David started Colorado Software Architects in 1996 in his basement as a one–man company. It quickly grew to three people as two of David's friends and fellow programmers, Kurt Godwin and John Gandee, came aboard and the three moved into office space in a bank building. "We kept referring to 'the end of the world,'" David laughs. "That meant the end of a contract with no other work in sight. First it was two months. Then we got another contract, which carried us for a year. Somehow we managed to keep generating new business as software consultants and stay afloat." When they completed their work for Philips, they consulted for Cheyenne Software.

Those early months were trying. Some weeks, everyone had to go home without a paycheck. But the three engineers believed in their ideas for data storage. Patience and perseverance paid off when, eight months after starting CSA, David reached an agreement with Microsoft to develop drivers for the Windows 2000 floppy disk and tape drive subsystems. The project earned David and his team a nice sum — $100,000 in gross revenues. More importantly, the relationship with Microsoft gave the small startup greater credibility and visibility.

Meanwhile, David and his colleagues developed his file management ideas into a solid, standard product, 1Disk, that they could sell. By 1997, the team wound down their consulting work to focus on launching and selling their new product. David founded 1Vision and brought along the core team plus one more engineer, John Moore, as business partners, with each holding equal shares of the company. They reached an agreement with Iomega, which soon started selling 1Vision's 1Disk bundled with Iomega's zip drives. Once again, the partners struggled through a rough initial period of no cash flow. But as the concept caught on with individual PC users and small businesses, 1Vision grew to 30 employees and $2 million in gross annual revenue. For a few years, David and his business partners settled into a comfortable niche.

With the current economic downturn, which has hit the engineering and technology industries especially hard, David is again re–inventing his companies to continue being in business for himself. He's had to lay off several employees — the hardest thing he's had to do as a business owner. With seven employees in CSA and six in 1Vision, David and his business partners are returning to software consulting in order to self–fund the launch of two new products, vNAS and vSERV, which are file management and backup products designed for large computer networks.

At the age of 47, David continues forward with his businesses, launching new products and taking new risks to keep working for himself. He put his oldest daughter through college and is about to do the same for his youngest. And despite the financial ups an downs and other uncertainties, David is a happy man. "Running my own company helped get rid of a lot of frustration stemming from the lack of control that I felt working for somebody else," he says. "I used to complain that management could be doing a better job. I wanted to prove that I could do it better, and I believe that I have. In terms of getting the right innovative products out, I've done a good job."

"It's also fun," he adds, "when running a small business, to see what tomorrow brings. It's exciting because you're the person who has to make it happen."

Take a Risk to Grow Your Dreams

"TRY DIFFERENT THINGS, AND BE CONFIDENT THAT YOUR OWN VOICE WILL EVENTUALLY TELL YOU WHICH WAY TO TURN. DON'T GET FRUSTRATED IF IT TAKES A WHILE TO FIND YOUR CALLING IN LIFE. DON'T BE AFRAID TO TRY DIFFERENT THINGS. IF YOU TAKE A WRONG STEP, WELL, LIFE IS LONG. KEEP TRYING THINGS, AND YOU'LL FIGURE IT OUT." — EDWARD BERGER, AIDS RESEARCHER (CHAPTER 9)

Chasing after any dream is bound to involve some risk. As the dream–achievers profiled in this chapter have shown us, there are many different kinds of risks we can take — artistic, financial, even physical. Only you can determine what kind of risk is right for you, and how big a risk you can take.

In weighing whether or not to take a risk, ask yourself the following questions:

1 *What do I stand to gain if this venture succeeds?*

2 *What am I prepared to lose if it fails?*

Write down your answers; they will help you gauge how much risk you're willing to take to reach your goal. Be realistic when looking at your potential losses. George Fullerton gave up his job in radio repair. But by taking that risk, he gained the chance to invent an exciting new guitar that would change the music industry, and ended up devoting his life to creating new designs and patents.

Dream CPR Journal

If you had one wish for yourself, for your loved ones, for your community, what would that wish be?

How would you go about making that wish come true?

Be honest with yourself about how much risk you're willing to take. Some risk is inevitable — nothing ventured, nothing gained. But decide how much risk is right for you, and understand all the pros and cons before you take a leap.

To let the Dream CPR essential element *risk* work in your favor, ask yourself the following questions:

1 *What's holding you back? Is it a fear of losing money, respect, or perhaps a stable job?* Build a safety net to cushion yourself in the event of that loss. George had enough experience working with radios that he probably could have returned to his former line of work if his venture with Leo Fender had proved fruitless. Yo–Yo excels at cello sonatas and concertos and could always return to his classical repertoire if his more adventurous musical projects failed. If you have a back–up plan, you'll feel more comfortable taking a risk. Think through your contingency plan and commit it to paper.

2 Once your safety line is in place, move forward with confidence. Take that risk, and don't hold back. Send your resume to your dream company. Apply for the job you've wanted for years. Learn that new skill that fascinates you.

Enroll in that class you've always wanted to take. Whatever it is, give it all you've got.

We can't possibly advance our dreams without taking some risk. But you can choose to take a carefully calculated risk rather than a careless, impulsive gamble. Know your dream, know the risk, and proceed with caution and confidence. Good things await those who reach for the stars.

Our next chapter showcases *responsibility*, the Dream CPR element that ensures that our dreams are aligned with our highest intentions and most noble purpose.

chapter 12

Responsibility: Choose Wisely

> "IN THE LONG RUN, WE SHAPE OUR LIVES, AND WE SHAPE OURSELVES. THE PROCESS NEVER ENDS UNTIL WE DIE. AND THE CHOICES WE MAKE ARE ULTIMATELY OUR OWN RESPONSIBILITY."
> — ELEANOR ROOSEVELT

It's up to us to choose what to do with our lives, so every Dream CPR essential element is connected to the final one, *responsibility*. We are responsible for discovering our passion, developing the confidence to pursue our dream, making a commitment to our dream, and taking a risk to set our dream in motion. Responsibility is all about the choices we make — as the saying goes, "If it's to be, it's up to me." If we choose to do nothing, then nothing will happen. By choosing to follow our dreams, we take responsibility for shaping our lives and ourselves.

Our choices also affect our family members, neighbors, co-workers, friends and associates. Our choices can affect people we've never met, even people who have yet to be born. We need to be aware of how our dreams and choices affect others, and take responsibility for dreaming dreams that will achieve the most good for ourselves and our communities. Nobody is an island; we're all in this together. To reach the dream of world peace, we need to achieve respect and nonviolence in our own homes and relationships. To reach the dream of ending world hunger, we need to feed the hungry in our own neighborhoods. Each of us has the power and responsibility to dream globally and act locally. Taken collectively, our responsible actions can create a better world for everyone.

In this chapter, you'll meet Doug Ishii, a researcher whose breakthroughs offer great promise for treating both diabetic neuropathy and brain disorders. Doug spent the first four years of his life in internment camps for Japanese–Americans, and the rest of his childhood in a low–income housing project besieged by gang activity. Yet Doug pursued an education, earning a Ph.D. in pharmacology, and today feels a sense of responsibility to serve humanity through his scientific research. His wife, Wendy, overcame her shyness to become a successful actress, thanks to a supportive mentor in high school. In gratitude for his help, she brings top–quality, thought–provoking theatrical productions to her community and helps acting students overcome their fear of auditions.

You'll also meet Mary O'Donnell, a mother and wife who saw that her community needed an alcohol treatment center for women — and took it upon herself to get one started. Christy Curtis moved forward with her entrepreneurial dreams, even after finding herself in a difficult place with an unplanned pregnancy. A single mom today, she considers what's best for herself and her child before making any business or personal decisions.

You'll learn things about Emmy–award winner Dennis Weaver that you never knew. The late actor enjoyed a successful television career, playing the lovable sidekick Chester in *Gunsmoke* during the 1950s and 1960s, and Marshal Sam McCloud in *McCloud* during the 1970s, among many other roles. But instead of slipping quietly into retirement, Dennis became a sought–after speaker and a champion for social and environmental issues. He founded the Institute of Ecolonomics to develop solutions for a sustainable ecology and economy. Dennis believed it was his responsibility, and ours, to give future generations the legacy of a clean environment and a healthy economy.

Remember the dual role that the Dream CPR essential element *responsibility* plays in our dreams. First, we're responsible for discovering and pursuing our most heartfelt dreams. Just as importantly, we're also responsible for dreaming dreams that will have a positive effect on ourselves and the world around us.

DOUG AND WENDY ISHII: MARRIAGE OF ART AND SCIENCE

> He's a medical researcher, she's an actor, but husband and wife share something important in common: a dedication to helping others. Dr. Douglas N. Ishii, professor and researcher at Colorado State University in Fort Collins, is applying his scientific discovery to develop revolutionary treatments for people suffering from advanced diabetes and brain disorders. Wendy Ishii, also a CSU instructor and the cofounder and artistic director of Fort Collins' Bas Bleu Theatre Company, presents theater as an artistic tool to foster and improve community dialogue.

Dr. Douglas N. Ishii's meticulous research in the field of neurobiology holds great promise for advanced–stage diabetics who suffer from painful, debilitating nerve damage. Hundreds of experiments finally led to Doug's key discovery: that a protein called insulin–like growth factor (IGF) helps maintain a healthy nervous system. The 59–year–old scientist dreams of using this discovery to prevent, and perhaps even reverse, the devastating effects of diabetic neuropathy, a form of nerve damage that plagues millions of diabetics worldwide, including 1.5 million Americans. Symptoms can include sharp, persistent pain, severe nausea and vomiting, and loss of bladder control. Some people with diabetic neuropathy may even lose the ability to walk or require an amputation.

Doug's dream is a personal one: His older brother has diabetes, and as he ages his chances of developing diabetic neuropathy increase significantly. Since his mid–1980s discovery that sheds light on IGF's vital role in nerve health, Doug has been racing against the clock to develop a safe and effective treatment for diabetic neuropathy before his brother suffers irreparable, painful nerve damage.

Doug, who works in both the department of physiology and the department of biochemistry and molecular biology at CSU, has shown that IGFs can prevent nerve damage in diabetic rats, and he's been awarded a patent for the treatment. Now he must synthesize IGF hormones along the strict guidelines of the Food and Drug Administration (FDA), a complex process that can cost several million dollars, before he can begin clinical trials. Clinical trials, in turn, will likely require three to four years to complete.

There's more: Doug also observed that IGFs can help repair nerve and brain damage from causes such as stroke, trauma, or Alzheimer's disease, and he has patents pending on these treatments. He discovered that IGFs can easily cross the often–impenetrable barrier between blood and brain. That means that it's possible to inject an IGF treatment directly into the patient's bloodstream — just like any shot — rather than having to drill a hole into the person's skull to get medications to the brain. But again, clinical trials and funding are needed before new treatments can become available. It's a slow, frustrating process, but Doug presses forward, working to overcome legal, clinical, and financial obstacles to bring effective treatments to the people who so desperately need them.

Obstacles are nothing new to Doug; they've been central to his life from day one. Doug's Japanese–born parents were living in San Francisco when the executive order that led to the unconstitutional internment of 120,000 Japanese–Americans was issued in 1942. Doug's brother was only a year old at the time, whereas Doug was not yet born: his mother was pregnant with him.

Doug's family had to leave their possessions behind to live in a converted race track in Santa Anita, California, which served as one of many "assembly centers," or temporary internment camps. "My family had no knowledge of what would happen," says Doug. "There were many rumors. People were afraid. The orders were that you could carry only that which you could hold in your hands. In one suitcase my mother carried diapers. She filled another suitcase with baby food. And that's how my parents arrived at the assembly center. I was born there."

The young couple and their two little boys were relocated first to an internment camp in Topaz, Utah, and then to a camp in Tulelake, California, where they remained until the end of the war. Altogether, Doug's family was held for four years.

Doug was very young, but he still vividly remembers the barbed wire, the common mess halls, the cold drafts, and the lack of privacy. But he also remembers playing games with other children and watching his mother teach his brother to read. Sitting on his mother's lap while she read to his older brother, Doug surprised her by learning to read English when he was only three. His love of reading has never left him.

When Doug and his family were finally released, they had nothing but $25 and four train tickets. Doug's parents had lost their home, their jobs, and virtually all of their possessions. The family returned to San Francisco but had to start from scratch. They ended up in a low–income housing project that had been hastily built for the city's Navy Base employees during the war. That's where Doug grew up. "It was meant to be temporary housing," he says. "The buildings were supposed to be demolished, but they never were."

Doug's parents tried to rebuild their lives, a difficult endeavor in the midst of continued anti–Japanese sentiment. His father fell ill with tuberculosis, brought on in part by the crowded, unhealthy conditions at the internment camps. Later, he developed schizophrenia. "I didn't have much contact with my father," says Doug, "but my mother was an enormous influence on me. She is one of the world's leading performance players of the biwa, a lute–like Japanese court instrument that dates back well before the 12th century. My father had excellent calligraphy and was always reading. So we grew up with this tradition of great respect for learning. Also, because of the isolation I felt living in our housing project, which had a lot of gang activity, I withdrew into a world of books." The public library became one of Doug's favorite hangouts. As a child he read at least three books a week, poring through the writings of everyone from Hemingway to Dostoevsky. Books gave him entry to a world beyond the confines of his neighborhood.

Earning outstanding grades in high school, Doug began his college studies in 1960 at the University of California at Berkeley. "It was an eye–opener for me," he says. "Coming from a very limited perspective at the housing project, I was suddenly thrust into a campus with 40,000 students with diverse backgrounds during a time of profoundly important social and cultural movements in the United States. It was like a great breath of clean, fresh air for me."

Initially he focused on creative writing and philosophy, but he soon became drawn to lab work and switched to a biochemistry major. Doug married his first wife, and the couple soon had children. He had to work full time to pay his way through college and support a family. "In my last year at Berkeley," he says, "I would work from midnight until 8 a.m. in a chemical plant. Then I would get off work and go to school until 5 p.m., then spend a few hours doing homework, sleep maybe two hours, and go back to work. That's how my final year there was spent."

After graduating, Doug obtained a temporary job with the U.S. Department of Agriculture on a project to develop nontoxic insecticides for forest use. Soon he was offered a permanent position. But Doug was disturbed by two requests on the government's job application form: fingerprints and an oath of loyalty.

Painful memories from the internment camps immediately surfaced. "There was the question of loyalty that had come up in the concentration camps, which greatly split the Japanese groups," Doug explains. "Everyone was requested to sign an oath renouncing any alliance to Japan. The problem was that, because of the U.S. laws at the time, the Japanese who immigrated to the U.S. were not allowed to become American citizens. Therefore, if they were to renounce any association with Japan, they would be people without a country. Children would have to turn their backs on their parents to prove their loyalty." Both requests clashed with Doug's concept of a free, democratic society. In the end, he chose levity. He left toe prints instead of fingerprints on the form. Next to the prints, he wrote the words "Hang Ten."

"Someone actually noticed that," he jokes. "So I did not get a government position, and I was requested to leave. I was down to the last 57 cents in my pocket. I had three kids to take care of. So I said to my wife, 'What are we going to do with 57 cents? Let's blow it all!' We went down to the corner store, and we actually spent a good 40 minutes looking through different colored bubble gum and candy bars and so on, trying to decide how to spend our last 57 cents."

The next morning, Doug began a job search by looking through the Yellow Pages; he found a place called the Biomedical Research Center. He dialed the number, talked with a couple of people there, and was asked to come in for an interview. He was hired on the spot. Doug was placed in charge of a substantial medical research project and was given the freedom to fill the lab with equipment, design and conduct experiments, and write research papers. He even got to name his own salary. In many ways, it was a dream job.

But after two years, Doug began asking himself what he wanted to do with the rest of his life. He enjoyed science immensely and toyed with the idea of going to medical school, but he wasn't sure he was ready to jump through more academic hoops. So he made a deal with himself.

"I decided to send an application to Stanford University," he says, "where the odds of getting in were one in 5,000 or so. If the medical school would take me, I would then see that as a sign to continue." Stanford did accept Doug, and so he entered graduate school in pharmacology in 1970. By the time he had completed his doctorate degree, Doug had dedicated himself to scientific research, particularly to the promising new frontiers of brain research. He completed post–doctoral studies in neurobiology at Stanford before crossing the country to accept a teaching post at New York's Columbia University.

While at Columbia, Doug and his first wife divorced, and he met and married Wendy. Doug began his research on nerve growth factors, which led to his important discovery that IGF hormones support the nervous system. Doug has been deciphering IGFs ever since, continuing his research at Colorado State University after he and Wendy moved to Fort Collins in 1985. At CSU, he has developed and tested countless theories to better understand the function of IGFs, speculating that in diseases such as diabetes, the number of IGF hormones are greatly reduced. Experiments validated his hypothesis.

"When I first started doing this," Doug says, "I approached it from the standpoint of a very dispassionate scientist looking at theories and testing new ideas. But then I began receiving letters from people who had seen an article about me in *The New York Times*, or the *Los Angeles Times*, and they would tell me about their friends, their family members, their husbands, their brothers, their sisters with diabetic neuropathy. And I would see students with this disease who would sit in the chair in my office, and from one year to the next, these young people would deteriorate to the point where they could not stand."

These experiences changed the way Doug looked at his research. Rather than taking a dispassionate, clinical approach, Doug began to feel a sense of having a mission and dedicated himself to finding a treatment for diabetic neuropathy. Doug's efforts may someday prevent the more than 80,000 amputations performed each year on Americans with advanced diabetes.

"Research is not a piece of cake. It's very difficult and requires intense work," says Doug. "You have to be willing to put in 12 to 14 hours a day, six days a week, sometimes seven, and you do this day in and day out, year in and year out. You often wind up with dead ends, which is extremely frustrating." Yet despite the frustrations and hard work, he says you have to live out your dreams.

"When I'm working," Doug adds, "I can lose all track of time. I don't get hungry. I get up in the middle of the night to write down the design of a new experiment I'm dreaming about. As a researcher, you run an experiment, the results come out, you look at them, and for a moment, you are the sole owner, the only person in the world who knows the answer. That, to me, is a thrill. That's what drives me."

Doug's wife, Wendy Ishii, is a versatile, accomplished actor who has performed major roles in more than 150 plays from classical and contemporary repertories. She has appeared in several television soap operas, including *All My Children, As The World Turns,* and *One Life To Live,* and on TV commercials pitching everything from Folgers to Geritol. And while Wendy likes the residuals from her TV appearances, her heart is in her dream of using theatrical expression to promote community dialogue. To that end, in 1992 Wendy and three other women formed Bas Bleu Theatre Company in Fort Collins, Colorado — the name, which literally translates to "Blue Stocking," is a reference to an 18th–century derogatory French phrase for an outspoken, intellectual woman. To date, Bas Bleu has given 700 performances in its renovated, intimate playhouse located in the city's quaint, historic district. Wendy's dream has come true.

"One of the things I love about our theater," says Wendy, "is that I'll be at the grocery store and somebody will come up to me and say, 'My husband is still repeating lines from one of your plays.' And I realize it meant something to them. We're telling stories for friends and acquaintances." Presenting plays that embody the breadth of the human spirit while dealing with real issues is a responsibility Wendy takes seriously. For example, Paula Vogel's Pulitzer Prize–winning *How I Learned To Drive,* which tackles the painful subject of incest with compassion and a touch of humor, made its regional debut at Bas Bleu.

"We try to bring social issues to the forefront, dramatizing them to help people connect to issues in their own lives," Wendy says. Bas Bleu's inaugural production, *Duet for One,* deals with multiple sclerosis. The company has revived it several times, with psychiatrists, people with MS, and caregivers participating in lively post–show discussions. "The response and gratitude of the community makes you realize, okay, we're doing something important," Wendy says. "We're giving people a forum to discuss these highly personal issues, we're giving them a safe place to deal with this. And that's something I'm just enormously proud of."

Born in Scarsdale, New York, in 1947, Wendy remembers a happy childhood with simple, quiet pleasures — catching fireflies, picking honeysuckle blossoms, and sitting by the radio listening to Dale Evans and Roy Rogers. Her high school years were spent in Vermont, where her 80–year–old mother still lives today. Wendy had a tremendous love of writing. She also was painfully shy. Overcoming her bashfulness has been one of Wendy's greatest hurdles in life. It took a mentor in the form of teacher John Stearns to discover her hidden acting abilities and guide her toward a career in theater.

It all started when Mr. Stearns caught Wendy writing a short story when she was supposed to be working on a science assignment. He confiscated the story and sent her to detention. But when he saw how well–written the piece was, Mr. Stearns made an unusual deal with Wendy. During sports, which she detested, he would send her to detention. But during detention, she had to write something, anything — a poem, an essay, a story. Wendy was ecstatic by this arrangement. It got her out of the competitive front line of sports and into a quiet room where she could write without distractions.

Then came one of those quirky turning points in life. During a major snowstorm, Wendy waited in the school auditorium for a friend to finish auditioning for a school play and give her a ride home. Mr. Stearns saw Wendy there and asked, "When do you read?" She replied that she was just waiting for her friend to finish. Her teacher then said, "Well, you're here. You might as well read a part." Wendy's shyness choked her with fear. She said no. She burst into tears. But she read the part and was cast in the lead role. "After he saw me audition, Mr. Stearns decided there was something there as an actor as well as a writer," she says.

He took Wendy under his wing, building her up as an actress while simultaneously trying to boost her self–esteem. Wendy did not want to go to college. While Mr. Stearns understood her fear of going away to a huge, impersonal college, he did not want to see her acting talent go to waste. Through patience, perseverance, and sometimes trickery, he convinced Wendy to consider Marlboro College, a smaller school in Vermont with an excellent theater program. "He told me that the only way to get into Marlboro was to have a two–hour interview with the entire faculty," she recalls. "'But let's just go over and talk to the dean,' he said to me. And I thought, 'Okay, I'll go. I have nothing to lose. That's not nearly as scary as the two–hour ordeal.'"

It turns out there was no such interview requirement; her teacher made that part up just to get Wendy to meet the dean. In the end, his efforts paid off. Wendy applied to and was accepted at Marlboro College. Much later, she learned that her mentor had gone to the campus to speak on her behalf. He told faculty members that she was enormously talented and that, while she would not do well in a large university setting, she would thrive there. "So I got in thanks to my mentor who pushed for me when I didn't have the guts to push myself," she says.

College gave Wendy the training and self–esteem to audition and get parts. After graduation, her career branched off in multiple directions — large theaters, small playhouses, even television. The more she immersed herself in acting, the more her self–esteem grew, enabling her to walk into auditions without fear and trust her acting skills to take over.

Wendy remembers well the fear and shyness that threatened to hold her back, and how Mr. Stearns's support and encouragement made all the difference. These days, Wendy advises her acting students to give themselves no less than 50 auditions before they start to re–evaluate themselves. "If you don't get a call back or a part after 50 auditions," she says, "then you might want to say, 'I need to revise my technique,' or 'I need to go learn more.' But don't decide after just one rejection because you really don't know what the other factors are. The main thing is that, if you're going out there and stretching yourself, going out on a limb each and every time, are trying your best, and are focused and prepared, you're gonna work. I think so much of the time we are such an instant–gratification society that if we get one 'No,' we take it so personally and beat ourselves up. And I think that's tragic."

Wendy feels a personal sense of responsibility to encourage her students to take risks. "I tell my students to ask themselves, going into an audition, 'What's the worst thing that can happen to me?' The worst thing that can happen in an audition is somebody calling you an idiot. Or, failing and not getting the part. Well, that's not life and death. You're trying something. If you don't take a risk, you'll never get the joy of going out there when the stakes are high and succeeding."

CHRISTY CURTIS:
FOLLOWING HER CONSCIENCE

Launching a business is challenging under the best circumstances, and it's not unusual for businesses to fail when something — or someone — unexpected comes into the picture. In the midst of struggling to grow her new business and get out of debt, Christy Curtis found herself with an unplanned pregnancy. She faced difficult decisions and a lot of hard work, but she made choices based on love and her sense of responsibility to herself, her child, and her dreams.

She had built a lucrative career for herself in pharmaceutical sales, but 30–year–old Christy Curtis was ready to take the plunge and pursue her dream of being her own boss. So she pulled together her entire savings, cashed in her stocks, and borrowed money, investing everything she had into her new home–based job placement firm. She named her new venture IPC — International Placement Consulting. She figured it would take three years to restore her original investment, but it was a sacrifice Christy was willing to make to reach her dream.

"I left a secure job to basically start over," she says. "I went from having a comfortable life to living from one month to the next on nothing but a dream. But I was ready." Without a steady paycheck and with mounting business expenses, Christy worked long hours to generate revenue, often spending 12 hours on the phone interviewing potential candidates and networking with managers and human resource specialists. During the first year, she focused just on establishing her business, earning little but running on faith and adrenaline and trusting that she was getting closer and closer to her first big placement.

Then came the unexpected twist. Christy, a single, career–oriented entrepreneur, found herself pregnant. She was in shock. "I remember tears filling my eyes," she says. "They weren't necessarily from sadness, because I was 31 years old and had always wanted a family some day." With an unplanned pregnancy, her future suddenly looked even more uncertain than ever. Christy was scared.

She faced difficult decisions. Would she keep her baby? Would she give it up for adoption? If she kept the baby, she realized she'd have to raise the child as a single mom, without help or support from the father. What about her dream of business ownership — how could she possibly raise a child and grow her business at the same time? She wasn't making enough money to support herself, let alone a baby. Would keeping the baby force her to give up her dream of self–employment and return to a secure, well–paying job?

Perhaps it would have been easier to give up her baby, or her business, or both. But right from the start, Christy chose to follow her heart. Christy wanted this child. But she also felt a sense of responsibility to her dreams. So she decided she would move forward with both parenthood and entrepreneurship, reaching both decisions the day her pregnancy was confirmed at a medical clinic.

Although at first she felt confused and overwhelmed, Christy soon felt reassured that she had made the right choices. "I came home from the clinic and prayed for the strength and the right mind–set to handle the changes and decisions that were going to affect my life and that of my unborn child for the rest of our lives," she says. "I had tremendous anxieties about finances. Amazingly, 10 minutes after I prayed, the phone rang. During that business call, I made my first big placement! It was enough money to pay bills and get me through at least two months. I started to feel that things were going to be all right."

Christy began to simplify her life to focus on her priorities. She moved away from draining relationships — like friends who expected her to socialize late into the night — and surrounded herself with people more supportive of her choices. She read every book she could find about pregnancy. She turned down invitations to social engagements, choosing instead to focus on her business, as well as on eating right and getting much-needed rest for both her and her baby's health. "While it used to be very hard for me to turn down an invitation to anything, I suddenly found myself content to stay home and enjoy quality time by myself," she says. "It took me a very small amount of time to realize that I was actually glad to not have draining plans and commitments."

Her faith and determination got her through the challenge of giving birth to a baby and a business simultaneously. Christy recalls that many times, she had to play the roles of mommy and professional recruiter at the same time, without her clients knowing. "Often I'd be on the cordless phone in the middle of a conversation with a client when my daughter would wake up from a nap," she says, "and I'd rush to take her out of her crib and start nursing before she began to cry. Many clients naturally assumed I was in a business suit working from a high–rise office; little did they know I was sitting at home with a baby at my breast." To meet the multiple demands of those early months, Christy would start each day at 4:30 in the morning. And sometimes, the only way she could make it to a business lunch was to bring her infant daughter along.

It was a juggling act, but she made it work, surviving two financially difficult periods — the early years while she was still building her business and the aftermath of September 11, when business temporarily ground to a halt. In 2001, Christy diversified to survive, expanding IPC's services to include seminars for managers and human resources personnel at Fortune 500 companies, and job coaching for professionals. Through it all, Christy persevered.

Today she's the proud mother of a beautiful, happy five–year–old girl, and the president and owner of a successful home–based business. She's learned that flexibility is key to success — and sanity. Christy takes her daughter to daycare when she needs to give her business undivided attention, and she gives herself a day off during the middle of the week when she wants extra time with her daughter.

"I have a new view and perspective of life," Christy says. "I have learned that the most positive and empowering choice I can make is to create a life of satisfaction and happiness." For herself, and her daughter.

MARY O'DONNELL:
PAVING A WOMEN'S ROAD TO RECOVERY

In 1971 Mary O'Donnell became a pioneer in her community when she opened La Vista Recovery Center, the first alcohol recovery facility available to women in California's Riverside County. Having served as the center's director for three decades, Mary has realized a dream born of a sense of responsibility, helping thousands of women of all ages create happier, healthier lives as a result.

During the 1960s, Mary O'Donnell's house served two purposes: home for her family, and a temporary shelter for women trying to recover from alcoholism who had nowhere to turn. In addition to being a wife and busy mother of five, Mary volunteered her time and energy to take care of these women and drive them to a recovery center miles away in another county. "I thought it was a terrible state of affairs that at the time, there were eight men's recovery homes in Riverside County and nothing for women," she says.

One evening Mary received an urgent call from the local hospital, just as she had many times before. This time it was a plea for help for a homeless woman who was drunk and badly beaten. Mary agreed to help, so she and her husband picked up the stranger at the hospital and drove her to their home. But when she took a closer look at the woman, Mary was shocked to see that her injured eye resembled a red–and–black golf ball, with the lid almost completely shut. Meanwhile, the intoxicated woman kept trying to take Mary's car keys and leave. Mary decided to take the belligerent woman back to the hospital so that her damaged eye could receive the medical attention it needed. She figured the lady would remain there at least overnight.

But just two hours later, close to midnight, the hospital phoned again to say that the woman had been treated and was about to be released — even though she was still heavily intoxicated, had nobody to look after her, and had nowhere to go except the streets. "I couldn't imagine such a thing," says Mary. "That's when I first saw the desperate need of the woman alcoholic." Exhausted, Mary contacted a friend, who fortunately was able to hurry to the hospital and assist the intoxicated homeless woman. But the experience left Mary longing to do more for women suffering the ravages of alcoholism.

Indeed, the U.S. Department of Health and Human Services' Center for Substance Abuse Treatment in 2000 found that 62 percent of homeless Americans who receive assistance from homeless programs across the U.S. have had an alcohol abuse problem, but 57 percent of those afflicted have never received treatment. In general, barriers to seeking help and staying in treatment are considered greater for women alcoholics than for men alcoholics, according to the Center of Alcoholic Studies (CAS) at Rutgers University in New Jersey. In the CAS paper "Facts On Women and Alcohol," Dr. Edith S. Lisansky Gornberg writes: "Barriers to seeking help for women include financial problems, child–care responsibilities, social stigma, and family pressures," and that "Attitudes toward female intoxication remain generally negative and a double standard prevails: an intoxicated woman is perceived as 'worse' than an intoxicated man."

Mary herself had struggled with alcoholism for ten years and had sought help in two recovery homes. She recalls the ordinary yet powerful encounter that set her on the road to recovery. "In the last recovery home I stayed in," she says, "there was a woman from the community who came in to volunteer. I looked at her and I thought, 'That's what I want to be.'" The volunteer gave

Mary a model for healthy living and a glimpse of what her future could hold if she stayed sober. After that defining moment, Mary was finally able to succeed in overcoming her alcoholism. In gratitude for her second lease on life, she opened her home to other women trying to achieve sobriety.

But after the incident with the homeless woman, Mary realized she could not meet the need by herself. Soon she developed a dream: To open the first women's recovery center in Riverside County, one staffed with professional drug and alcohol counselors and compassionate caregivers, to provide a safe place for women to begin the road to recovery.

Mary knew that she first needed the community to accept the idea of having a women's recovery center. Cautiously, she approached members of her predominantly conservative community, holding house meetings with prominent women and giving presentations to local churches and service clubs. She asked, "Do you think this community would support a women's recovery center?" Much to her surprise, and relief, the answer was a resounding "Yes!" Service clubs, churches, many individuals, and sober members of Alcoholics Anonymous volunteered to help. Along the way, Mary, who had previously held clerical jobs, had to learn many new skills, like how to form a corporation, become licensed and certified, and handle contracts. She even launched her own public speaking campaign to educate members of the community, stressing the stigma placed unfairly on alcoholic women.

In 1971, Mary's dream came true: She opened La Vista Recovery Center and became its director. La Vista was a six–bed facility with a single bathroom, and for ten years it operated beyond its capacity with every bed full and women sleeping on couches. Then in 1981, Mary moved the center to a 7,500–square foot facility in San Jacinto, California, which immediately doubled the number of women Mary could help. The center has continued to expand and today serves 250 women each year.

The recovery center treats any woman addict who needs help, but Mary has developed programs for specific populations as well. First is what Mary calls the "hidden woman alcoholic" among senior citizens. Depressed elderly women — often widows living alone — sometimes turn to alcohol in a futile attempt to fill a void. "The phenomenon is labeled late onset alcoholism," says Mary. "A woman could have handled alcohol without any problems all her life, but due to changes in her body, in her metabolism, and in her life roles, she can quickly become a chronic alcoholic, much to the surprise and anguish of her family." So Mary expanded La Vista to meet the specific needs of older women. She also started a program called SOARx, Success Over Alcohol and Rx (prescription medicines). Mary took the SOARx message into the community to educate people about the dangers of mixing prescription drugs with alcohol, something that, Mary had come to see, many seniors did.

Then Mary turned her attention to alcohol– and drug–addicted pregnant women, and added a perinatal unit to La Vista. "We've had clean and sober babies who show no evidence of alcohol or drugs, which is very encouraging," Mary says. "And we've seen that when a mother gets sober, she's not going to let her child get into all kinds of mischief that she experienced herself." Mary also started an outreach program called AWARE (Any Woman's Alcohol Recovery Education) to teach young women and men about the dangers of drinking and using drugs during pregnancy, such as an increased risk of the baby being born with brain damage or physical deformities.

Mary's work with recovering women benefits not only the women themselves but also their children and families. "I've watched many children visit their mothers at La Vista," Mary says. "Often they think it's their fault that Mommy drinks. So we encourage each mother to write to her children and describe her disease to them, letting them know what is really happening. A couple of weeks later, we see those same kids return with a healthier and more positive attitude. They have gained the understanding that Mommy is not a bad mom, but a sick mom who is getting well, and that they are not bad kids." Mary happily reports that a child's self–esteem grows enormously when he sees his alcoholic mother taking steps to improve her health and well–being.

Mary's sense of responsibility bred a dream 30 years ago that, put into action, has met a very real need for recovering women, from teenagers to the elderly. She continues to speak in the community to educate and inspire people. "Action is the magic word," she says, "and spirituality is the ultimate answer. In our recovery program, we emphasize that everyone seek and find a power greater than themselves." By acting on her sense of responsibility, Mary met a need and is proud to have planted the seed of recovery in 10,000 women.

DENNIS WEAVER:
LEADING MAN FIGHTS FOR THE BACKDROPS

Comfortable in a cowboy hat whether acting in front of cameras or relaxing on his ranch, Dennis Weaver is remembered for bringing the spirit of the rugged American West to television viewers through his sincere performances in "Gunsmoke" and "McCloud." Later in life, Dennis worked to preserve that spirit by protecting the natural environment that provided the beautiful backdrop for so many of his roles. We were fortunate to interview this soft–spoken gentle soul and write his story before he passed away in February, 2006, at 81.

Dennis Weaver wanted to be an actor ever since he was a cute four–year–old reciting "Little Jack Horner" in a Christmas program. He proved to be a good actor in high school plays, but almost nobody supported his acting dream; in fact, his principal tried to discourage him. "It was very unusual in those days," he says, "for someone from Joplin, Missouri, to have that dream and to feel like it was something that was possible to fulfill. The support for that sort of thing was not terribly strong."

Fortunately, Dennis did receive encouragement at home. "The community that supported me was basically my family," he says, "particularly my mother, who told me that I could do anything." His mother's words stayed with him as he majored in drama at the University of Oklahoma. They followed him to New York where he studied with the best drama teachers he could find. And they accompanied him on stage as he accepted an Emmy in 1959 for his role as Chester in television's longest–running series, *Gunsmoke*.

Many other accolades and accomplishments have followed. Dennis' versatility, talent, and dedication as an actor have earned him prominent roles in movies and television. His work on the TV series *McCloud* earned Dennis three Emmy nominations. He received an award for outstanding service to his fellow members as president of the Screen Actors Guild, and he can boast his own star on the Hollywood Walk of Fame.

Most admirably, however, the fame and fortune that came with his childhood dream coming true have not changed the values that Dennis and his wife, Gerry, hold dear. Dennis' dedication to service has earned him several humanitarian honors, including the Presidential End Hunger Award for his work with Love Is Feeding Everyone (L.I.F.E.), a hunger relief organization he co–founded. Acting may be Dennis' realized dream, but serving others, growing spiritually, and protecting the environment are the dreams he pursues today.

"If we could just understand that we're truly one, that we're all connected, and that when we hurt somebody else we either directly or indirectly hurt ourselves; if we could just understand that we share each other's pain and joy, the world would change overnight!" Dennis says. "All of these problems we see outside of us that we have constructed and made, they would totally disappear. We wouldn't hurt somebody if we understood we were hurting ourselves. We would bring others joy and laughter and peace and love, because that would immediately come back to us. That's the secret of finding the happiness we're all looking for."

The determination and strength that propelled Dennis into acting when few supported him now take him around the world to talk about how businesses today have the power and responsibility to create profitable industries in harmony with the environment. His desire to help humanity and our planet inspired Dennis to start the Institute of Ecolonomics (IOE) in 1993, a nonprofit organization that strives to create beneficial alliances between the ecology and the economy.

"Ecolonomics is a word that I coined to represent the truth that our ecology and our economy are two sides of the same coin," Dennis explains. "Supporters of each, whether it be the environment or business, can come together to form alliances, form partnerships, and bring benefits both to our environment and to our economy. Because we realize that if we are to have a sustainable future — and that is what the institute is about, its mission is to create a sustainable future — we've got to have at least two things. One is a sustainable environment, and the other is a sustainable economy. And if we fail in achieving either, we will suffer, and suffer greatly."

The institute works with businesses and universities to create ecolonomic industries to provide a strong economic base without damaging the earth — in other words, making money while also cleaning and protecting the environment. Businesses that have teamed up with IOE include Alpha Fibre International, which turns agricultural waste straw into a strong, natural fiber that can replace certain plastics, and SpiritMoney, a mortgage company that offers financing and expertise in home energy efficiency, alternative building materials, and sustainable real estate development. "There's power in profit and in business that we just can't stick our heads in the sand and ignore," Dennis says. "We've got to use the power that's there in a very beneficial way — beneficial to the earth, beneficial to human beings and all the inhabitants that live on earth, beneficial to business, and beneficial to our economy. It can be done. We have the wherewithal to do that. We have the technologies to do that."

Dennis applied his environmental beliefs to his personal life. He and his wife built a unique home in southern Colorado that functions as an independent sustainable living space. Designed by New Mexico architect Michael Reynolds, the home is constructed of recycled materials including cans and used tires, but you would never know that simply by looking at the beautiful home the Weavers named Earthship. With large picture windows, it is solar–powered and uses neither forced air heating nor air conditioning.

"I wanted a wonderful place in which to live," Dennis says, "and I wanted it to be an example of how we can be more energy–efficient and kinder to our environment, and create a living model. It's been just a joyous place to live. You feel like you're walking into nature when you walk in here." Part of the reason is that Dennis and Gerry grow much of their own food inside their home — everything from spinach to tomatoes to Swiss chard.

Dennis enjoys a productive, fulfilling life, but he's first to admit that obstacles surface at every major juncture. He credits prayer and meditation with helping him get through obstacles, and he has found that looking within provides the necessary guidance in challenging situations. "I've been practicing meditation since 1958," he says. "And my life would be a shambles without it. It's that stillness, it's that moment of quietness where you are able to receive inspiration or guidance, and the awareness that there is a love that is available to you that is absolutely unconditional."

Dennis has not retired from acting — he recently appeared in remakes of *The Virginian* and *High Noon* — but he devotes most of his time and energy to Ecolonomics. In 2003 he participated in the "Drive to Survive," a caravan of hybrid and clean–burning, renewable fuel vehicles (including hydrogen–powered cars) that drove from California to Washington, D.C., to raise public awareness and deliver a petition to lawmakers requesting them to actively promote the development and use of renewable energies.

As a sought–after speaker, Dennis encourages people to nurture their creativity, dream boldly, and help create a bright, sustainable future for everyone. "It's really important that we retain goals in our lives, that those goals also bring benefit to others as well as to ourselves," he says. "And there's great satisfaction in achieving those goals, or even pursuing them."

Take Responsibility for Your Dreams

"IF WE CHOOSE PROPERLY, LIFE TREATS US WELL. WE ALL AFFECT ONE ANOTHER."
— GEORGE FULLERTON, FENDER GUITAR CO—INVENTOR (CHAPTER 11)

You've read about dozens of people who have achieved dreams and continue to reach for dreams. You've seen that every-day people can and do overcome obstacles, challenges, and limi-tations to create the lives of their dreams. The people featured here have been through discrimination, debt, job loss, personal tragedy, illness, rejection, addiction, abuse, doubt, and ridicule and yet, they've overcome. They've taken the responsibil-ity to dream and to follow those dreams, and the rewards speak for themselves.

Now it's your turn to take that responsibility. Like every-one else, you're facing your own set of obstacles and chal-lenges. But you need to realize something very important: You already have, inside of you, every Dream CPR essential element we've discussed. Whether these elements are still seeds or fully developed, or a lit-tle of both, you already have them.

Dream CPR Journal

What do you believe in now? What causes do you hold close to your heart?

If you could do one thing today that would help change the world, what would it be?

As Wendy Ishii put it, "I believe that when people do have dreams, somewhere they know they have it in them to realize it. Somewhere, they know they can make it." And as Dennis Weaver explained: "I think it's important that we face those challenges and know that we have the wherewithal within us and the strength to overcome them."

In the next chapter, you'll find the keys that will help you unlock the door to the Dream CPR essential elements within yourself so you can apply them to your dreams.

chapter 13

Nine Keys

> **"THE BEST BOOKS ARE YET TO BE WRITTEN; THE BEST PAINTINGS HAVE NOT YET BEEN PAINTED; THE BEST GOVERNMENTS ARE YET TO BE FORMED; THE BEST IS YET TO BE DONE BY YOU!"**
> — JOHN ERSKINE

You've learned how people from different walks of life overcome obstacles to follow and reach extraordinary dreams. You've seen how they tap into the ten essential Dream CPR elements. Now it's your turn: It's time to empower yourself with Dream CPR and begin to create the life of your dreams.

In this chapter, we'll show you nine keys to unlock your Dream CPR essential elements and bring them to light. These keys will help you open the gateway to your dream quest, whether you are resuscitating a dream from days gone by, hoping to discover new dreams, or ready to take your first steps toward a dream close to your heart. With each key, you will find questions, ideas, or suggestions to explore with your *Dream CPR Journal*.

Some of the suggestions that follow may seem obvious, even simplistic. But very often when we're stuck, the way to get unstuck is to try the path that's right in front of us. False starts or blunders will be inevitable on any dream quest. It's when you feel most frustrated that you need to get back to basics and turn to these pages. When you find your dream quest halted by a barred door, these keys will unlock a window that you can slip through.

1.   Trust your intuition

Intuition is a direct perception of truth independent of any reasoning process. It's a moment of *absolute* knowing. In that intuitive moment you access information that you've neither gleaned from a book nor heard somewhere, but that you just know. Our intuition can telepathically and via "gut feelings" present us with important messages like *Don't go there* or *This person is trustworthy*. Your intuition can also help you along your dream quest by acting as a wise, discerning guide that reveals what you must do to align with your Dream CPR essential element *purpose*.

When you're standing at a crossroads in life, not knowing which way to turn, your intuition helps you choose a direction, just as it helped Beverley Berlin Mas (Chapter 7). Following a series of painful personal tragedies, she didn't know where her life was headed. But her intuition told her that living through these experiences put her in a unique position to compassionately counsel others in similar circumstances. Perhaps it made no sense logically — after all, Beverley was 59 years old and didn't have a counseling background — but she knew that her intuition was guiding her to a greater *purpose* in her life. So Beverley chose to go back to school to study psychology with classmates young enough to be her grandchildren, and follow her new dream of counseling people grieving deep losses.

Jimmy Carter's life (Chapter 7) also changed in a moment of intuitive insight. He and Rosalynn had been praying and searching for purpose to their post–presidency lives, for work that was more meaningful to them than simply putting together a presidential library. One night Rosalynn woke up to find a wide–awake Jimmy sitting straight up in bed. For a moment she worried that he might be sick, but she quickly discovered that he was having an epiphany. Jimmy shared with Rosalynn his idea to de-

Key	Essential Element(s)
Intuition	Purpose
Feeling	Passion
Imagination	Creativity
Verbalization	Commitment, part 1
Focus	Commitment, part 2
Action	Courage, Risk
Process	Persistence, Resilience
Belief	Confidence, Responsibility
Growth	Responsibility, Creativity

velop a place where leaders of nations could resolve disputes. Thus, a moment of intuition gave birth to a dream that led to the creation of the Carter Center — and led the Carters to fulfill their purpose of serving as global ambassadors for peace and human rights.

You, too, can discover your purpose by listening closely to your intuition. Practice by doing the following exercise:

Find a tranquil spot in your home or perhaps outside in your yard or at a park where you can sit quietly for a while. There, relax, breathe comfortably, and quiet your mind. Gaze at a beautiful sight, such as a grove of trees, a pond, a floral arrangement, or a scenic painting, to generate positive feelings like awe, joy, wonder, and peace. Internalize these feelings and become aware of how good they make you feel.

With a quieted mind and a joyful heart, you're ready to access your intuition — your internal guidance system. Breathe in and out comfortably as you picture possible career and life directions. For each scenario, pause and listen. *What is your intuition telling you? Which way is your intuition advising you to go? Which direction feels right? What images bring you a sense of peace* and *purpose?* Your first impressions generally come from intuition. But be patient. The answers may come right away, or they may arrive later in a burst of inspiration.

Many people find it helpful to pray about which direction to take, as Beverley and the Carters did when seeking their purpose. Meditation also helps people find answers, as does sleeping on it — asking yourself a question before going to sleep, then waking up with answers. Whatever method works for you, trust that you can find your purpose with help from your intuition. Learn to work with and trust your internal guidance system.

2.   Get emotionally involved

To breathe life into your dreams, you must invest not only time and effort but also your emotions. You have to *care* about your dream. The most carefully contrived plans fizzle out if we fail to put our heart and soul into the endeavor. But when we get emotionally involved, energized, and excited about our dreams, we fuel them. We bring the Dream CPR essential element *passion* to the surface to fire ourselves up to pursue our dreams in earnest. Automobile entrepreneur Walter Chrysler, founder of the Chrysler Corporation, once said, "The real secret to success is enthusiasm. Yes, more than enthusiasm, I would say is excitement. I like to see people get excited. When they get excited, they make a success of their lives."

Actor Michael Clarke Duncan (Chapter 8) was excited about acting. He put his heart and soul into breaking into Hollywood, even though his experience was as a ditch digger and nightclub bouncer, not as an actor. The odds were stacked against him, but Michael invested his emotions into the dream, wanting to reach it so badly that he didn't let the odds stop him. The prospect of acting made Michael feel *alive* with excitement, desire, intrigue, and joy. In the end, his passion led him to fulfill his dream and receive widespread recognition for his acting abilities, including a nomination for an Academy Award.

Discover what moves you — whatever you're most emotionally involved in is your passion. Start by taking an honest look at where your time and energy go. Find a quiet spot where you can relax without distractions. There, think about your past and present jobs, hobbies, pastimes, volunteer positions, causes, vacations, and projects. Write down everything you do or are involved in, or have done, and then spend a moment thinking about each item. As you contemplate each, gauge your emotions. *Which interests bring up the strongest emotions? Which activities generate enthusiasm, excitement, and joy for you? Which causes do you feel passionate about? Is there anything not on the list that you feel passionate about — something you're not involved in but wish you were?* Answers to these questions will help you discover your passion and develop dreams born of passion.

3. Imagine your life

In his bestseller *Conversations with God, Book 1,* author Neale Donald Walsch writes: *"Thought* is the first level of creation." We may not realize it but thoughts hold tremendous power. Before we take action, we picture our dream in our mind — the first step, the process, the outcome. When you envision the life you want to lead, you assimilate the information gathered with your intuition and your emotional investment, and so take the first step toward creating the reality you want.

Personal chef industry creators Sue Titcomb and David MacKay (Chapter 6) imagined a life that offered more quality time to spend as a family. David, an entrepreneur, wanted to create a business that would give him the financial security to make his own hours. His wife, Sue, loved being a chef but wanted to spend her evenings and weekends with her family. So they worked together to envision a new way to create income. First Sue began working as a personal chef. Then David and Sue imagined an entire personal chef industry to support this new concept of the personal chef. In the end, they successfully took this concept from idea to reality. Today Sue and David live the lives of their dreams and head the United States Personal Chef Association, which now boasts thousands of members.

When you imagine your future, you release your Dream CPR essential element *creativity.* Dissatisfied with his engineering job, Science Guy Bill Nye (Chapter 6) turned to comedy for a creative outlet. And then he realized that he could actually combine comedy, science, *and* television. First he imagined himself hosting a show as the "Science Guy," then he took action to make it so. One thought unleashed a creative process that led to action, culminating in a successful TV series.

The first two keys help you tap into your intuition and feelings to discover — or remember — your purpose and passion. They help you pinpoint what gives you joy and a sense of meaning. The third key helps you use this information to form an idea about the life you want to lead. Keeping in mind the answers you wrote down earlier, ask yourself: *What kind of life do I imagine for myself? What lifestyle could I create to bring me joy and meaning? If I could do anything in the world, what would it be?*

4.   Say it out loud

"Words are the second level of creation," Walsch writes in *Conversations with God, Book 1.* Words are powerful because they take thoughts and ideas from your head and release them into the world. By attaching words to your ideas, you have formulated your dream and taken your first step toward committing to that dream. You have found your Dream CPR essential element *commitment.*

Teacher and abolitionist Barbara Vogel (Chapter 5) understands the power of words. Barbara will talk with anyone who asks about her classroom's cause, and she shares her two primary dreams: to help her students become active humanitarians, and to help abolish slavery once and for all. She knows that by stating her dreams out loud she deepens her commitment to both. And of course, she accomplishes her heartfelt goal of bringing much–needed global attention to the plight of modern–day slavery.

By saying our dreams out loud, we commit ourselves to them, and commitment is key to bringing a dream to fruition. When Tiger Woods (Chapter 5) told himself he wanted to be the best golfer ever, he made a commitment to that dream. His commitment has carried him to a level of success and international acclaim unmatched by any other professional golfer.

The first three keys helped you journey from intuition to feelings to idea. Now, put it all into words. *How can you verbalize your dream?* Write down different possibilities. Once you know how to put it into words, say it out loud. This gives your dream power and helps you dedicate yourself to the dream. When you're ready, find someone you trust who won't discourage you. Tell that person your dream. In the meantime — and throughout the process of your dream quest — continue to tell yourself your dream out loud.

5. *Focus your mind, heart, and energy*

This key represents "Part 2" of commitment to a dream, which is long–term and ongoing. It requires that you put everything you have into your dream. As the wise Jedi Master Qui–Gon Jinn said in *Star Wars: Episode 1,* "Your focus determines your reality." Indeed, whatever you put your mind, heart, and energy into is what you'll reap. Isn't it tragic to see people stuck in a mode of resentment, bitterness, even hate because their minds and hearts remain focused on past slights and failures? To break free from such a self–imposed prison, one has to consciously shift the focus to something positive and productive — like a vision for a bright future. Focusing on our dreams leads us away from counterproductive thinking and toward a mind–set of success.

Psychic Cynthia Hess (Chapter 5) carved a rewarding, successful career despite ridicule and even persecution, showing that commitment is crucial to making breakthroughs in life. "You can't divide yourself," she says. "You have to put everything you have into it." How do we do this? It takes practice.

Set aside time every day to direct your thoughts, feelings, and energy to dreaming. Unless they require your immediate attention, ignore distractions while you focus on your dream. Turn off the TV, put aside the newspaper, and let the answering machine pick up the call. Enjoy just thinking about your dream, getting excited about it, and devoting your full attention to it.

Then, begin to increase the length of time you devote to your dream each day. Ask yourself: *Where can I cut back on the rest of my schedule to work more on my dream? How can I expend more energy to the dream?*

To help you focus, write your dream on sticky notes and post them throughout your home or office as reminders — on your bathroom mirror, by your computer, on the refrigerator door, on your wall calendar. And every day, extend the length of time you focus your mind, heart, and energy on your dream.

6.   *Take action*

This is the next logical step. To launch your dream, you must take action. Do something — anything — to set your dream in motion! When you take action, you bring out the Dream CPR essential elements *courage* and *risk*.

Cyclist Lance Armstrong (Chapter 4) was in a frightening, uncertain place when he was going through surgeries and chemotherapy for cancer. He had no idea what the future held, or if he would even survive. But he mustered the strength and courage to take action, getting up on his bike between chemo cycles and riding — even if only for a few blocks — to keep alive his dream of competing again.

To take action, we need to tap into courage to overcome our fears and insecurities. Risk is inherent to launching a dream; we know that there are no guarantees. More importantly, we know that if we don't try, we'll never find out how high we can soar.

Take a look at your dream. *What can you do, this week, to launch it? What action can you take to get started on achieving your dream?* Taking action will create the momentum you need to keep going, which leads to the next key.

7.   *Take one step at a time*

Accomplishing a dream is a process. Taking one step at a time divides that process into finite, doable stages. "If one focuses only on the journey's end, completion always appears in the distance," writes Dan Millman in his book, *The Laws of Spirit: Sim-*

ple, Powerful Truths for Making Life Work. "This leads many to abandon their goals when obstacles arise or the path grows steep. You know that every journey begins with a single step, but you also have to take a second step, and a third, and as many as needed to reach your destination."

When you take it one step at a time, you tap into your essential Dream CPR elements *persistence* and *resilience.* Moving forward requires persistence. You develop persistence by trying again and again, maybe from different angles or approaches, and not giving up. During those difficult stages when we find ourselves taking two steps backward for every step forward, resilience comes into play. We become more resilient when we get back up each time we fall and continue toward our dream.

Convincing auto manufacturers and legislators to enact changes to make car trunks safer was a daunting task. But Janette Fennell (Chapter 9) approached her dream one step at a time. She began by doing research, much of it on the Internet. Then she compiled a database on car trunk entrapment cases, since one didn't exist. Armed with previously unavailable statistics, she sent letters to legislators and auto manufacturers. Had she tried to bypass those important first steps and approached lawmakers without any facts to support her claims, nobody would have listened. But she was armed with enough information to get a few people on her side. By taking the process one step at a time, Janette was able in five years to achieve her dream of making car trunks safer.

At this moment, don't try to see the end of the journey. Instead, concentrate on the next step. You've taken action to launch your dream. *Now, what can you do to get one step closer?* Each step you take is another successful milestone on the path to achieving your dream.

8. *Believe*

You have to believe that you've got what it takes to make your dream come true, and that you will achieve that dream. Period. If you don't believe it, who will? Perhaps a mentor will believe in you before you can believe in yourself. Ultimately, however, you have to believe to achieve. In her book *If Life is a Game, These are the Rules,* Chérie Carter–Scott writes: "It is not our external resources that determine our success or failure, but rather our own belief in ourselves and our willingness to create a life according to our highest aspirations."

Writer and skier Cale Kenney (Chapter 3) believed, despite a tragic accident that took her leg and dashed many of her hopes and dreams. Cale clung to her dream to return to college. She not only hoped she would go back, she believed this with all her might. Her belief turned to conviction and determination that got her back on campus.

Believing in yourself and in your dreams brings out your Dream CPR essential elements *confidence* and *responsibility.* Believing in our ability to reach a dream elevates our confidence level, enabling us to overcome criticism the way young Harrison Ford (Chapter 3) overcame a producer's scathing remarks. And by believing that we *can* accomplish our dream, we take responsibility for ourselves so that every time we hear "You can't," we refuse to buy into it. Every time an obstacle pops up, we take responsibility to move forward regardless of challenges.

How do we believe in ourselves and in our dreams? Affirmations can help greatly. Write this down: *"I have set my dream into motion. I am moving forward. I am living the life of my dreams. Each day, I am closer to attaining my dream."* Say this every day — memorize it and repeat it whenever you need a lift. Feel free to modify the phrase to suit your personality. But definitely practice positive thinking. And picture yourself reaching your dream. Bring that image up daily. The more you see it, the more you'll believe it, and the more real it will become.

9. Never stop dreaming

The day will come when you fulfill your dream, and what a marvelously satisfying day that will be! But after you celebrate your achievement, *what next?*

Dream achievers keep dreaming. Doug Ishii (Chapter 12) achieved his dream of going to college, then reached his dream of conducting research in neurobiology. In his early 40s he made a breakthrough discovery. Did Doug stop there? No, he kept conducting research to learn even more about nerve growth, and he began to pursue a new dream: to use his discoveries to help patients with diabetic neuropathy and brain disorders. Doug shows us that when we reach one dream, we can then use that momentum to help us dream even bigger.

Dennis Weaver (Chapter 12) enjoyed a satisfying, successful career as an actor, but his dreams didn't stop there. Dennis' love of nature and respect for the earth propelled him to launch Ecolonomics, a concentrated effort to develop businesses and eventually an economy that function in harmony with our environment, not in opposition to it.

Dream CPR Journal

Even as you approach the end of this book, your work in your *Dream CPR Journal* is only beginning. Take some sage advice from Phil Vischer (Chapter 6):

"Draw more. Write more. Daydream more. The key to changing the world is picturing it differently in your head, and then thinking up ways to make your dreams real."

When we keep dreaming, we uphold the Dream CPR essential elements *responsibility* and *creativity*. We are creative beings with the ability to continually dream wonderful new dreams. Once we've attained one dream, that accomplishment can serve as a springboard that launches us to the next dream. It is our responsibility to take that opportunity. Because when we keep dreaming, we keep growing. Dreaming and doing are what life is all about — the ticket to our own personal bliss.

chapter 14

Do It!

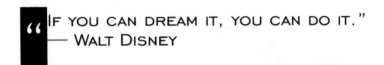
You now have a collection of tools at your disposal to use along the road to your dreams — the elements of Dream CPR, stories of successful dream achievers, nine keys to unlock the secrets to making dreams come true, and just as important, your own *Dream CPR Journal*. Here's the exciting part: Now that you've done the homework, you are ready to define your dream.

Open your *Dream CPR Journal* and review your answers to the questions posed throughout this book. *What trends do you spot? What themes appear again and again in your life?* It's no accident that similar themes keep popping up. Your heart knows your dreams, and your journal now reveals traces of these inner-most dreams. The trends you've uncovered point to a dream you want to achieve.

Now that you've re-read your journal — which really is your personal story, written in your own words — you're ready. Listening to your intuition, write down your dream, as best as you understand what it is at this point. Don't worry about getting it perfect. It's preliminary, and that's okay. You will refine it as you go.

BREATHE LIFE INTO YOUR DREAM

> "IF YOU WANT TO REALIZE YOUR DREAM, NEVER GIVE UP. CONTINUE TO PERSEVERE, EVEN WHEN YOU FAIL... IT TAKES CONSTANT RE-EVALUATING, CONSTANT ANALYZING OF WHAT'S WORKING AND WHAT'S NOT IN ORDER TO GET SOMETHING OFF THE GROUND." — DAVID MACKAY, FOUNDER, UNITED STATES PERSONAL CHEF ASSOCIATION (CHAPTER 6)

You now have a preliminary dream — *your* dream! It may evolve over time, and that's fine. But it's time to breathe life into your dream. If you're not sure where to begin, pick something from this list. It doesn't matter where you start. What's important is that you start *today.*

1 *Seek resources* such as books, training seminars, or courses that can help you move in the direction of the life of your dreams. Visit your local library — a terrific, *free* resource. If you want to change jobs or launch a new career, talk to a career guidance counselor.

2 *Get rid of stuff* that's cluttering your life or holding you back. Clean out your closets and give or throw away what you don't need. Cancel subscriptions to magazines or newspapers that you're not reading. Set email controls and don't even bother with spam!

3 *Allocate space* at home for the practical needs of your dream, such as in your office or study, your workshop, a spare room, the corner of a room, or on your kitchen table.

4 *Make time* for your dream. Wake up an hour earlier (or for night owls, stay up an hour later) to work on your dream. Recruit help from family members or, if your budget permits, hire help for things like housecleaning, laundry, cooking, yard work, child care, or car maintenance to give you more time for your dream. Allow yourself to daydream about your dream and where you're going with it.

5 *Acquire the equipment* you'll need to achieve your dream, such as a computer, sewing machine, guitar, reading lamp, or filing cabinet. If you can't afford to buy the equipment right now, start setting aside a certain amount of money each week until you have saved enough to make the purchase.

6 *Reach out to other people.* Share your dreams with someone you trust, or find and join a support group of like–minded people.

> *Dream CPR Journal*
>
> Complete these two sentences:
>
> 1. Based on what I've discovered about myself, I believe my dream is …
>
> 2. To begin my dream quest today, I will …

7 *Seek out a mentor.* Find somebody who's doing what you want to do and ask her how she got started.

8 Finally, *remember to nurture yourself* throughout your dream quest. Make a point of treating your body, mind, and spirit well to promote your own health as you follow your dream. Try taking a walk every day to recharge your batteries and think about your dream.

Go For It!

> 66 PEOPLE DON'T REGRET WHAT THEY DO NEARLY AS MUCH AS THEY REGRET WHAT THEY DON'T DO. SO DO IT!" — BILL NYE, THE SCIENCE GUY (CHAPTER 6)

You are ready. You must dream, and you must live your dreams. Don't forget to live them. As Albus Dumbledore, the wise wizard in J. K. Rowling's *Harry Potter* series, says in the first book: "It does not do to dwell on dreams and forget to live."

The choices we make today shape our future. Indeed, a single action can completely alter the course of the future — for better or worse. You have a say in what kind of world you leave for loved ones and future generations. By dreaming and doing responsibly you help build the future, bring yourself closer to fulfilling your true destiny, and pave the way for dreamers and doers yet to be born.

Confidence. Courage. Commitment. Creativity. Purpose. Passion. Persistence. Resilience. Risk. Responsibility. Hold these close to you. They will serve you well on your dream quest.

Now go out there and start making your dreams come true! Do it today.

Appendix A

Voices of the Future

In a climate of uncertainty — war, terrorism, nuclear proliferation — and in a pop culture of instant gratification, young people need inspiration to dream and guidance to follow and reach their dreams. Young people today need mentors and role models, and they want to know real people who have faced challenges, overcome obstacles, and followed their passion to create the life of their dreams

We talked with young people across America and asked them about their dreams. Here's a sampling of what they had to say.

WHAT DO YOU DREAM FOR YOURSELF?

"I dream of being an architect or an engineer. I like to draw buildings and decorate." — Kelsey, 13, Montana

"I want to go to college and major in television broadcasting, be successful in that field, and eventually get married." — Katie, 16, California

"My dream is to become a star athlete in volleyball and soccer. I also want to be a positive, wonderful, and inspiring role model for young kids." — Michele, 16, California

"My dream is to become an RN when I get out of school and work in pediatrics." — Anthony, 15, California

"I love weather and watching storms, they're exciting. My dream is to be a teacher or a meteorologist." — Karrin, 15, Montana

"I want to go to college and major in art and maybe fashion design." — Amelia, 12, Connecticut

"I want to be a professional snowboarder or a professional baseball player." Steve, 12, Connecticut

"My basic love is dance. I want to pursue dancing." Taylor, 12, Connecticut

"I want to be a paleontologist. We had a dig at school. I thought I found teeth but I found part of a tail." — Scarlett, 6, California

"My dream is to become a neonatologist." — Lisa, California, 17

"I would like to become a police officer and an elementary school teacher. I would like to make a difference in many people's lives. I also want to be there for all my loved ones in their happiness and sorrow." — Griselda, 17, California

"I want to be a writer. I like writing stories and telling what my point of view is. I want to be supportive like my mom." — Melinda, 12, North Carolina

"My dream is to succeed. To help the people that are less fortunate than me, and spread my knowledge throughout a world of peace and love. To help fight against the brutal killings of innocent animals of the world. To keep my own goals while helping others to achieve their own." — Matthew, 15, California

"I want to be a medical doctor helping people." — Hemali, 13, Connecticut

"I've always liked flying. I've been thinking about building a jet to strap on your back to fly. I have graphed it out already." — Nick, 13, Connecticut

"For now, my dream is just to be happy." — Hollie, 16, California

"I want to be a gymnast. I think and dream about going to the Olympics all the time." — Ryan, 13, Connecticut

"I like helping little kids out because I have always been good at that. I want to be a teacher." — Erin, 12, Connecticut

"My dream is to help, in some way, my fellow man." — Courtney, 15, California

WHO DO YOU ADMIRE?

"I want to be a fireman like my dad. My dad is my hero." — Brian, 12, Connecticut

"My grandmother is my role model, she gives so much." — Rachel, 14, Montana

"I admire my mother and my reading teacher. I like the way he teaches." — Bailey, 13, Connecticut

"When I was little, Michael Jordan was my hero. Now I want to be an engineer like my dad." — K.C., 14, Connecticut

HOW CAN ADULTS HELP YOU REACH YOUR DREAMS?

"From the adults in my life, all I need is a smile to motivate me, a hug to inspire me, and a 'hello' to relax." — Lindsey, 16, California

"Adults need to realize we are not all bad. We are good teenagers making a difference." — Kara, 15, Montana

"It makes me feel good when people compliment me and tell me I am doing good. It makes me want to strive harder." — Ben, 12, Connecticut

"Adults can help us by taking more time with us and by helping us to better understand how life works." — Kellie, 13, California

"Please do not judge, but instead inspire us." — Tory, 14, North Carolina

"I'd like for adults to stop telling us younger generations that things are impossible." — Matthew, 15, Montana

"I would like my parents to continue being supportive and my teachers to continue to be as helpful as they are." — Kathryn, 14, California

"I would like for society to let me be the person I want to be." — Nivia, 17, California

"I'd like to ask adults to support us in what we want to do. Give us love and hope." — Caitlin, 13, Connecticut

"I feel happy when I'm told I can do it." — Liz, 13, Connecticut

WHAT DO YOU DREAM FOR THE FUTURE OF OUR WORLD?

"For the future, I hope no one pollutes the earth, nobody fights, nobody hurts anyone and that no one brings dangerous stuff into their homes." — Alex, 7, Oregon

"My dream is that there would be no pollution and people would not litter." — Kristen, 9, Kentucky

"One of my dreams is to stop all wars on earth. I want everyone to throw away their guns and swords. And no more bombs." — Spencer, 7, Colorado

"My dreams for the future are that we could have clean air, unpolluted water, no hatred, and nice homes for everyone." — Kyle, 10, Oregon

"I wish that people would stop abusing and misusing dogs. For the world, I want it to be a cleaner place and a place where no dog has to be without a home." — Susanne, 9, Colorado

"My dreams are that all the rain forests would be alive as much as they were in the beginning, and that not many animals would be extinct or endangered." — Kimberly, 10, Kentucky

"I would like peace and greater protection for everyone." — Tanya, 12, Connecticut

"People should have freedom just like me. There should be no owners for others." — David, 9, Colorado

SEND US YOUR STORY!

Please share with us your own story of a dream come true. Write to:

Dream It Do It
Planning/Communications
7215 Oak Avenue
River Forest, IL 60305

Or send an email to:
graciela@dreamitdoit.net
or to
sharon@dreamitdoit.net

Appendix B

For More Information...

These web sites offer additional information about the inspiring individuals and organizations featured in *Dream It Do It*.

Maya Angelou: http://www.mayaangelou.com

Nancy Archuleta: http://www.mevatec.com

Lance Armstrong: http://www.laf.org; http://www.lancearmstrong.com

Edward A. Berger: http://www.niaid.nih.gov/dir/labs/lvd/berger.htm

Richard Bloch: http://www.blochcancer.org

Rosalynn & Jimmy Carter: http://www.cartercenter.org

Eileen Collins: http://www.jsc.nasa.gov/Bios/htmlbios/collins.html

Christy Curtis: http://www.ipclegalsearch.com

Gloria Estefan: http://www.gloriaestefan.com

Janette Fennell: http://www.kidsncars.org

George Fullerton: http://www.glguitars.com

Cynthia Hess: http://www.cynthiahess.com

David Howard: http://www.the1vision.com

Doug & Wendy Ishii: http://www.colostate.edu

Carl Karcher: http://www.ckr.com

Cale Kenney: http://www.howlings.com

Marigold Linton: http://www.kuconnection.org/2004jan/people_2.asp

Yo–Yo Ma: http://www.sonyclassical.com/artists/ma

The National Mentoring Partnership: http://www.mentoring.org

Binh Nguyen Rybacki: http://www.childrenofpeace.org

Bill Nye: http://www.billnye.com

Sue Titcomb & David MacKay: http://www.uspca.com

Phil Vischer: http://www.bigidea.com

Barbara Vogel:
http://www.iabolish.org/activist_ctr/stop/curriculum.html

Barbara Walters: http://www.abc.go.com/theview

Dennis Weaver: http://www.dennisweaver.com;
http://www.ecolonomics.org

Doug West: http://www.dougwestart.com

Tiger Woods: http://www.tigerwoods.com

Credits & Permissions

All photos are reproduced by permission of the copyright holder named below. All rights reserved.

Back Cover

Gloria Estefan photo: © Mitchell Gerber/CORBIS

Harrison Ford photo: © Mitchell Gerber/CORBIS

Tiger Woods photo: © Reuters NewMedia Inc./CORBIS

Chapter 2

Michael Clarke Duncan photo on page 10: © Rufus F. Folkks/CORBIS

Barbara Walters photo on page 11: © Ronald Reagan Library

Chapter 3

Harrison Ford photo on page 19: © Mitchell Gerber/CORBIS

Harrison Ford quotes from the 1986 article "Harrison Ford on Harrison Ford," written by Kirk Honeycutt and published by the Daily News in Woodland Hills, California.

Cale Kenney photo on page 25: © Bruce Benedict

Nancy Archuleta photo on page 30: © MEVATEC/Photo by Jennifer

Chapter 4

Marigold Linton photo on page 41: © University of Kansas

Lance Armstrong photo on page 45: © Graham Watson

Stephanie Ngo Pham photo on page 48: © Larrry Pham

Chapter 5

Barbara Vogel class photo on page 57: © STOP Campaign/Barbara Vogel

Tiger Woods photo on page 62: © Tim Pade/Desert Golf
Magazine

Tiger Woods quotes from The Tiger Woods Foundation web site,
http://www.tigerwoods.com. Used with permission.

Cynthia Hess photo on page 65: © Intuitive Visions, Inc.

Chapter 6

Bill Nye photo on page 73: © Hayley Sumner Co.

Sue Titcomb & David MacKay photo on page 76: © USPCA

Phil Vischer photo on page 82: © Big Idea Productions, Inc.

Big Idea Productions, Inc. proprietary information of Big Idea
Productions, Inc. All rights reserved. Used with permission.

Chapter 7

Beverley Berlin Mas photo on page 90: © Karyn LeVine

Binh Nguyen Rybacki photo on page 97: © Craig
DeMartino/Children of Peace

Rosalynn & Jimmy Carter photo on page 102: © The Carter Center

Chapter 8

Gloria Estefan photo on page 110: © George Bush Presidential
Library

Gloria Estefan quotes (except those as specified from 1999 Larry
King interview) from Gloria Estefan: Queen of Latin Pop, by
David Shirley. Chelsea House Publishers: 1994. Used with
permission.

Michael Clarke Duncan photo on page 115: © Rufus F.
Folkks/CORBIS

Eileen Collins photo on page 118: © NASA

Carl Nicholas Karcher photo on page 123: © Carl Karcher
Enterprises

Chapter 9

Barbara Walters photo on page 131: © Ronald Reagan Library

Edward A. Berger photo on page 136: © Edward A. Berger

Janette Fennell photo on page 139: © TRUNC

Chapter 10

Richard Bloch photo on page 147: © R. A. Bloch Cancer Foundation

Maya Angelou photo on page 154: © David Umberger/Purdue News Service

Doug West photo on page 158: © Doug West

Susanne Blake photo on page 163: © Shevaunn Williams & Associates

Chapter 11

Yo–Yo Ma photo on page 169: © ICM Artists/J. Henry Fair

Yo–Yo Ma quotes as specified from February 2, 2000, live Internet chat with barnesandnoble.com. Used with permission. Other Yo–Yo Ma quotes from Quintet: Five Journeys Toward Musical Fulfillment, by David Blum. Cornell University Press: 1998. Used with permission.

Connie Brady photo on page 174: © Joe Brady

George Fullerton photo on page 176: © George and Lucille Fullerton

David Howard photo on page 183: © 1Vision Software

Chapter 12

Doug & Wendy Ishii photo on page 195: © Bas Bleu Theatre

Christy Curtis photo on page 200: © Yuen Lui

Mary O'Donnell photo on page 204: © The Memory Photography Studio/Ron Barker

Dennis Weaver photo on page 207: © Alice Billings

About the Authors

Sharon Cook photo on page 238: © Bryan Salmans

Graciela Sholander photo on page 238: © Derek Shoaff–Bembry

Carpe diem!

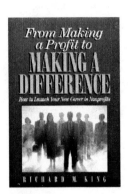

Ready to revive your dreams?
Ready for a job or career for which you have a real passion?
Ready to help others help themselves?

You'll find a wealth of affordable resources to help you map your path to the job or career you've always wanted when you go online to http://jobfindersonline.com. We offer more than 500 of the most effective career and job–search books, videos, and software that will help you:

- 👍 **Decide which career or job is right for you**
- 👍 **Switch to a new career at any age**
- 👍 **Find the job of your dreams**
- 👍 **Write effective resumes and cover letters**
- 👍 **Interview and negotiate salary with success**
- 👍 **Prepare for and choose college or graduate school**

Save 20% on our Job Finders when ordering online. During checkout, simply type JFONLINE in the coupon code field and you'll save 20% on the books we publish (they all appear on our home page). You can also order by mail. For a free copy of our printed *Job Quest Catalog*, call us toll–free at 888/366–5200 (weekdays, 9 a.m. to 6 p.m. central time) or write to us at Planning/Communications, Dept. DIDI, 7215 Oak Avenue, River Forest, IL 60305–1935.

Visit http://jobfindersonline.com today!

About the Authors

Sharon Cook's previous book, *Return to the Child of Light,* has empowered thousands of people to break free from addictions. A motivational speaker and the co–founder of a sober living home for recovering women, Sharon conducts "Movement Meditation" classes designed to motivate people to live joyful, healthy lives. She has appeared frequently on television and radio in addition to speaking extensively at conferences, workshops, clinics, treatment centers, and hospitals. She lives in the Palm Springs, California, area. Her website is: http://www.lifecoachingdreams.com.

Freelance writer Graciela Sholander has written more than 250 feature articles on such diverse topics as self–esteem, coping with dyslexia, family camping, and Feng Shui. Her work has appeared in publications ranging from *Women's Circle* and *Family Magazine* to *New Mexico Magazine,* as well as on web sites, including KidsHealth.org and experienceonline.com. Before becoming a writer, Graciela was an electrical engineer. She lives in Colorado with her husband, Kevin, and their two children.